MAKING WORK, MAKING TROUBLE: PROSTITUTION AS A SOCIAL PROBLEM

Why have our efforts to 'clean up' prostitution failed? Even new programs, such as 'John Schools' for customers and training in life skills for service providers, have been ineffective. Deborah Brock asks if our approach to prostitution is fundamentally flawed. We generally think of it as a social problem, but prostitutes see it as a work relation.

Anti-prostitution campaigns and attempts to regulate the sex trade have been made and re-made over the past few decades. In the 1970s and 1980s urban development and new policing strategies displaced workers from established prostitution strolls. Movements for social and sexual liberation turned the business of selling sex into a complex political issue. The Canadian state was confronted with a range of regulatory approaches, advocated by competing interest groups. Deborah Brock examines how prostitution in Canada has been *produced* as a social problem. Contending that 'social problems do not exist objectively,' Brock interprets the role of various actors in mounting the urban sex-trade spectacle: the media, feminist organizations, rights advocates, residents' groups, and state agents and agencies such as the police, politicians, the courts, and government commissions.

Making Work, Making Trouble is the first critical survey of prostitution in Canada. It provides much needed context to all groups enmeshed in the melée over territory and rights and should become a standard source in Canadian criminology.

DEBORAH R. BROCK has taught sociology and women's studies at Ryerson Polytechnic University, Wilfrid Laurier University, and Trent University.

DEBORAH R. BROCK

Making Work, Making Trouble: Prostitution as a Social Problem

UNIVERSITY OF TORONTO PRESS
Toronto Buffalo London

ISBN 0-8020-0976-x (cloth)
ISBN 0-8020-7935-0 (paper)

Printed on acid-free paper

Canadian Cataloguing in Publication Data

Brock, Deborah R. (Deborah Rose), 1956–
    Making work, making trouble : prostitution as a social problem

    Includes bibliographical references.
    ISBN 0-8020-0976-x (bound)   ISBN 0-8020-7935-0 (pbk.)

    1. Prostitution – Canada.   I. Title.

HQ148.B76 1998   363.4'4'0971   C98-930144-3

University of Toronto Press acknowledges the financial assistance to its publishing
program of the Canada Council for the Arts and the Ontario Arts Council.

This book has been published with the help of a grant from the Humanities
and Social Sciences Federation of Canada, using funds provided by the Social
Sciences and Humanities Research Council of Canada.

FOR MY MOM AND DAD

Faye Dawn Ruth Winnifred Walz Brock
1932–1993

Chuck (Charles Herbert) Brock
1932–1971

Contents

Acknowledgments

This book was once a PhD dissertation, although it has undergone considerable transformation since then. I hope that it demonstrates my commitment to write in a way that people without university educations, let alone specialization in a specific discipline, can comprehend. The people who I believe will find this book useful include sex-trade workers, members of residents' groups, journalists, social workers, policy makers, students, academics, and people with a general interest in the topic. I have attempted to negotiate the tricky business of writing a book that is useful to the very people whom I write about, yet passes the scrutiny of my colleagues. I worked with this tension by publishing my earlier work in both the popular and academic press, and by keeping in mind that my mother was also a part of my audience. I wish that I could have produced this book sooner, while she was here to read it.

I am indebted to many people who provided advice and support during this book's earlier development as a PhD dissertation. Bob Gardner, Alice DeWolff, Gary Kinsman, Jennifer Stephen, Lorna Weir, and Cynthia Wright proved invaluable, particularly during the final push to transform it from draft form to defence ready.

I would like to thank all of those women and men who were students at the Ontario Institute for Studies in Education while I was undertaking my doctoral work there. I was extremely fortunate to find myself in the kind of learning environment that the sociology department at OISE provided from 1984 to 1989. I was also fortunate to be associated with the Centre of Criminology at the University of Toronto as a junior research fellow while undertaking my PhD, and as a postdoctoral fellow after having completed it. Thanks also to all of those who were on my PhD committee at one time or another. Alison Prentice, Dorothy Smith, Philip Corrigan,

Roxana Ng, and Gord West all provided advice at various stages of this project.

Cynthia Wright and Lorna Weir both provided astute advice during the time that the thesis underwent significant transformation into book form. When I was ready to pull the draft manuscript back out of the filing cabinet, their support and encouragement kept me from throwing it back in. They helped me to re-evaluate what I was doing and determine what I needed to do. Their excellent advice got me going again, and I wish that I had been able to incorporate more of it while still managing to get the book out before the end of the millennium. But there are other projects ...

Becki Ross, Mary Louise Adams, Carolyn Strange, Karen Dubinsky, Margaret Little, Julie Guard, and I met regularly as the Sex History Study Group. In addition to sharing the latest gossip and eating copious amounts of food, we managed to discuss one another's work through the long process of churning out theses and books. These are times that I recall with much fondness and a little nostalgia.

I would also like to acknowledge Carolyn Strange for drawing to my attention a number of criminology books that have been published recently, all of them 'Making' something. However, because none of the friends whom I called upon could manage to come up with a better title, I decided to live with trendiness.

Mariana Valverde provided an encouraging critique of the draft of an earlier book on prostitution, and although I did not find the time, energy, and self-confidence to proceed with that project, I know that her comments and support made *Making Work, Making Trouble* a better book. Ed Jackson, Tim McCaskell, Tom Warner, and George Hislop shared with me their memories of the lesbian and gay community in Toronto in the 1970s.

Stella Westcott has been a dear friend for about twenty-five years. She has helped to keep me grounded.

My sister, Janet Brock, has provided encouragement and support while I have headed in new directions. I also want to remember my grandmothers, Jesse Moore Walz (d. 1993) and Hilda Brock (d. 1997), two very different women who nevertheless exemplified the position of women of their times.

Sandy Chu always lent an ear, and learned more about book publishing than she ever wanted or needed to know.

Activists in International Women's Day Committee/Toronto Socialist Feminist Action and the Ontario Coalition for Abortion Clinics taught me about political struggle, and helped me to keep my work relevant and meaningful.

Thanks to the women and men of the Canadian Organization for the Rights of Prostitutes for taking the risks entailed in speaking out about their work and their life experiences, and for helping to build a movement. Peggy Miller, CORP's founder, Val Scott, Ryan Hotchkiss, the late Danny Cockerline, Alexandra Highcrest, and Gwendolyn were the organization's early movers and shakers.

I would also like to remember just a handful of those people in the sex trade who were murdered on the job during the time that I was writing this book. Pamela George, Shawn Keegan, 'Deanna' (Thomas Wilkinson), and Brenda Ludgate are all mentioned here; many more are not.

Thanks to the staff at Street Outreach Services (SOS), particularly Julia Barnett, who told me that I should work there. SOS continues to provide a critical service for young men working in prostitution.

I would like to remember David N., whose 'high support worker' I became during my too short months as a contract worker with the agency. Although my job was eliminated as a result of budget cuts, I was able to carry on my work with David as his buddy at the AIDS Committee of Toronto until his death in 1994, at the age of 26. Like most street youth, David knew both a lot more, and a lot less, than other people his age. David taught me a lot about the streets, and gave me a crash course in the skills needed to work with street youth, as I constantly tried to stay one step ahead of him. He sometimes outsmarted me. But he kinda grew on me.

Dorothy Chunn warrants thanks for being so generous with her time through her support of my work. She is a fine feminist academic.

Andie Noack provided excellent editing assistance, funded by a Book Preparation Grant from Wilfrid Laurier University. I was really fortunate to have Andie's help.

Colleen Whelan of Venture Consulting provided superb technical assistance for my computer-related minor complaints and major crises.

Finally, thanks are due to the Social Sciences and Humanities Research Council of Canada for its support for this work when it was being undertaken as part of my doctoral research.

I would also like to acknowledge the efforts of Margaret Williams and Virgil Duff of the University of Toronto Press, in getting this book into print.

DEBORAH R. BROCK

Credits and Sources

The cover image is public domain clip art. It was used by CORP in its campaign for prostitutes' rights.

Canadian Criminal Code statutes and numbers are listed as they were at the time of the events being reported on. For current Canadian Criminal Code numbers and statutes, see Appendix C.

Permission has been secured to include portions of the following previously published material:

'Prostitutes Are Scapegoats in the AIDS Panic.' *Resources for Feminist Research* 18:2 (June 1989): 13–17. Reprinted from: 'Scapegoating Prostitutes for AIDS Transmission.' *Broadside* 10:4 (February 1989): 6–7.

Brock, Deborah, and Gary Kinsman. 'Patriarchal Relations Ignored: An Analysis and Critique of the Badgley Report on Sexual Offenses Against Children and Youths.' In *Regulating Sex: An Anthology of Commentaries on the Findings and Recommendations of the Badgley and Fraser Reports*, edited by John Lowman, M.A. Jackson, T.S. Palys, and S. Gavigan. Vancouver: School of Criminology, Simon Fraser University, 1986. Reprinted from 'Patriarchy Ignored: A Critique of the Badgley Report.' *Canadian Criminology Forum* 8 (winter 1987): 15–29.

Thanks to all of these original sources for reprint permission.

MAKING WORK, MAKING TROUBLE: PROSTITUTION AS A SOCIAL PROBLEM

1

Sexual Regulation and Sex Work

Late one morning in May 1977, 'Liz'[1] was making her way downstairs to the kitchen, still in pyjamas, when two policemen walked in her front door. Others followed and searched the house, while she was taken to the police station and charged with being an inmate of a 'common bawdy-house.' In all, about twenty-five women were arrested on the same charge that morning. After their release from jail in the evening, they found the contents of their homes in disarray as a result of a police search, and their bank accounts and safety deposit boxes frozen. Their places of work – four Calgary massage parlours – had been shut down by the police. Some of the women immediately applied for welfare assistance. Some began to work out of hotels and bars, others on the streets. Within a year, 'escort services' would begin to open, filling the space left by the disappearance of massage parlours.

What took place in Calgary was also occurring in other Canadian cities, such as Vancouver, Toronto, and Montreal. Massage parlours, 'nude encounter studios,' and other places for 'adult entertainment' were under attack as obvious fronts for prostitution. How is it that at this particular moment, the sex trade, which had been operating in relative privacy, had come to be considered a social problem worthy of national attention?

This is a story about the making of social problems. Rather than beginning with the assumption that social problems exist as social facts, as objectively discoverable conditions in a society, I explore them as the creation of a complex interplay of economic and social forces at particular historical moments in specific locations. We need to ask *why* prostitution in our time is considered to be a problem, and *for whom* (for example, police, residents' groups, feminists, and the media). This may seem an odd pursuit, given that, in our collective historical memory, prostitution has always appeared to be a social problem, for reasons that depend on one's ideological and analytic framework. For example, from a theological standpoint, the sale of sexual services offends Judeo-Christian morality, particularly as it flies in the face of the ideals of monogamy, fidelity, and chastity. From the mainstream feminist standpoint, prostitution represents women's subordination and degradation in patriarchal society. Through prostitution, women (and young people of both sexes) are bought and sold as commodities, according to the sexual whims and desires of men. The purpose here is neither to explain these positions, nor to debate their relative merits – prostitution as a sin against God versus prostitution as our society's clearest expression of the sexual domination of women and young people. Rather, it is to demonstrate how, regardless of approach, prostitution takes on greater social meaning at some times than others, and becomes the target of public, media, and state action. Prostitution as a social problem is clearly not a new concern. My focus, however, is on how particular forms of the business of prostitution were *produced* as visible and regulatable social problems from the 1970s through the 1990s.

Chapter 2 describes how indoor forms of prostitution, particularly massage parlours, became problematized in Toronto and other Canadian cities as a result of economic shifts, urban development, policing practices, and local state interests. Economic interests and local state interests worked to develop the idea that these forms of prostitution constituted an urban social problem, a process exacerbated by media participation in the organization of a moral panic. In the wake of the murder of a young boy in Toronto, public support for the elimination of these places was galvanized. Police were therefore mandated to act, and local business interests were addressed as Yonge Street was cleared of its indoor sex trade.

Chapter 3 describes how, with the resulting shift of prostitutes onto the streets, some residents' organizations, police, and city officials allied to 'inform' the federal government of the problem of street solicitation in Canadian cities and demand that it be resolved through criminal legislation. Some of the contradictions, which existed within the branches and levels of the state in addressing what to do about prostitution, are discussed. These led to the appointment of a government commission whose task was to provide recommendations for improvements to state regulatory mechanisms regarding pornography and prostitution.

Chapter 4 briefly analyses the work of this Special Committee on Pornography and Prostitution (the Fraser Committee) on prostitution. The committee's mandate – reform of the Criminal Code of Canada – produced a legislative 'solution' to the 'problem.'

Chapter 5 discusses Bill C-49, a new, punitive regulatory tool enacted in response to the interests of the alliance of residents' organizations, police, and city officials. The legislation, restricting communication for the purpose of prostitution, failed to clear the streets of prostitutes despite record arrests, and caused contradictions within the courts about how such legislation should be employed. Emergent tensions about the use of this law for the policing of prostitutes arose not because of the abrogation of prostitutes' rights, but because of the expansion of the rights of the affluent to determine the character of a city and its public spaces. Tension also grew as criticism of the continual expansion of police resources and powers increased.

Chapter 6 analyses how juvenile prostitution was produced as a social problem through its redefinition as a form of the sexual abuse of children. This was accomplished through the work of the Committee on Sexual Offences Against Children and Youths (the Badgley Committee). The committee's mandate structured this outcome and provided the directive to produce a new system of criminal classification of sexual offences, organized around a distinction between adults and youth. As well, the committee, without questioning the shortcomings in the organization of social services, recommended that they be expanded.

Chapter 7 shows how the deployment of this new understanding of juvenile prostitution via the media used the Badgley Report and police as 'expert' sources in a manner that produced a moral panic about juvenile prostitution. This panic further legitimated and expedited the implementation of the recommendations of the Badgley Committee, namely, an expansion of criminal law and social services, despite the questionable adequacy of these measures in meeting the needs of young prostitutes.

The Making of a Social Problem

In the decades following the Second World War, Canada's economic growth brought with it sweeping social and political changes.[2] The realm of the 'sexual' was in a process of renegotiation, and the Canadian state was forced to take an increasingly active role to maintain its hegemony in the face of movements for social and sexual liberation. Matters concerning sexuality and gender became prominent social issues. Abortion, homosexuality, pornography, and prostitution, as well as increasing awareness of sexual violence and abuse (for example, rape, incest, and other sexual abuse of young persons), came to comprise a contested terrain through which established sexual boundaries and moral codes were challenged, renegotiated, and shifted.[3] The feminist and lesbian and gay rights movements confronted sex-power relations predicated on the privileging of heterosexual activity within the context of the patriarchal nuclear family. These struggles for greater sexual freedom[4] took place during a period marked by the intensive sexualization of consumer capital (the use of sexual imagery to sell products). As Jeffrey Weeks has commented, the destabilization resulting from these occurrences means that Western industrialized nations no longer have 'an agreed upon moral framework.'[5] Now, more than ever, sexual matters are recognized as contested political issues. 'Sex' does not refer simply to a constant, unchanging force or drive, but to a site of socially constructed power relations whose history needs to be uncovered. It is in the context of this renegotiation of sexuality that an overhaul of sex- and morals-related statutes in the Criminal Code of Canada was initiated, particularly since the late 1970s, on a scale not seen since the early twentieth century. It is also within this context that the most recent reconfiguration of prostitution as a social problem occurred.

Feminist organizations challenged the double standard at work in the regulation of prostitution, which punished prostitutes for the sex work that they were compelled to do, but, for most of this period, left their customers untouched by the law. Most of these organizations ultimately favoured the elimination of the sex trade, while in the more immediate term advocating, along with prostitutes, the decriminalization of prostitution. At the same time, prostitutes were beginning to organize and develop a political voice, asserting their right to work, free from harassment. The question of what was to be done about prostitution was a politically complex issue, and in the meantime, the available urban space for prostitutes to work in was rapidly shrinking as redevelopment of downtown cores increased. Throughout the 1970s and 1980s prostitutes were continually displaced from established working areas through inner city renewal practices and policing strategies. Police, residents' organizations, and city officials demanded both the legal tools and financial support for the control of the streets and of off-street prostitution.

It is the latter group of interests, supporting legal sanctions against street-level prostitution, which has had the greatest resonance in the media. The inclusion of a morally laden activity in the Criminal Code of Canada predetermined a 'common sense' perception of prostitution as a social problem requiring a legislative response. Marginalized through this process was an alternative approach: prostitution is work, and it must be treated as such. As Joseph Gusfield comments, to talk about a problem 'is to already assume the character of a phenomenon ... and to define it as having such and such a shape.'[6] People, groups, and organizations then propose solutions based upon their definition of reality, and in keeping with their degree of access to the mechanisms of political power. By looking at how social problems are actually made, we can locate alternative possibilities for their resolution.

Advocates of criminalization and legalization strategies regard them as realistic and practical responses to street solicitation, by assuming that regulatory strategies will stem the transmission of HIV and sexually transmitted diseases (STDs), eliminate noise and traffic congestion from downtown (particularly residential) streets, and protect property values. Critics of these regulatory strategies point to how these laws are used to condemn and discipline a population of predominantly working-class women for the work that they do, while doing nothing to address the reasons why prostitution becomes an occupational choice for women and young people.[7]

Criminalization is what we have now. While prostitution itself is not illegal in Canada, legislation regulating prostitution-related activities like street solicitation is so broad that it may as well be. Although criminal legislation is not expected to lead to the abolition of prostitution, it is intended to control the trade and keep it as invisible as possible. It places moral judgments upon women's sexual conduct. It is only in recent years that customers and male prostitutes have been recognized as culpable in acts of solicitation in Canada, although the double standard continues since female prostitutes are more likely to be arrested and convicted than male clients. Those who uphold this view regard punitive legislation as necessary for defining and enforcing a society's moral code, a code that is considered the essential glue for holding a society together. The function of the law is therefore as important for its symbolic implications as for its practical application.

Advocates of legalization generally also support the stringent regulation of prostitution. A certain form of prostitution might be permitted, subject to licensing, taxation, and rigid codes determining what is and is not allowed, while other forms of prostitution, particularly street solicitation, remain illegal. The legalization of brothels in Nevada is evidence of the unsuitability of this tactic. Women employed in these brothels may leave the brothels infrequently for time off, and may only shop in nearby towns on certain days and during specific hours. The women may work fourteen-hour shifts (as no union or labour code exists for them as a basis for arbitration), during which they service ten to fifteen customers, in whose selection they are allowed no part. They are subject to mandatory medical inspections, and until the AIDS panic, they were not permitted to use condoms for protection against venereal disease. They are photographed and fingerprinted, and this information is kept in police files. In addition, on top of giving a percentage of their earnings to the brothel owner, they must pay for room and board and for the use of linen, and use personal care facilities like hairdressing and laundry services provided on the premises, all of which take a sizeable chunk from their weekly earnings. Although their work environment is at least more secure than where prostitution is conducted in a clandestine fashion, equally secure conditions could be arranged in other contexts, were prostitution not a criminal activity. Through legalization, prostitution may also be limited to certain areas of a city, the so-called red-light districts. Keeping prostitution concentrated within a particular area institutionalizes the control of women by profiteers and police, and many women justifiably refuse to work in these areas.

Decriminalization is the approach most favoured by feminists as it eliminates state interference into and control of the affairs of the prostitute. From a liberal or civil libertarian standpoint, we may question the legitimacy of prostitution laws, since they violate civil liberties like freedom of speech and the right to privacy. These kinds of arguments have been used (unsuccessfully, so far) in Canada to challenge the constitutionality of the legislation. The provision of sexual services by adults is considered to be a victimless crime in the legal sense, in that it is a crime without a complainant; it does not cause harm to others, is an act undertaken by consenting adults, and therefore should be outside the purview of the law. Some feminists also consider the legislation to be blatantly discriminatory, since it implies that the individual prostitute is responsible for prostitution, rather than society as a whole. Women should not be prosecuted for work which they do as a result of social and economic constraints.

Decriminalization would lessen the control of prostitutes by more powerful males: police could no longer demand pay-offs, and, where pimping does occur, their status as so-called protectors would be undermined. The lopsided application of the law, through which street prostitutes, particularly those who are Black, Native, or other women of colour, are more frequently arrested and imprisoned, would be eliminated through decriminalization. The state need neither condone prostitution, nor act as pimp through profiteering and stringent regulation. Finally, as legislation implies that prostitutes are responsible for prostitution, decriminalization would reduce the focus and blame placed on the prostitute, and would make it easier for women to leave the business should they choose to do so, as they would not be branded with a criminal record.

What feminists most commonly mean when they advocate the decriminalization of prostitution, however, is partial decriminalization. It is the legislation which most directly affects a woman's ability to work – soliciting and bawdy-house laws – which most feminists want to see repealed, while, at the same time, supporting the strengthening and more rigorous enforcement of legal sanctions against procuring and living on the avails of prostitution. Some also want customers to be liable to charges, as they now are in Canada.

I want to go beyond this legal analysis by demonstrating not only why problems appeared at the times that they did (for example, how popular fears are mobilized), but how regulatory procedures can actually *create* that which is being regulated. As Brophy and Smart find, 'the effect of law is never gender neutral.'[8] Women stand as 'legal subjects and sexual objects' in relation to the law, and 'it is legislation and legal practice informed by specific ideologies of female sexuality which serves to construct prostitute women as mere "sexual objects." In turn this sexual objectification of prostitute women reinforces their special status as denigrated legal subjects.'[9]

The regulation of prostitution is structured, through criminal code provisions, as sexual regulation, because it is the sexual character of the activity which makes it a target of regulatory strategies. However, we must be clear that from the standpoint of prostitutes themselves, it is not their own sexuality which is being regulated, but their work. 'Sexual regulation' is produced through the practices I describe. Arguments advanced by police, politicians, and residents' organizations for the more stringent regulation of prostitution are not always expressed in moral terms. What may be at issue in the development of regulatory strategies are the assertion of property rights, shifts in policing practices, or the making of a news story through the construction of newsworthy events. Nevertheless, the sexual character of prostitution remains determinate in that prostitution is subject to special regulation, distinct from that of other indoor businesses or street vendors. The regulation of prostitution undoubtably remains a form of *moral* regulation.[10]

Prostitution is designated as a social problem. Subsequently its regulation is affected by a concatenation of social relations and practices (albeit shaped by the economic context), including the production of legislation, changes in policing practices (often but not always connected to changes in the law), the work of government commissions, and the work of the media – the everyday process of 'making news.' These are organized to the constitution of social classes and the determination of property rights in a changing urban environment. Clearly, it is not state power alone that determines how prostitution is problematized and regulated. For example, in the policing of prostitutes, the power of the police is accomplished as much through an alignment of police interests with the media and residents' organizations, as through the provision of a legal mandate to act through the federal state.

The following study demonstrates the difficulty of conceptualizing state power as always having a unified structure or purpose. For example, criminal legislation regulating prostitution may be in place, but the means by which police interpret and enforce it in Canadian cities varies by locale and time period. Similarly, judicial interpretation may vary by province and within a province's court system. Police and local-level officials may demand the passage of more stringent legislation in order to increase police powers of arrest, while federal-level politicians who are responsible for creating new legislation are reluctant to do so in an uncertain political climate. A federal government can establish a commission of inquiry to investigate the dimensions of a social problem (for example, pornography, prostitution, or the sexual abuse of children and youths) and direct it to make recommendations for changes to social policy and criminal law, but the government is not bound to act on those recommendations, and may in fact proceed with quite a different agenda. As well, while 'the state,' with its often diffuse and contradictory agencies and actors, clearly has the central role in moral regulation (indeed, the state is looked to as the site for the codification and enactment of rules), it is not the only source. Citizens' groups (for example, residents' groups and feminist organizations) compete to define the nature of the problem and determine the method of its resolution by convincing the rest of the public, as well as state agents, of the rightness of their position.

The media, which Stuart Hall refers to as 'the dominant means of social signification in modern societies,'[11] plays an important role in forming the contemporary public identity of the prostitute: as the brazen, loudmouthed women who work residential streets until early in the morning, depriving respectable citizens of their sleep; as the lazy 'Josies' of the Yonge Street massage parlours; or as the young girl picked up by a pimp in the Eaton Centre and forced to work the streets. Part of this process entails reporting the perspectives of 'average citizens' whose lives are in some way affected by prostitution. These standpoints, along with those of 'authorized knowers'[12] (including police, social workers, politicians, and government commissions), whom the media consult for their expertise, can be assembled in ways that have the effect of organizing social problems and, at times, creating crisis situations, legitimating new initiatives to regulate prostitution and thus reorganize it into new relations. As summarized by Ericson, Baranek, and Chan, 'News not only articulates the knowledge structure of society, it actively contributes to the constitution of that society and to the changes occurring within it.'[13]

Those who do not play a role in the organization of prostitution as a social problem and in suggesting strategies for its resolution, are those persons actually being named as the problem. Indeed, their definition as 'the problem' keeps them outside of the debate, silenced by groupings that can claim a more legitimate interest. Ironically, without the contributions of those who work in prostitution, there can be no resolution.[14]

The Standpoint of Prostitutes

The delineation and regulation of prostitution do not take place in a moral vacuum, and prostitution is specifically subject to special forms of regulation because of the sexual nature of the transaction. As Foucault noted, the sexual has become identified as the source of 'truth' about the individual.[15] For women who work in prostitution, this 'truth' is unflattering. Women working in prostitution *become* prostitutes in the eyes of others; that is, publicly they are more identified with their work than are people in other jobs.

I use the standpoint of women working in prostitution as a point of entry, in order to describe the impact upon them of having their work relations continually reorganized. Describing how prostitution is organized shows how prostitutes' public identities are constructed and how prostitutes are oppressed.[16] Simply taking the basis of the oppression of prostitutes with gender, class, race, and age as starting points, is not a given. Rather, the ongoing constitution of these categories occurs through active social processes like the work of the media, policing, and the determination of legally constituted rights.

In this chapter, non-activist prostitutes speak about their conditions of work, relations with their customers, and the stigma of their jobs. Occasionally, throughout the study, prostitutes' rights activists also discuss the treatment of women in the business at the hands of police, the impact of criminal law on their work, their interactions with feminists, and safe sex. Both activist and non-activist prostitutes regard prostitution as work, albeit work that is heavily regulated by the state. Their comments, regardless of how they feel about their jobs (good, bad, or ambivalent), demonstrate that they want to gain more control over their working conditions.

To state that prostitution is a form of work may appear to be trite, but it is a statement that activist sex trade workers find that they must assert over and over again. Widely held perceptions of the prostitute as sinner, sexual deviant, or sexual slave suggest that prostitution is not addressed as a work relation, but as a social problem. Women working in prostitution who act as political agents and attempt to speak about their work come up against an identity assigned to them by their audience. Prostitutes have been prevented from entering into the discourses that determine their work and construct their identities.

When we treat prostitution as simply a social problem, relying uncritically on knowledge derived from 'authoritative' sources like the police, the courts, and the media, we unwittingly participate in the silencing, marginalization, and control of prostitutes. For this reason, and in order to disrupt the reading of prostitution as a social problem and replace it with a reading about regulatory practices and their impact on the work relations of prostitutes, I will now discuss prostitution as a work relation. This allows us to look at the concrete ways in which state power gets involved in the regulation and policing of prostitutes, an approach that is often neglected in feminist research on prostitution, or limited to challenges to the sexist organization of legal and social policy. The following interviews with two women working in prostitution provide a starting point for accomplishing this.

Prostitution as a Work Relation

It is difficult to conceptualize sex work as a viable occupation for women, given the feminist rejection of the use of women as sexual commodities to which men have right of access. Negotiating these viewpoints is not an easy task; it is one that I have grappled with for years. But I can, through this study, demonstrate the organization of prostitution as a work relation not so different from other kinds of jobs that women, particularly working-class women, take up. When I try to work through this I consider the context of the work; the social and economic power relations of living under capitalism that determine how women may be 'freely compelled' (to borrow a phrase from Marx) to find work in prostitution.[17]

The first step is to make an analytic separation of prostitution as a form of female labour from the institution of prostitution itself; social institutions and the people who fill particular places within them are not the same thing. For example, we can do a support picket for factory workers striking for a better contract, but that does not mean we lend legitimation to the corporation that employs them. This may seem an obvious point, but in the context of prostitution it is often elusive. The resulting conflation lends itself to standpoints which portray a prostitute as either a helpless victim or a social pariah who embodies what we perceive as the worst features of the institution. The second step of this process entails drawing directly from the experiences of women who work in prostitution, and comparing them with the experiences of other women in the workforce. We can explore how prostitution is not so different from other jobs that women do in a social formation where race, class, and gender, rather than individual choice and initiative, are the primary determinants of the kind of work one does.

Consider the following accounts of two women, whom I will call Liz and Donna. They are white women who were in their mid-twenties when I interviewed them in the early 1980s. Liz is from a working-class background and Donna is from a lower-middle-class background. They had been in the business for three or four years, and as their stories demonstrate, Liz 'sort of happened' into street prostitution after dropping out of high school in Toronto and working in numerous unskilled jobs before deciding to try her luck on the east coast. Donna, on the other hand, made a more deliberate decision to work in massage parlours. By the time I interviewed them they were co-owners of an escort service.[18]

Liz

I went to work in a fish factory. I didn't last long. Two days. My first day I was grading eggs for twelve hours ... good eggs, mediocre eggs, bad. Good eggs, good eggs, fuck I hate these eggs! After my first night, a guy came around looking for what girls they were going to pick to work in the guys' section. Like a meat market. You get picked just like you're in a fucking meat market anyway. So I end up going. Now I got to weigh the eggs; I didn't have to grade them anymore. I'd fill the bucket up to 44 lbs, lift it off the scale, lift up another one. There would be 38 lbs left by the time I got it over to where it was going. I hated it! I was so tired I was ready to faint! The next day I faked a back injury and went to the hospital. Then I went to work in the city. I was staying in a really sleazy hotel because I didn't have much money. The fishermen's compensation gave me a little bit. I bumped into Bonnie, who was hooking. When you're staying in a sleazy hotel, you're bound to work, especially in that city. So I ended up hooking with Bonnie, and moving into an apartment with her. I never worked nights and had $300 by the end of the day. I was on the street. I could have ended up better places but I didn't know.

Donna

I got into it slowly, actually. My first glimpse of this was when I was sixteen and I had been working my butt off as a waitress. I was really uncoordinated, a very poor waitress. I was working really hard and not doing well. This was across the street from a massage parlour and I was barely aware that it existed. A girl came in for a coffee and she saw how harassed I was. She asked me to have a coffee with her when I was done, and so I did. She told me I could make better money giving massages for like ten bucks for half an hour, or whatever the rate was at the time. She didn't mention anything about extras. She said it was a little easier than waitressing. Then she asked me how old I was, and said, 'Oh well, forget it.'

I forgot about that for a couple of years, but I guess I didn't really forget about it. Then I started working in record stores. I was working at this one store. My eighteenth birthday had passed. The manager let me go. He said they were overstaffed, but everyone knew there was money missing from the till. I didn't do it. And I was doing my job.

So I got really pissed off. And I thought, fuck the straight world, the straight world is bullshit; you just get screwed. And then I thought about what I could do to make some money, and I applied at a massage parlour. I found in that job there was more honesty than there was in a lot of the straight jobs I had. I had worked a lot of straight jobs, I think thirty different types of unskilled labour through temp manpower. They [the parlours] were more open. They'd say take it or leave it. And when you go to a lot of straight jobs they'll say very nice and it's this and that, and it's not so nice. And its a meat market. Have you ever noticed how waitresses get their asses pinched for a fifty-cent tip?

I worked in a massage parlour for quite a while before I would even give a hand job. I would either work topless or nude. I'd give a massage and make terrific commissions ... and I didn't feel that I was doing anything wrong. I gave a hard massage and thought that I was earning my money quite honestly. But I would always get grabbed. You get a harder time if you don't do extras.

I was working the reception desk for a while. That's when I got sick of rubbing these creeps. But I'd watch these girls making all this money. They'd be flashing it and wearing all of these nice clothes. Then it got to the point where even just answering the phones or booking the sessions you'd end up talking to so many of these perverts that I thought I may as well go back to rubbing them again. I knew what these other girls were up to but I thought I was making pretty good money and could live on what I was making. I thought all the other girls were slutty and seedy.

I didn't realize then that people paid to screw with a safe. I thought that if you had to screw you'd become a walking scumbag. And I didn't care for that. I thought that these girls who even then (the mid-1970s) were walking around in $700 outfits, well, still they're walking around with fifteen guys' cum in them.

And then finally I was working at this other place. One of the girls there was a university student studying interior design. It helped her subsidize her education. This girl looked nice and healthy and sweet. All the other girls at the last parlour had looked like hookers and I thought that if I'd start doing it I'd look like them. She was just jerking people off. And I thought she's doing it and her hands aren't falling off and she's not turning into a complete tart, so I'll do it too. It was a few years later before I started screwing. I thought, what the hell? So the money sort of got me into it. It took me a long time to get into it.

If I had other options, like, if I was a guy, an option would be to go work on an oil rig in Calgary and make good money. But seeing as the way I'm built, and where I live ... I didn't have options like that. This was the most obvious option. If massage parlours hadn't worked out financially, I would have tried something else, and maybe I would have tried to start a business even then. Though it takes money to start a business.

It was really a lucky break for me. In my position, where I didn't have money opportunities, that was one genuinely good opportunity. The public image of the job stinks, but the money was for real. It's true that in the last six years I could have done better. It's only in the last year that I've come out ahead; that I've started to do more than break even. The past five years have been up and down, but mostly down. So I don't know if it was worth it. But the whole time that seemed like it was my fastest opportunity to reach my goal, which was money. So that's different than desperation. The girls that start out in desperation will wind up on the street. Or girls who aren't very pretty, or don't have the resources. This is like any other business. It takes money to make money. But if you've got clothes on your back and you're not desperate and you know there are better ways of doing it, then you'll go and search them out. And some people will know people.

I've never been a really exclusive call girl, but I never met those people. I've always worked at something I could find in the phone book. I had to look up massage parlours in the phone book just like any customer. So you depend on your resources and your luck and determination when you start out.

When we see how women get into prostitution, we can see it is not so different a process from the way in which working-class women find working-class jobs, generally. Women do not often grow up wanting to become prostitutes. However, they do not often grow up wanting to become factory workers or domestic servants either. Given the low pay and limited range of jobs open to women, prostitution may appear to be the best available option. In this context, fifteen minutes of sex with a man for a minimum of $80 is perhaps no more exploitive or degrading than working eight hours a day at a sewing machine in a sweatshop for minimum wage, while the profits accrue to a multinational corporation. As Marx asserted, 'Prostitution is only a *specific* expression of the *general* prostitution of the *labourer*.'[19]

Liz: It's such a disgusting job, and you're only doing it for the money! Sometimes I wish there were condoms that covered their entire bodies!

Debi: You really contradict yourself. Sometimes you say, its such an easy job, a clean job.

Donna: With a customer who lays there on his back and doesn't even lay a hand on you, and lets you do your thing and jump off ... there is less contact than you have with a tampon applicator. Half the time they don't take much longer than a tampon does to insert. And I make $120 for it. Like, you've got to admit that's clean and easy and fast.

So you try to develop your clientele to be more of the type that you can tell them, 'Lie on your back and let me pamper you.' And what you really mean is, 'Lie on your back; don't you fucking touch me, and let me do my job my way so that I can get to have the least amount of contact with you. You just sit. Play dead.'

Touching them is better than them touching you. Because a dentist has to touch people, a doctor has to touch people that he's not attracted to ... You get used to it. Once you get used to touching them you realize how much easier it is for you to touch them as if they were an object, rather than them touching you. There's no getting around it; them touching you is like mauling if you don't like it. But I take into consideration all of the other things I could be doing for a hell of a lot less. And some of those other things I find even more distasteful, cause I've tried them. You've got to judge how much you're willing to put up with and how much it will take for it to be less distasteful.

Liz: I'll be teaching Sharon [a woman new to the business, who will be working at Liz and Donna's escort agency]. She was really anxious to do a call today. I was going to send her to see Mike. In and out in ten. That could even include giving him a bath. But he didn't call back.

Sharon has two children and a sister she takes care of. She's not on her feet, financially, right now, and her nerves are shot. When she was on the phone I was telling her how much to ask for and it was like, 'Glory, glory, hallelujah!' I felt like she was humming that while I was telling her.

Donna: You pay for everything. You pay for Exlax, you pay for TV, you pay for entertainment, so he'll pay for that ... he thinks he's got a need and it's throbbing and it hurts ... It's buying a service. Except for the odd one who rips you off. They don't think of it as buying a service. They think of the girl as a slut who deserves to be ripped off ... And as far as the girl who is willing to do that for money ... Probably a girl who does that for money wants to make a living somehow, thinks of what she has available to sell, her snatch has crossed her mind as a commodity she has that is marketable, and it doesn't gross her out so much that she refuses to consider it, so she considers it and goes out and sells it for whatever she can market it for.

As this interview reveals, prostitutes competently assess the advantages and disadvantages of their jobs in relation to other forms of work. Eileen McLeod's interviews with prostitutes in London, England, resulted in similar findings. As 'Rose' stated, 'The pay is good and the hours fit in with the kids.'[20]

Prostitution can take a heavy physical and emotional toll on women, particularly where they must work in unsafe conditions. Anyone who is labelled a social outcast is going to be susceptible to those who are more powerful, and legal control only reinforces and exacerbates prostitutes' vulnerability. Nonetheless, the incentives for women to work in prostitution, when compared with those of other jobs, are considerable, as the following example shows. I was working as a chambermaid in a hotel at the time that I conducted my interviews, and if Liz had come to regard men as 'pigs,' I was beginning to feel that way about almost everybody whom I had to clean up after. I wrote that summer, 'spend enough time cleaning up after other people, scrubbing remnants of faeces off of toilet bowls, and you may change your opinion about how one "chooses" to earn one's money.'

Sometimes Liz would do an 'escort' at the hotel where I worked. One day I cleaned a room after she and her customer had vacated it. She had just made $200 for a half hour's work; I made $2.30 in the same amount of time. On another day, I met Liz at 4:45 P.M. after working an eight-hour day that included cleaning twenty bathrooms, and earning $30. Liz had only been working since noon and already had $450 in her pocket (though of course not all her days were that good). I questioned who it was who was being exploited. I believed too that all women experience their subjectivity as objects to some degree, and that I was not accorded a great deal more respect working as a chambermaid in my green smock than she was as a prostitute in her silk stockings.[21]

Given the education and employment limitations facing working-class women and girls, women who work in prostitution are more likely to come from working-class backgrounds than middle-class backgrounds.[22] Working-class girls are not streamed through the education system to take up a postsecondary education and a career. They are presented with a limited range of options, such as clerical or low-skilled service work. Moreover, given the intensive use of sexualized portrayals of women as a commodity, and women's (particularly working-class women's) educational streaming and position in the labour market, it is perhaps surprising that more women do not work in the sex trade. It is a telling comment that prostitution may appear to be the best available option for some women, and that women can receive more money for supplying sex than for almost any other work that they do in the segregated female job market. Women who lack educational or job skills training find themselves supporting families in minimum wage jobs or on social assistance, as Liz's sister did, in conditions far more restrictive than prostitution.

When we compare work in the sex trade with other forms of female labour, however, we need not be limited to working-class jobs alone. For example, after leaving prostitution as a result of the social stigma of the job, Liz took up a sales career. She told me that whatever sense of oppression she felt in prostitution was nothing compared with that felt in her new job. Not only does Liz have to deal constantly with sexual harassment in her work, but the business practices of the people (primarily men) whom she deals with are ruthless and parasitical. She feels used much more than she ever did in prostitution, while her income is lower and less stable. Further, regardless of women's economic class, the subordinate position of women in the labour market means that middle-class women may also find themselves underpaid or unemployed.[23]

Finally, when we talk about prostitution, we are actually referring to quite a broad range of experiences and incomes. Prostitution has its own internal hierarchy, from the women who work the streets, to those who work as escorts or from indoor businesses, to women who maintain a relatively small number of steady and sometimes affluent clients. Some of the latter group of women may even disassociate themselves from prostitution and its attendant stigma by referring to themselves as something else entirely (such as 'companion'). Along with the job hierarchy are different degrees of job satisfaction. Any job will be subject to a range of opinions on how satisfactory it is. One key to job satisfaction is the degree of control one has over working conditions. Incomes also vary widely, depending on the type of work and whether it is practised full or part time. Women who work the streets are paid less for their services than are women who work from indoor locations (where earnings also vary). Some women who support children on welfare may only work during the last week of the month, if they cannot make ends meet.[24] When we try to make sense of how women enter prostitution and the working conditions that they face, we must keep this diversity in mind.

To label women working in prostitution as victims of these processes would be to deny them the right to speak; we would silence them as surely as if they were objects. The following extracts from interviews with Liz and Donna reveal the existence of relations of female subordination; for many of their customers, a whore is a whore is a whore. However, they also reveal their own agency in attempting to determine the conditions in which they work, as skilled practitioners of their trade.

The Defence of Work Relations

Debi: When you are in a room with a guy, who do you think is in the power position; the customer, because he has the money, or ...

Donna: If you let him have the power position you're fucked. Mentally, physically, and financially, if you don't control the whole thing from beginning to end. That's where beginning girls get into trouble. A guy will quickly sense who's running the show. If he thinks he is running the show, he'll get a lot out of you and then rip you off.

Liz: Cause he thinks it's nothing for you to do it.

Donna: Even a guy who has never stolen in his life will rip off a working girl if he feels that she isn't on her toes. The risk is so high. You have to appear so professional. If they're ill at ease, you take advantage of it; if they're not, you can make them, but in a certain way so that they know that they can't get by you. So you imply that you have brute force behind you. [While Liz and Donna were running their own escort service, they pretended to be managing it for someone else – a male – to keep competing escort services from attempting to run them out of the business.]

If you said, 'This is my first time,' they'd fucking screw your brains off and then either forget to pay you or rip you right off, including whatever money you brought in with you. I've heard of people who rip your clothes off. You can't even leave the hotel room.

So I appear like an aggressive, mouthy bitch, especially considering my size, cause I can't wave brute strength in front of them. Some girls can; there's some strong girls around. It really helps if you can take care of yourself, physically. You have to command respect, or they'll screw you and tattoo you. Like, they don't feel that they should be paying for this anyway, and you're just a slut.

Liz: But some guys who pay all the time, like the guy I saw last night, some of them, and very few of them, don't mind giving you the money at all.

Donna: They've finally adjusted to the fact that it is a commodity that they have to pay for if they want to get it. But the other ones still think, 'Well, damn, like I can't get laid so I have to bribe this girl to fuck me.' It's the same way that they mislead a girlfriend. Like, they're screwing them under false pretences. They'll mislead or rip off a whore and think all is fair in an effort to get laid. Plus a whore can't really complain about being raped. Hell, a librarian can.

Women who go on the bar-hopping scene can get themselves in a lot of trouble. At least here [with the escort service] we realize that there is an element of risk involved. We try to take as many precautions as possible. Half hourly phone calls, phone calls every fifteen minutes; someone has the guy's name and address, and knows exactly what time you should be there. You realize that you could meet your maker. But a secretary who goes bar hopping can get in even worse situations. She's got no precautions, she doesn't have her guard up. At least we've got a few deterrents. The guy knows that the police will know where to look in half an hour.

Liz: You don't look at it so morbidly, because if you're gonna go, you're gonna go. And the risk element is not very much.

Donna: We practically live on repeat customers. Nine out of ten people we've seen before.

Liz: And the ones who are weird you can pretty well tell on the phone. They'll call and they won't ask the rates. They'll say send me a girl no matter what. Those guys don't get a girl.

Donna: We don't go looking for trouble by going to guys who are obviously drunk, either. And with one guy you can talk your way out of trouble. You can tell him about Bruiser who is waiting outside [there is no 'Bruiser']. But two guys is very dangerous. One guy you can persuade to behave himself. But two guys ... they don't want to back down, they egg one another on, their friend is pushing them. So two guys a girl can never handle. When two guys call and pretend to be just one they always give themselves away. They'll share a joke with the other guy in the background, or make a few comments, and you'll hear someone in the background laughing. We try to be very careful with where we're going. Meanwhile, someone can be very meticulous and sound very straight on the phone, and you could be going to your deathbed.

Liz: It's pretty safe, actually ...

Donna: Most guys don't want to kill you, they just want to get fucked.

Clearly, prostitutes must attempt to maintain control over their work relations with their customers if they are to survive in the business. It is difficult for them to call the police when something goes wrong; to do so would be to expose themselves to criminal charges for the work that they do. The criminalization of their work makes prostitution potentially dangerous, and prostitutes must provide their own defence, since they cannot rely on the law or the police to do this for them.

Prostitutes and other sex trade workers can use their sexuality as power, in situations where they, as other women, would otherwise have little. It can be argued that women's only social power has been achieved through their sexuality; therefore, what kind of power is that? Nevertheless, prostitutes can assert a control over their relations with men so commonly denied to women. Men may think that their ability to pay gives them unlimited rights, but they may also feel that having to pay for sex is an affront to their masculine dignity. Those who pay for sex must ultimately recognize that the object of their 'affections' regards them as a source of income, not sexual pleasure. Women who work in prostitution know that while their customers are paying for sex, they as providers of the service merely go through the motions in a detached and dispassionate ritual. Sex with customers is kept quite separate from their own sexuality; no acquiescence here. They learn to manipulate masculine power skilfully, as many women have learned to do as a matter of survival.

Power operates at the level of the individual experience, although clearly it is shaped by the way power works at the social/institutional level, whether we, as individuals and collectivities, react with acceptance, resistance (including attempts at self-definition), or something in between. The institution of prostitution in the contemporary world may be a product of female oppression, but that does not prevent women from using it as a source of power.[25] Women are, after all, not simply the objects of control. We are active subjects who attempt vigorously to exert control over our own lives, whether it be through the individual homemaker's refusal to pick up one more dirty sock off of the floor or through our active participation in feminist, antiracist, and lesbian and gay rights movements. This dialectical relation between subject and object is also articulated by Mariana Valverde: 'Our bodies and our lives are not hopelessly determined by patriarchal oppression – but neither are they capable of complete individual autonomy. We need an approach which does not presuppose a rigid opposition between necessity and freedom, but rather sees sexuality as an open terrain in which the powers of the state, of the scientific and moral establishments, and of the sexist ideology of male-defined pleasure are constantly meeting resistance from individuals and groups. The experiences of such individuals and groups give them a starting point to challenge the ideas and power of those who have created the oppressive institutions.'[26]

In summary, prostitutes demonstrate a 'practical consciousness' about their work, and hence, about how their lives are organized. As Eileen McLeod discovered in her study of prostitutes, I too have found women who work in prostitution to be assertive and independent. They express resistance to forms of oppression in, for example, refusing to be poor, and by attempting to maintain control over their working conditions. While mainstream feminists decry the institutionalization of patriarchy and its expression through commercialized sex, women working in prostitution are, like the rest of us, living within the realities of a capitalist economic system. One has to earn a living. And more money is better than less money.

The labelling of the prostitute as 'victim' is an affront to the many assertive, independent, adult women who state that they would not subject themselves to the more 'respectable' female job ghetto. It ignores the fact that they may regard their jobs as a form of self-empowerment that provides them with a degree of financial well-being, and therefore more control over their own lives. Their reclaiming of the label 'whore' certainly attests to this. Victim analysis can disempower prostitutes, since it denies women's ability to make choices and promote changes. Valerie Scott, of the Canadian Organization for the Rights of Prostitutes (CORP), has commented that when feminists label prostitutes as victims, it means that prostitutes can't deal with them on an equal footing. Many prostitutes are now claiming a political voice that challenges the victim analysis of their work. Since the mid-1970s they have formed political organizations to defend their right to work and to improve their working conditions. The decriminalization of prostitution is fundamental to achieving their goals.

Beginning with the formation of COYOTE (Call Off Your Old Tired Ethics) – the first prostitutes' rights organization – in California in 1973, prostitutes and other sex-trade workers have been forming political organizations to improve working conditions, while raising their public profile. These organizations now exist internationally, and network through the

International Committee for Prostitutes' Rights (ICPR), which held its first 'Whores' Congress' in 1985.[27] These organizations demand for prostitutes the same human rights and civil liberties accorded to others; control over their working conditions, including the ability to determine where they will work (and live) and to pay taxes on the same basis that other businesses pay taxes; and, correspondingly, access to the same social benefits as other citizens. Foremost, control over their work necessitates the decriminalization of prostitution. In addition, they call for programs for the prevention of prostitution involving young people, and access to job retraining programs for those who want to leave the sex trade.[28]

By speaking for themselves, sex workers are asserting that they are not mere victims of a patriarchal society, who must be protected from their work (and from themselves) by feminists and social workers. Their central premise is that prostitution is a legitimate occupational choice for women.[29] These organizations commonly combine a libertarian view of sexuality with an assertion that feminism and prostitution are compatible positions. For example, Margo St James, the founder of COYOTE, identifies prostitutes as the first feminists, because prostitutes challenge codes of acceptable female sexual behaviour and refuse to be the sexual property of any one man.[30] The 'Statement on Prostitution and Feminism' issued by ICPR at the Second World Whores' Congress in 1986 acknowledges a link between the condition of prostitutes and that of women generally. Listed among the goals of prostitutes are financial autonomy for women, occupational choice, the development of alliances between women, bodily integrity and sexual self-determination, the right of sex workers (including porn models) to control their work, and the development of a women's movement that accounts for the rights of all women, including prostitutes.[31] The sexual division of labour, as well as differences in race and class, are acknowledged as factors that shape the organization of prostitution as an institution. However, the main thrust of their agenda is to challenge the coercive aspects of the state, which continually disrupt and reorganize their work relations. For prostitutes, the social reality of their work relations is that the intensive regulation of their jobs puts them at risk. The state *is* patriarchy. As one women who worked in prostitution commented at a conference on pornography and prostitution, 'We've heard a lot about patriarchy at this conference. We know about this. We call it "the man."'[32]

Sex-trade workers have sought out feminists as potential allies in the struggle for prostitutes' rights, asserting that the women's movement must be broad enough to include the perspectives of sex-trade workers themselves.[33] In Canada, this has resulted in the intervention of members of

CORP into the work of Toronto's March 8th Coalition (1985), and feminist events such as the 'Challenging Our Images: Politics of Pornography/Politics of Prostitution' conference in Toronto in 1985, where sex-trade workers turned a debate from one among feminist academics and activists to one between feminists and sex-trade workers.[34] CORP also engaged in important interventions into the politics of the National Action Committee on the Status of Women (NAC), Canada's bi-national feminist umbrella organization, comprising over 500 member organizations. At NAC's annual general meetings, beginning in 1986, CORP instigated the approval of controversial resolutions asserting the legitimacy of prostitution. Their participation resulted in the formation of the NAC Prostitution Committee, whose goal was to maintain a dialogue between feminists and women working in prostitution.[35]

My research is a product of a dialogue with activist as well as non-activist prostitutes. If feminist sociologists are to develop a sociology for women, as Smith advocates,[36] we need to account for differences among women, whether that difference is a result of geography, race, ethnicity, class location, or subcategorically, occupation. We need also note the following caution issued by Griffith and Smith: 'The relations between a generalizing discourse and those whose experience it proposes to represent are unequal. It is all too easy for us as feminist sociologists to fall into speaking for women in the terms, contexts and relevances of a sociological discourse, a discourse which the women we claim to speak for have no power to shape. It is all too easy for us to find ourselves replicating in new forms precisely the relations we had sought to escape.'[37] This is especially relevant given the hegemonic accomplishments of mainstream feminism, particularly its association of the sex trade with the exploitation of women. Mainstream feminism must now be located as a namer of social problems and as a moral regulatory force, having some (however nominal) influence on the organization of social life and on state-imposed 'remedies.'

2

Campaigns and Moral Panics

From 'Permissive Moment' to 'Social Problem'

The 1960s have been widely heralded as a decade of 'permissiveness.' Social values and moral standards became more open and state regulation of sexual behaviour appeared to loosen. The postwar population bulge known as the baby boom generation came of age in a period of economic growth, a rising standard of living, and an increasing level of disposable income. The market forces of industrial capitalism were provided with a sizeable market for the growth of the mass consumer society.

As Barbara Ehrenreich has pointed out in her book, *The Hearts of Men*, the growth of *Playboy* magazine typified, and in some ways set, the standard for shifts in postwar consumer culture.[1] Beginning in the late 1950s, Hugh Hefner, founder of *Playboy*, not only made 'girlie' magazines respectable enough to display on household coffee tables, but launched the 'playboy ethic' of the hedonistic male consumer. The principal objects of consumption were to be women, but Hefner's strategy accomplished more than this. As sexual imagery became more explicit, particularly with the emergence of *Playboy* competitors such as *Hustler* and *Penthouse*, pornography eroticized aggression and power in men.[2] The 'playboy ethic' became part of the broader sexualization of consumption in all forms, and the advertising and entertainment industries were able to capitalize on it. The sex industry burgeoned.

As established moral boundaries were brought into question, staid Canadian cities such as Toronto were introduced to public nudity through contemporary theatre and the opening of strip clubs.[3] The musical *Hair* came to the Royal Alexandra Theatre in the late 1960s, backed by members of the Toronto establishment (for example, the Eaton family), and police dared not shut it down for its inclusion of nude performances. This opened the door to full nudity in strip clubs. The sex industry was not a new way for women to make money, but its expansion certainly opened up more jobs, and some of these jobs, the most notable being the 'playboy bunny,' even took on an air of respectability.

The same social and economic conditions that gave rise to the intensive commodification of female sexuality also provided for the emergence of the feminist and lesbian and gay rights movements. In the postwar period, the moral framework of western capitalist societies was destabilized, as issues related to gender and sexuality were beginning to be renegotiated. These shifts were integral to the development of a climate of social and legal reform. The 'just society' of late 1960s Canadian liberalism promised a more equitable division of social rewards, as poverty was 'discovered,' regional disparities recognized, and the welfare state expanded, particularly health, education, and social programs. Emergent social movements exerted pressure on the Canadian state apparatus to lessen the legal control of sex-related matters, including homosexuality, birth control, and abortion. It was during the establishment of this 'permissive moment' that Justice Minister Pierre Eliott Trudeau made his famous statement, 'the state has no place in the bedrooms of the nation.' In 1969, the Canadian Criminal Code was reformed to legalize homosexual activity in private between persons over twenty-one, and to legalize abortion procedures when conducted in hospitals and approved by a therapeutic abortion committee.[4]

Under pressure from the women's liberation movement, the federal government announced the appointment of the Royal Commission on the Status of Women in Canada (RCSW) in February 1967. Feminists in Canada were developing an understanding of how the state served to enforce and entrench patriarchal privilege, and called for a weeding out of sexist bias in social policy and criminal law. The commission was to investigate the impact of federal laws and practices on women. Its mandate included a review of criminal law, federal labour laws, marriage and divorce legislation, and federal tax laws, the position of women in the labour force, education and job skills, immigration and citizenship policy, and any other matter found relevant to women.[5] The appointment of the commission was the federal government's first significant attempt to address gender inequality, and marked the beginning of the definition of the term 'status of women' included in a state-coordinated approach to feminism in Canada. The commission released its report in September 1970.

A critique of legislation regulating street prostitution was an important feature of the commission's study of criminal law and women offenders. Prostitution was treated as a form of vagrancy under section 164 (1)(c) of the Criminal Code. 'Vag C,' as it was known, specified that 'Every one commits vagrancy who, being a common prostitute or night-walker is found in a public place and does not, when required, give a good account of herself.'[6] This section was found discriminatory since it applied only to women, not to mention the blatant moral condemnation it exhibited in its assessment of aberrant female sexual behaviour. The commission charged that 'Vag C' restricted the freedom of women in public spaces, allowed the arbitrary use of police powers, and labelled women as prostitutes through the imposition of a criminal record, thereby making them more difficult to 'rehabilitate.' Women were prosecuted 'not for what they do but for what they are considered to be,' a judgment which the commissioners asserted should not be within the mandate of criminal law.[7] The RCSW drew on the findings of the Prevost Commission,[8] which had found that while the public believed prostitution to be morally wrong, they were not in favour of imposing legal punishment. Rather, briefs to the Prevost Commission stated that prostitution was 'fundamentally a social, not a criminal, problem.'[9] The RCSW also took into account Britain's Wolfenden Report, which had explored the regulation of homosexuality and prostitution, in stating that prostitution had never been eradicated through legislation. They recommended the repeal of 'Vag C,' and the use of bylaws dealing with matters such as 'disturbing the peace' where warranted to deal with the possible nuisance effects of street solicitation. They also advocated the development of government programs for the 'rehabilitation' of prostitutes, which would include the provision of alternative job training.

An important influence on the liberalizing trend in the federal state came from abroad. The general liberal legal philosophy articulated in Britain's *Report of the Committee on Homosexual Offences and Prostitution* of 1957 (the Wolfenden Report) has been credited with setting the terms for liberal legislation in several nations. The Wolfenden Committee questioned the place of morality in the functioning of criminal law governing homosexuality and prostitution.[10] The key to the impact of the Wolfenden Report was its reformulation of the relation of the law to private consensual sexual matters: it determined that while it may be in the interest of the state to control public displays of sexual behaviour, certain activities between adults, when conducted in private, were not the law's business. Homosexuality was regarded as a matter for psychiatric and medical professions, not legislatures, as long as it did not interfere with public order and decency. Stuart Hall states:

The key to the Wolfenden Report's 'permissiveness,' and the real index as to the specific character and limits of its reformism, is thus the tendency it exhibited towards the privatisation of selective aspects of sexual conduct. The philosophical rationale which it employed was the distinction between crime and sin, illegality and immorality – a blurred and indistinct boundary within the English criminal law which, by selective reiteration, Wolfenden immeasurably strengthened. But the mechanism by which this distinction was practically implemented was the drawing of a sharper distinction between 'public' and 'private' – between the spheres of the state and civil society.[11]

The 'permissiveness' of the report has been characterized as a 'double taxonomy in the field of moral regulation,' according to Hall,[12] by, on the one hand, creating greater penalties and control and, on the other, increased freedom and leniency.[13]

Gary Kinsman has documented how the Wolfenden Report's philosophy shaped Canadian legislation governing homosexuality through the 1969 Criminal Code reforms in Canada. An accomplishment of the legalization of homosexual activity between consenting adults in private was the intensified police persecution of gay men in public spaces.[14] Similarly, the liberalization of the abortion law was double-edged. Abortion was legal when performed in a hospital with the approval of a therapeutic abortion committee, but governments did not provide the funds and facilities necessary to ensure equal access. Therefore, despite the apparent permissiveness of this period, state control over the public's moral conduct did not disappear. Rather, new strategies of social regulation emerged in response to changing social conditions, as well as to the demands for sexual and reproductive freedom.

The same analysis cannot be applied to the impact of the Wolfenden Committee's recommendations on prostitution, as there was very little pretence to liberalism about them. The committee called for tougher legal action against public prostitution by recommending the elimination of the need to prove that acts of solicitation caused annoyance, and steeper penalties for prostitutes convicted of solicitation (but not their customers). This was consistent with a long-standing interest in preserving 'public order and decency,' articulated throughout the report. It also contained some implicit sanctioning of private prostitution, stating: 'It is right that the law should guard against the congregation in any one place of undesirables of any type [but] too rigorous enforcement of the law in this respect might well have the effect, in some places, of driving prostitutes whose conduct at the present time is inoffensive, on to the streets, where their very presence would offend.'[15]

Nonetheless, the comittee recommended broadening the scope of the law covering tenants and owners of bawdy-houses. Liberalizing legislation on the operation of brothels, it believed, would encourage their use and the recruitment of women to them, thus providing an increased market for those who traffic in women and children. However, the committee saw little point in closing an existing loophole in the law, whereby a woman could use her place of residence for the purpose of the prostitution of herself alone. The committee acknowledged that, 'as long as society tolerates the prostitute, it must permit her to carry on her business somewhere.'[16]

The private/public distinction articulated by the Wolfenden Committee was in direct contradiction to that advanced by the Royal Commission on the Status of Women in Canada over a decade later. The Wolfenden Committee demonstrated what they believed to be a protectionist stance toward women in refusing to liberalize legislation governing brothels, while further punishing the visible prostitution-related activities of women. However, it managed to avoid a prohibitionist approach by recommending the maintenance of a very limited private space for the prostitution of individual women to occur.

The Royal Commission on the Status of Women went beyond the Wolfenden Committee's general philosophy in implicitly challenging the position that prostitution could be tolerated in some private spaces but not in public.[17] That the RCSW did not take a position on the decriminalization of bawdy-house legislation was, it appears, also a protectionist measure to prevent potential third-party exploitation through the operation of prostitution businesses. However, for the RCSW to adopt a punitive stance toward public prostitution would be to both demonstrate a double standard for sexual conduct for women and men, and to punish prostitutes for the very social and economic inequalities the commission was appointed to address. Thus the RCSW came up against contradictory discourses on the private/public distinction; those of liberalism and of feminism. Liberal legal philosophy was based on the distinction between spheres of political action, the public, regulatable sphere and the private domain (permitting more limited intervention), which corresponded to the idea of separate spheres for women and men. In seeking equal opportunities for women, the RCSW challenged the double standard of sexual behaviour and sought to increase the 'protection' of women in the private sphere, as well as to improve opportunities for women to move beyond it.[18]

The enforcement of 'Vag C' was running into some difficulties in the courts in any case. Police were abusing their powers of arrest and detention, as women arrested under this section were detained in custody overnight and subjected to mandatory medical exams. The courts did eventually rule that the legal and medical systems had no authority to require such examinations, but this alone was not sufficient to correct the shortcomings of the statute. In 1972 'Vag C' was finally repealed in the context of the repeal of all vagrancy legislation, as part of a parcel of legal reforms under the Criminal Law Amendment Act (Bill C-2). Justice Minister Otto Lang noted that the repeal was in keeping with the recommendations of the RCSW, but rather than leaving the regulation of the nuisance effects of prostitution to the purview of other legislation, a new statute referring specifically to the act of street solicitation was passed by the House of Commons. Section 195.1 specified that 'Every person who solicits any person in a public place for the purpose of prostitution is guilty of an offence punishable on summary conviction.'[19]

Feminists were expected to be appeased by this statute because it did not legally define prostitution as a 'status offence,' as the vagrancy provision had done through its identification of the 'common prostitute.' As well, it was gender neutral, as the term 'common prostitute' had previously implicated only women in judicial practice. This implied gender neutrality was to be extended to the 'living on the avails of prostitution' statute, meaning that women too could be charged for living on the prostitution earnings of another person. One (male) member of parliament referred to this change as 'a noble victory for man's liberation.'[20]

The statute therefore accommodated formal equality rights before the law, while doing nothing to recognize that discrimination against women runs much deeper than distinctions between female and male behaviour in the expressed intent of legislation. Politicians who supported the statute did not question why women became prostitutes in the first place, or the role of prostitution legislation, gender neutral or not, in regulating women on the streets. A gender-neutral statute could not significantly alter the *application* of the law, and as time would tell, it continued to be overwhelmingly women who were arrested by police and prosecuted by the courts, while some judges refused to even recognize that the solicitation legislation could apply to male customers.

We must therefore question both the character and extent of the perceived permissiveness. Certain feminists have questioned how beneficial this period really was for women specifically. They have pointed out that a shift had taken place from a time when women were unable to say 'yes' to one where they could not say 'no.' Although 'the pill' lessened the risk of pregnancy for women, sexually active women again came face to face with their lack of control over their own bodies when potential harmful side-effects of the birth control pill were revealed. The loosening of sexual boundaries intensified the definition of women as sexual objects as much as it opened up a wider potential range of experiences and pleasures. However, women did indeed slowly come to assert their own sexuality and their right to erotic pleasure. Lesbian and gay historians have also revealed how it opened up space for the development of lesbian and gay identity, and ultimately, of their community.[21]

The establishment of permissiveness through shifts in federal policy in this period was of a limited and double-edged character. Indeed, the state continued to play a key role in sexual regulation and the organization of prostitution. State regulation of prostitution, particularly at the local level, was to intensify throughout the 1970s, as the apparent permissiveness of the 1960s was called into question. What follows is an account of the making of a social problem requiring state response, as Toronto's indoor prostitution trade came under the spotlight of public and media scrutiny.

The Emergence of a Moral Panic

The sex industry was expanding in Canadian cities in the early 1970s. Tensions were particularly high in Toronto, where Yonge Street was developing a reputation as the 'sin strip' of Canada. Strip clubs, adult movie houses, pornographic book stores, massage parlours, and other fronts for prostitution were appearing everywhere along the section of Yonge Street extending approximately from Wellesley Street to Queen Street. The first of the 'body rub' parlours opened on 'the strip' in December 1972. These establishments were blamed with attracting women to work the street as well, given the ample market for prostitutes' services as men came to Toronto's main street to access the sexual entertainment industry.[22]

Some Toronto residents, politicians, and police pointed to Yonge Street as evidence that the sexual permissiveness of the 1960s had gone too far, and prostitutes, and later gay men as well, were scapegoated for causing its most blatant abuses. Although there was some concern about conditions on Yonge Street when 'red tory' David Crombie became Mayor of Toronto in 1973, that concern was not sufficient to prompt a clean-up campaign, despite the popular mayor's support for such a program. Crombie's efforts to sanitize the city resulted in a negative public reaction, indicating that he had stepped beyond his mandate in attempting to govern people's moral conduct.[23]

However, the economic conditions of the early 1970s, most notably the embargo of Saudi Arabian oil and the growing rate of inflation, had set the conditions for a creeping conservatism in social and political affairs, as

Canada and other Western capitalist nations entered a period of recession. In Canada, the recession motivated an intensified struggle concerning wage and price controls and state spending. While this economic climate cannot be held solely responsible for the decline in permissiveness taking place over the course of the decade, it did at least help to shape the moral climate of social relations, and sexual and moral issues became important rallying points in the conservative agenda. Economic interests did play another, more direct role.

By the mid-1970s, plans were well under way for a renewal of commercial development on Yonge Street. A massive indoor shopping mall, the Eaton Centre, was to be the focal point for this transformation, and politicians were anxious to make the area appealing once again to middle-class shoppers. The Downtown Business Association supported the idea of a clean-up, and the Toronto police, who were anxious to re-establish control over the area, added incentive by claiming that organized crime from the United States was taking over Toronto's sex industry. The sex shops were blamed for having driven reputable small businesses off of the street. Yet, according to researcher Yvonne Ng, officials and business people were well aware that sex-related businesses were among the few that could survive the inflated real estate market on Yonge Street. Redevelopment plans had resulted in an escalation of real estate values as speculators bought up land and properties, and rents increased to the extent that most small businesses were squeezed out of operation or forced to relocate. The fact that it was the holders of financial capital forcing these businesses out, and that sex shops had merely set up in the aftermath of this squeeze, was conveniently ignored.[24]

Two daily newspapers, the *Toronto Star* and the *Toronto Sun*, played a key role in garnering public support for the clean-up campaign, which identified body rub parlours as the ruination of Yonge Street. By 1975 public sentiment was beginning to shift. That year the Conservative party ran for re-election in Ontario on a 'law and order' platform that included a promise to clean up Yonge Street. The emergence of law and order campaigns in Canada and other advanced capitalist nations at this time signalled a shift toward the curtailment of permissiveness through 'the rule of law.' This reassertion of state authority over the social order took place, not coincidentally, at the same time that the state's inability to manage the economy had become apparent.[25]

The Tories won the election, and their campaign helped to further the cause of the clean-up campaign. The Conservatives soon began implementing their promise through amendments to the Municipal Act and Theatres

Act in July 1975 that expanded municipal legislative power over body rub parlours. As a result, city politicians were able to pass a bylaw to license and limit the number of body rub parlours in Metro Toronto. This measure proved to be largely ineffective. While only five operators had their licences accepted, over sixty other establishments continued to operate. Owners simply averted the bylaw by offering 'nude encounter sessions.' Despite the law and order campaign waged by the Conservative party, the building up of Yonge Street as a problem in the press, and the sex trade's flagrant outmanoeuvring of politicians, there was still not the substantial public support required to launch a full-scale 'clean-up.'[26]

In February 1977 a special committee (including members of Toronto City Council, the Chief of Police, and legal council) was appointed to investigate conditions on the 'sin strip' and to come up with some hard data to legitimate the efforts of police, politicians, and business people. The *Report of the Special Committee on Places of Amusement* was released in June of 1977. The inclusion of police and politicians on the committee had from the start guaranteed that the report would produce the kind of recommendations the city wanted. The report stated that 'Yonge Street should be an acceptable and appealing street for people of all ages and interests to shop and visit ... it should be an attractive place for a wide variety of businesses ... it is absolutely necessary that appropriate levels of government take action to minimize the offensiveness to the general public of adult entertainment establishments in particular.'[27] Police used the report to claim that prostitution-related businesses were being used to finance more serious types of crime, for example drug distribution. And they used the alleged presence of organized crime in these businesses to prod a public that was reluctant to regard the existence of prostitution alone as a serious threat to the community.

Within the 'reasonable' or 'common-sense' framework of the report, the fact that there had been no appreciable rise in the crime rate since these businesses had opened was acknowledged but not addressed.[28] Although the report stated that there was not a rising level of decay on the street, it went on to suggest that a 'psychological crisis' was developing because of the activities on Yonge Street. A 'psychological crisis,' it was argued, could easily become the real thing.

The work of the committee was itself part of the production of a 'psychological crisis,' so much so that it even made the questionable assertion that the sex industry in Toronto was creating a demand for itself, as if it were leading otherwise respectable citizens astray. The structure and composition of the committee, and its resultant research, was articulated to the interests of the local state, including politicians and police, in order to produce just such a crisis, legitimating further state action.

The Yonge Street businesses identified as a source of the crisis were labelled by the committee as 'adult physical culture establishments.' These included 'any establishment which offers or purports to offer any form of physical encounters whether or not there is a direct physical contact between an employee of said establishment and a patron or guest where either the employee or patron or guests' specified sexual areas are less than opaquely covered.'[29] 'Specified sexual areas' were defined as 'human genitals, pubic region, buttocks and female breasts below a point immediately above the top of the areola.'[30] The body of the sex-trade worker was thereby identified as the site of the offence against public decency and therefore the site of regulation. The committee recommended that Toronto police 'act vigilantly to curtail on-street solicitation by prostitutes and employees of nude services ... and incidently by panhandlers.'[31] Increased fines were proposed for breaching licensing conditions (fire, health, and building regulations were already being tightly enforced through frequent inspections), as well as for employees found guilty of providing prostitution services. For better control, it recommended the establishment of a 'special class' of licences for adult entertainment establishments, using a reverse onus: the applicant would have to 'show cause' why a licence should be issued, and then be informed of the legal repercussions if licensing conditions were breached. Unlicensed places were to be considered a public nuisance and closed.

They also recommended that no new adult physical culture establishments or adult movie arcades be permitted to open except in specified zones. In a move that would expand police powers far beyond their prescribed role, police were to be given the right to act as licensing inspectors. Where establishments were permitted and licensed, the owners and employees were not to be visible from the street; nor were they to encourage, on or off the premises, the public to use the services of the premises.[32] The voices of prostitutes, who stated that closing the massage parlours would put women back on the streets, went unheard.[33]

These and other recommendations were quickly acted upon by city hall. A 'war room' and 'war council' were put in place, and the Yonge Street Implementation Committee was formed to implement the report's recommendations.[34] The crackdown was under way. Body rub parlours found their licence fees increased to $3,300 per year, and exotic dancers and body rub attendants found themselves placed in the same licensing category with a fee of $55 per year.[35] To apply, they were required to complete questionnaires asking whether they had a criminal record, which served to screen out women who had previously been convicted of a prostitution-related offence.[36]

Toronto city officials predicted that it would take five years for the clean-up campaign to be completed. However, events spurred the campaign along much more quickly than they had dared hope. On 1 August 1977, a twelve-year-old Portuguese youth, described as a 'shoeshine boy' in the media, was found dead on a roof beside Charlie's Angels, a Yonge Street massage parlour named after the popular 1970s 'T and A' (tits and ass) format television show. Emanuel Jaques had been sexually assaulted and reportedly drowned in a sink during what *Maclean's* magazine described as 'a 12-hour orgy of abuse by homosexuals.'[37] One of the four men charged with the murder was a part-time employee of Charlie's Angels, and lived in rooms above the massage parlour. And the key figure in the killing, Saul Betesh, was a gay man. Betesh had persuaded Jaques to go with him to the apartment, and later informed police of the murder and led them to Jaques' body. Whatever resistance there had been to a clean-up was silenced. Yonge Street was now proclaimed 'the meanest street in the nation.'[38] The street itself was blamed for Jaques' death, and overnight, sex shops were raided and owners prosecuted.[39]

Lawyer Morris Manning was appointed as a special crown assistant to clear up the backlog of morals cases awaiting trial and file writs of injunction to padlock the parlours under the Disorderly Houses Act. This little-used act gave county court judges the authority to close a premise if the occupants had been charged under the bawdy-house laws in the previous three months. While its constitutionality was questionable, this 'padlock law' proved to be the most effective legal strategy available.[40] Many massage parlour owners simply closed themselves down, recognizing that staying in business would be impossible. In addition, the bawdy-house statute was enforced vigorously. The Criminal Code statute relevant to bawdy houses specified that:

193. (1) Every one who keeps a common bawdy house is guilty of an indictable offence and is liable to imprisonment for two years.
(2) Every one who
(a) is an inmate of a common bawdy house,
(b) is found, without lawful excuse, in a common bawdy house, or
(c) as owner, landlord, lessor, tenant, occupier, agent or otherwise having charge or control of any place, knowingly permits the place or any part thereof to be let or used for the purposes of a common bawdy house, is guilty of an offence punishable on summary conviction.

(3) Where a person is convicted of an offence under subsection (1), the court shall cause a notice of the conviction to be served upon the owner, landlord or lessor of the place in respect of which the person is convicted or his agent, and the notice shall contain a statement to the effect that it is being served pursuant to this section. (4) Where a person upon whom a notice is served under subsection (3) fails forthwith to exercise any right he may have to determine the tenancy or right of occupation of the person so convicted, and thereafter any person is convicted of an offence under subsection (1) in respect of the same premises, the person upon whom the notice was served shall be deemed to have committed an offence under subsection (1) unless he proves that he has taken all reasonable steps to prevent the recurrence of the offence.[41]

Between mid-July and 2 September 1977, 224 charges against 'inmates' and 'keepers' of common bawdy-houses were laid, as opposed to only 16 from June to July 1977.[42] Women were literally rounded up and loaded into paddy wagons by police. By November 1977, only four adult entertainment establishments remained on Yonge Street, where there had been forty in July. In December 1978 the last body rub parlour on Yonge Street closed its doors.[43]

The anger and outrage expressed following the boy's death were further fuelled by graphic media accounts of his last hours (unrivalled for gruesome detail until the 1995 Bernardo murder trial in Toronto), and sensationalist stories of conditions on Yonge Street and in other Canadian urban centres. Jaques' death provided the rationale for other cities to clean up their sex industries before they met the same fate as Toronto. As then Mayor Volrich of Vancouver stated, 'it *can* happen here.'[44] In cities such as Calgary, Ottawa, and Montreal, clean-ups already under way were further legitimized by the events in Toronto. For example, John Lowman reveals that the closure of certain indoor places of business (cabaret clubs) had occurred in Vancouver in 1975–6. This will be discussed in the following chapter.[45] In the spring of 1975, same-sex escort services in Ottawa were raided after police alleged that they engaged in child prostitution and 'white slavery,' although no evidence of either ever materialized.[46]

The tenor of mainstream media coverage in the period following the murder is succinctly expressed in this *Maclean's* magazine report:

After a decade and more of slow surrender to the siren song of the permissive society, Canada's biggest cities are fighting back against prostitution and pornography, mainstays of what has become a multi-million dollar sex industry. For the moment, at least, the cities appear to be winning – mainly through the use of licensing and zoning restrictions enforced by gung-ho municipal police forces. The counterattack has been spurred by civic survival instincts as much as by outrage at the ever-increasing brazenness of the flesh peddlers. In the past few years, bodyrub shops, sleazy bookstores, nudie movie theatres and 'escort' agencies have been proliferating throughout urban Canada with the grim determination of lymphatic cancer and, civic officials fear, unless curtailed will ultimately kill off the areas they infest.[47]

The media was not simply a vehicle for expressing public outrage; it served to mobilize a moral panic, as in the above association of commercial sex with deadly disease, and to therefore organize public consent for repressive state action. Stanley Cohen defines a moral panic as follows:

Societies appear to be subject, every now and then, to periods of moral panic. A condition, episode, person or group of persons emerges to become defined as a threat to societal values and interests; its nature is presented in a stylized and stereotypical fashion by the mass media; the moral barricades are manned by editors, bishops, politicians and other right-thinking people; socially accredited experts pronounce their diagnoses and solutions; ways of coping are evolved or (more often) resorted to; the condition then disappears, submerges or deteriorates and becomes more visible. Sometimes the object of the panic is quite novel and at other times it is something which has been in existence long enough, but suddenly appears in the limelight. Sometimes the panic passes over and is forgotten, except in folklore and collective memory; at other times it has more serious and long lasting repercussions and might produce such changes as those in legal and social policy or even the way the society conceives itself.[48]

As Stuart Hall notes, moral panics come into effect when anxiety and traditionalism connect with the public definition of crime by the media and are mobilized.[49] Richard Ericson states that the news media typically merely reproduces popular myths about crime, how it is caused, and how it can be controlled.[50] Voumvakis and Ericson suggest that 'newsworkers' tend to report on events that can be fitted to an existing newsworthy theme, and through this process, 'all crime themes have the potential to become crime waves.'[51]

The police are a major source of journalists' information on crime. As 'authorized knowers' they can contribute to the perception that crime waves are occurring in order to gain public support for their legislative and other interests. In addition, as Ericson states, 'While not alone, the police force is instrumental in ensuring that currents of opinion about "law and order" are stirred into tidal waves, and that their organization rides along at the crest of the waves to gain maximum advantage.'[52]

The working up of a moral panic about crime can even occur at times when the violent crime rate has not statistically increased, as was noted earlier. The 3 August 1977 issue of the *Toronto Star*, the day after the paper first reported the boy's murder, contained three front-page articles about the case. The same issue also contained an article titled 'Violent crime rate decreases' buried on page E12.[53]

As Yvonne Ng has discussed, the Jaques murder *was* a tragic event, but that should not detract from understanding how it was also used as a convenient excuse for accomplishing what politicians and police had sought to do for some time. She points out that a similar murder had taken place just off Yonge Street in 1973. Why was there not a massive public outcry when this young boy was found sexually assaulted and murdered? His death was no less tragic. It was simply not politically useful.[54]

The clean-up campaign also contributed to the further identification of homosexuality as a problem at a time when the lesbian and gay liberation movement was growing in strength and numbers, and same-sex couples becoming more publicly visible, particularly in large urban centres like Toronto. Toronto was now home to a significant population of lesbians and gay men, many of whom had established the Church–Wellesley area as their neighbourhood. A lesbian and gay liberation journal, *The Body Politic*, had been launched in 1971, and expanded to an international circulation. Numerous political organizations, including the Canadian Homophile Association of Toronto (CHAT), the Gay Alliance of Toronto (GATE), and the Coalition for Gay Rights in Ontario (CGRO) were in existence, with the purpose of challenging both stereotypes and social marginalization. In response to lesbian and gay pressure, the week prior to Jacques' death, the Ontario Human Rights Commission had released a report recommending the inclusion of sexual orientation as a prohibited ground for discrimination. This recommendation was vehemently attacked by some members of the press. For example, in the 22 July 1977 edition of the *Toronto Sun*, Claire Hoy, notorious for his homophobia, stated, 'I don't want the state teaching my kids the wonders of being a fag. Do you? I believe homosexuality, like alcoholism, is to a large extent a psychological problem, a sickness, and should be treated like one.'[55] The murder of Emanuel Jaques added further vitriolic fuel to the fire, and was regarded by many as the perverted act of homosexual men. The conceptualization of gay men as perverts and pedophiles was reinforced in public discourse, as media coverage of events surrounding the murder and the subsequent trial demonstrated amply. The consequences were immediate.

Where the *Toronto Star* had previously focused on the presence of heterosexual commercial sex in the city, in 1978 it began to report on establishments and services for homosexuals.[56] Now, it seemed, there was a new problem in town. In December 1977, *The Body Politic* published an article by Gerald Hannon entitled 'Men Loving Boys Loving Men.' The following month, police raided the journal's offices. Its publisher, Pink Triangle Press, and its officers were charged under Section 164 of the Criminal Code with the use of the mails to distribute immoral, obscene, indecent, and scurrilous materials. In December 1978 Toronto police began to raid bath houses used by men for sexual encounters (the raids were to continue into the 1980s). Employees and found-ins were charged under bawdy-house legislation, which broadly included the designation of a bawdy-house as any place used for 'acts of indecency.' Police claimed that the sexual activities taking place in the baths included acts of prostitution, an argument used to legitimate the raids and circumvent the supposed reduction in police powers created by the 1968 Criminal Code reform legalizing homosexual activity between two people over the age of twenty-one in private.[57] While the moral panic following the Jacques murder cannot be said to be directly responsible for the raids on *The Body Politic* and the baths, it clearly helped to foster a climate that legitimated repressive police action against gay men. These raids, however, were met with massive resistance from gay men and their supporters, and have been credited with sparking greater cohesion and solidarity among gay men in Toronto. As gays were radicalized by these events, they founded a community.[58]

The Impact on Prostitutes and Reorganization of Prostitution

Prostitutes were scapegoated as sharing a responsibility in the death of Emanuel Jaques; the 'common sense' perspective produced through the moral panic was that if there had not been the prostitutes on Yonge Street, there would not be the men who killed Jaques. As immoral women, prostitutes spread disease and decay wherever they went. Hence the deterioration of Yonge Street. Women arrested for a prostitution-related offence in the aftermath of the Jaques murder found themselves denied bail and detained in the Don Jail before going to trial.[59] Police called for a return of the repealed vagrancy legislation, which would give them the power to pick up women simply for being on the street, and also for the return of capital punishment.[60] While their bid for a return to the vagrancy legislation was unsuccessful, Ericson points out that criminal law is only one of the tools available for the purpose of policing. The moral panic, which the police themselves had helped to produce, legitimated the more intensified policing of prostitutes through existing mechanisms, with the courts and the media acting in concert.[61]

The press used stereotyped characterizations of women working in the sex trade for the characterization of the street itself, as was illustrated in the September 1977 *Maclean's* article, 'Mean Streets':

Call her Josie. In the work-a-night world of commercial sex real names don't matter anyway: Josie is as good a name as any ... The Josies of Yonge Street, predictably, run to a type: young, undereducated, flashily attractive, greedy and, like most whores ... lazy as sin.

The Josies mostly toil one flight up, in sleazy clubs with unimaginative names such as Relaxation Plus, Skin Deep, Venus, or Charlie's angels. There, in their tacky nighties or their wired-up bras and their drop-down panties, they work their shifts. They may pose in the nude for incompetent 'photographers' or sit in the nude and pretend to discuss a client's sexual problems or they may stand in the nude and half-heartedly rub baby-oil on their client's body. But this is all beside the point. The point is extras – masturbation, oral sex, and copulation – which no one connected with the 'industry' really tries to deny anymore. Josie's earnings depend on how many extras she can persuade her client to buy, and how much cash she can extract from him for the service. When she's not 'working' Josie often rationalizes: 'Well, uh, you know, these guys have their problems and we sort of help. I mean, it's like we're all social workers or something.' Or she complains: 'This crackdown won't really change anything, except it's makin' it harder for me to make a buck.' Or she snarls: 'Get stuffed, we've had enough trouble with reporters.' Or she smiles sweetly and says: 'You know, I kind of like the work and the money's good, and besides nobody really gets hurt.' Prostitution is sometimes described as a 'victimless crime.' The Josies of Yonge Street suggest otherwise.[62]

Clearly, this reporter was not implying that the 'Josies' themselves were the objects of repression. However, sex-trade workers were also speaking out, although their perspective had little impact. A woman who worked as an attendant at Charlie's Angels was quoted in the *Toronto Star* as saying, 'It could have happened in Scarborough and nobody would jump, but now a lot of people are going to be I-told-you-so's and want to close us all down ... We all feel terrible about it. But it isn't our fault. You don't get rid of kooks and weirdos who would do things like that by shutting us down.'[63]

As a response to the attack on the sex trade, and the targeting of prostitutes themselves, Canada's first prostitutes' rights organization was formed in Toronto, modelled after those set up in the United States throughout the

1970s. BEAVER (Better End All Vicious Erotic Repression, a name chosen for its acronym) was formed in November 1977. Its mandate was stated straightforwardly on its business card: 'Legitimize the female sex. Decriminalize prostitution.'[64]

Some Toronto feminists also posed an alternative critique of the clean-up campaign and intensified policing of prostitutes. The Toronto Wages for Housework Committee, a feminist organization which was attempting to forge links with prostitutes by comparing the status of homemakers with the status of prostitutes, spoke out against the treatment of the women in the sex trade.[65] This comparison of the roles of the wife and the prostitute drew upon early marxist tradition. As Fredrick Engels had stated in 1884, the wife 'differs little from the ordinary courtesan only in that she does not hire out her body, like a wage worker, on piecework, but sells it into slavery once and for all.'[66] Spokesperson Judith Ramirez stated that 'Less money for women' was what the crackdown was all about.[67]

Ramirez also questioned why Emanuel Jaques was working as a shoeshine boy on Yonge Street in the first place. The fact that the young son of immigrant parents, living in the economically depressed Regent Park area of Toronto, found it necessary to earn money shining shoes on the street said a great deal about the structural organization of class and ethnicity in Canada. Just as women in the sex trade, faced with systemic discrimination on the basis of their gender, their social class, and for women of colour, their race, found a source of income on Yonge Street, so too was Jaques' work on Yonge Street determined by his family's class and ethnic location.

Thousands of people, many from the Portuguese and immigrant communities, marched on Yonge Street after Jaques' death in support of the clean-up campaign. But as Ramirez reported in the Wages for Housework Bulletin, this was not the only issue: 'The issue for most of the immigrants marching ... was the right of any immigrant boy to earn his money on the streets of Toronto. When you come halfway across the world to feed your family, and even young children must help earn the family's wage, the right to safety on the streets is the right to economic survival. And nobody knows what that's all about better than the women of all races and nationalities who are earning their living on the Yonge Streets of Canada.'[68] Ramirez astutely charged that the same politicians who were enforcing the crackdown did nothing to increase the wages of immigrant women working in sweatshops so that their children would not have to work on the streets.

Although the women's movement had long recognized the economic reasons for women entering prostitution, it subordinated this focus to that of viewing the institution as the most direct consequence of patriarchal oppression. As a result, feminist political involvement has been directed toward the need to extract women from the sex trade, rather than working to improve conditions for women within it. Ramirez's analysis was insightful because it began not from the position of prostitution as the sexual degradation of women, but as work that women did because they refused to be poor. She implicitly supported the right of women to work in prostitution, given the social and economic conditions facing them. At the same time, she asserted that sex work was becoming a source of concern for politicians because it was becoming acceptable and visible. Said Ramirez; 'the politicians' primary aim is clearly to bring hookers back in line because prostitution is losing its stigma. Hookers have become too visible, too upfront, and too *numerous*. Housewives are doing it for extra spending money. Students are doing it to put themselves through school. And young girls are getting into it because it beats being a cashier or a file clerk.'[69]

Similarly, Carol Smart has noted of the moral panic around street solicitation in late 1950s Britain: 'The prostitute could no longer be held as a class apart from respectable women; the separate spheres were merging, and in this way the prostitute became more of a threat to respectable family lifestyles.'[70] Both Ramirez and Smart direct our attention to the problematization of prostitution within the context of shifting gender relations, particularly women's growing autonomy, a shift that had intensified into a serious split by the late 1970s.

In her own work on moral panics, Smart notes that events concerning prostitution in 1950s Britain developed in two phases; the first leading to the inclusion of street solicitation in the Wolfenden Committee's agenda. This phase was a product of concerns about the potential disgrace to the nation that would be brought on by the spectacle of street solicitation, as tourists gathered in England for the Queen's coronation. Following this, increasing allegations that non-white men were living on the avails of the prostitution of white women, linked prostitution and immigration as related social problems. The racial, immigration, gender, and class fears of the dominant English white group fused to create an urgent new social problem. The second phase began with the release of the Wolfenden Report, which justified an expansion of police powers in order to curb the problem of street solicitation. Smart's interpretation of the role of a government commission as both intended cure and springboard for further campaigns against prostitution is an important one for the forthcoming analysis.

The moral panic about the indoor sex industry in Toronto and other Canadian cities changed the form of the business of prostitution, as massage parlours and other establishments were regulated out of existence. It was precisely because prostitution is work that women in prostitution were compelled to find alternative places to conduct their business. From the standpoint of those who supported the campaign to shut down sex-related businesses, the campaign was successful in removing a moral stain on the face of the city. From the standpoint of prostitutes, however, the campaign reorganized their work relations, requiring them to find other indoor venues, and more problematically, shifting many of them onto the streets.

The analysis presented here does not underestimate the importance of economic forces in the organization of social relations. I have also attempted to demonstrate the critical character of ideological shifts around sexuality and sex-related conduct that brought the moral framework of society into question. The murder of a young boy provided a trigger for various agencies and levels of the Canadian state to act in concert in reasserting control over the sexual affairs of the nation.

3

The Problem of Street Solicitation

The indoor sex industry did not collapse with the closing of massage parlours and encounter studios. As quickly as these enterprises closed, escort services began to appear in Canadian cities. These services were somewhat more discreet in advertising the type of service provided, although a quick glance through the Yellow Pages would leave no doubt as to their intent. Because the services themselves were not provided in fixed locations, but in places arranged between the escort and customer, these businesses were more difficult to prosecute under bawdy-house legislation than the massage parlours had been. The scrutiny of prostitutes by police, the courts, politicians, and the public returned to those working the streets of major Canadian cities. As the 'battle' over the streets heated up, debate focused on the adequacy of the Criminal Code of Canada in regulating the sale of sex in public streets.[1]

By the time that street solicitation began to be regarded as a major urban problem, the economic downturn of the early 1970s had become a deep economic recession. Global economic conditions were such that capitalism was regarded as being in crisis. Politically, the forces of conservativism were on the rise in Canada, as they were in all western industrialized countries. High unemployment, increasing inflation, declining real income, a growing government deficit, cutbacks in social service programs, and fear of crime characterized this period, as new global economic forces initiated the restructuring of national economies.[2]

Given the crackdown on indoor businesses and the impact of the economic recession on female employment, it is not surprising that street solicitation should appear to increase in urban centres. The key issues became the *visibility* of prostitution and the *control of the streets*. A single legal decision was blamed by police and politicians for causing the problem of street solicitation in Canadian cities from 1978 onward. The following discussion demonstrates that a change in the law was but one (and certainly not the most important) reason why street level prostitution came to be considered a major social problem in this period. After exploring the legal struggles surrounding street solicitation, I will introduce more pertinent elements in the trouble-making process, particularly policing decisions, the role of the media, and the constitution of social class, not to mention the effects of the economic recession. The power of the law can only be understood within the context of these related institutional and economic power relations that, as we shall see, actually determine the shape of law.

The Struggle over Law

In 1978 the Supreme Court of Canada ruled in *Regina v. Hutt* that street solicitation must be 'pressing and persistent' to constitute an offence. A single proposition was no longer sufficient grounds for arrest. Furthermore, the court ruled that the act of solicitation must occur in a public place, and that the interior of a motor vehicle could not be considered as such.[3] This ruling effectively gutted the solicitation legislation under Section 195.1 of the Criminal Code, and severely limited the powers of police and their practice of entrapping prostitutes in unmarked cars (entrapment is not illegal in Canada).[4]

Angry police, local level politicians, and a much publicized residents' association combatting street solicitation in their Vancouver neighbourhood – The Concerned Residents of the West End (CROWE) – asserted that the ruling resulted in a growth of street solicitation in their communities. Municipal governments in Calgary, Vancouver, Toronto, Montreal, Niagara Falls, Regina, Saskatoon, and Halifax attempted to take control at the local level through the introduction of city bylaws prohibiting street solicitation. However, these bylaws were found to contravene the constitutional division of powers, which granted the federal government sole authority in the administration of criminal law. The *Hutt* decision had not overturned the existing legislation; rather it had made it much more difficult to enforce.

A 1981 Alberta Supreme Court ruling established that such bylaws were beyond the power of the provinces. In the *Westendrop* appeal, defence council succeeded in overturning the conviction of a woman charged with unlawfully using the streets for the purpose of prostitution under the Highway Traffic Act of the city of Calgary. While the purpose of this bylaw was said to be the control of the streets, notably absent were other forms of disturbance such as swearing or fighting. The defence counsel was thus able to establish that the bylaw's real intention was to prosecute prostitutes. This bylaw and Section 195.1 of the Criminal Code shared the same purpose, and the bylaw could not 'stand in the face of Section 195.1.'[5] As a result the defendant's conviction was overturned on the grounds that the bylaw was *ultra vires*. Numerous other cities had or were considering similar bylaws but put further action on hold while awaiting the results of Calgary's Appeal to the Supreme Court of Canada. During 1982, the most prevalent debate on prostitution in the Canadian mainstream press was whether the regulation of street solicitation was best left to local-level legislation or to Criminal Code provisions controlled by the federal government.[6] The Supreme Court of Canada eventually upheld the Alberta decision. Chief Justice Bora Laskin stated in his subsequent ruling on the case in January 1983: 'however desirable it may be for the municipality to control or prohibit prostitution, there has been an over-reaching in the present case which offends the division of legislative powers.'[7]

Following the Supreme Court of Alberta ruling, the federal Liberal government once again had to address the regulation of street solicitation as a result of limitations in the enforcement of S.195.1 created by the *Hutt* decision. In 1982 however, in anticipation of the Supreme Court of Canada decision on the use of city bylaws, Justice Minister Mark MacGuigan referred the issue to the House of Commons Standing Committee on Justice and Legal Affairs for public discussion. This move was taken in an attempt to reach a compromise position that would resolve the mounting tensions between federal, provincial, and municipal levels of the Canadian state. The mandate of the committee was a narrow one, addressing only the regulation of street solicitation, rather than the regulation of prostitution generally.

Two opposing positions appeared in the briefs presented to the Standing Committee. The procriminalization camp consisted primarily of chiefs of police, city mayors, and members of CROWE, who argued that further criminal legislation was needed to regain control over the streets. Those opposing criminalization were primarily representatives of feminist organizations, as well as civil libertarians and lawyers, who were concerned about the impact of restrictive legislation on women in prostitution, and potentially, on civil liberties.

Police complained that they were unable to intervene on behalf of the residents of affected neighbourhoods because of the *Hutt* decision. In 1979 the Canadian Association of Police Chiefs had recommended that the powers of Section 195.1 be expanded by eliminating the need to prove that solicitation had been pressing and persistent, considering a motor vehicle to be a public place, and prosecuting men as well as women for soliciting. This position was supported in submissions to the Standing Committee from the Mayors of Vancouver, Calgary, Niagara Falls, Regina, Victoria, Halifax, and Edmonton, and the Progressive Conservative Party of Canada. However, it was Vancouver that dominated the media spotlight and CROWE that spoke as the main voice of the affected public during the committee's deliberations. Indeed, through the attention of the national media, CROWE was to play a significant role in the constitution of street solicitation as a social problem during the early 1980s.

CROWE stated that up to 100 prostitutes frequented the West End on a regular basis, depending on the time of day and weather conditions.[8] Beyond the alleged decrease in property values, they argued that street prostitution was responsible for increased traffic and trespassing problems, and that residents were being harassed by prostitutes and their customers. Further, such visible prostitution gave local young people a bad example. There was, they claimed, a decrease in police authority and an increase in crime and violence. Finally, street prostitution was detrimental to local businesses since sex shops, strip clubs, and related businesses were moving into the area.[9] CROWE's 1982 submission to the Standing Committee included an article entitled 'Broken Windows' by James Q. Wilson and George L. Kelling, just published in the March issue of *The Atlantic*. CROWE asserted that 'Each prostitute is like a broken window that says no one cares.'[10] They stated that inadequate police control of a neighbourhood heightened anxieties among residents, as the perception arose that the area was fair game for criminal activity. This ultimately led to the disintegration of the neighbourhood and the declining morale of its residents.

Residents claimed that they were being 'held hostage' by prostitutes and their clients, and that the streets were now dangerous because of the type of people who had been attracted to the area. Because of this, some residents were themselves beginning to resort to violence. The committee was told that vigilante actions on the part of residents would likely have occurred had CROWE not been established to address the concerns of residents.[11] Despite the campaign launched by CROWE, a January 1984 survey of Greater Vancouver residents indicated that only 20 per cent believed that prostitutes should be 'run off the streets.' Although the vast majority believed that some curbs should be put on prostitutes' activities, they also believed that prostitution was a necessary service.[12]

By contrast, feminists and civil libertarians advocated the partial decriminalization of prostitution, through the repeal of the soliciting legislation and amendments to the bawdy-house legislation, so that women working in prostitution could remain indoors. These groups included the National Action Committee on the Status of Women, the National Association of Women and the Law, the Elizabeth Fry Society, the Vancouver Coalition for a Non-Sexist Criminal Code, the Status of Women Action Group (BC), the Women's Caucus of the British Columbia Law Union, the British Columbia New Democratic Party Women's Rights Committee, as well as Ottawa Mayor Marion Dewar. The committee also heard from the British Columbia Civil Liberties Association, civil rights lawyer Clayton Ruby, and barrister Priscilla Platt. They took the position that street solicitation is not in itself a criminal activity, just as prostitution itself is not a crime. Rather, any problems created by street solicitation could be regulated by other sections of the Criminal Code, including S.171 – Causing a Disturbance, Indecent Exhibition, Loitering, etc.; S.169 – Indecent Acts; S.305 – Extortion; and S.381 – Intimidation; as well as through the use of municipal bylaws concerning residential tenancy, motor vehicles, and zoning. They asserted that in any case it was mainly customers and onlookers who caused the disturbances associated with street solicitations. Feminist organizations did not challenge the procuring and living on avails legislation because it was considered a useful tool for the prosecution of men who financially and sexually exploited women. Prostitution involving young people could also be addressed through S.166 – Procuring Defilement, and through the expansion of provisions for social service delivery and educational programs.

In the Standing Committee debates, both the pro- and anticriminalization advocates made occasional references to the need to address prostitution involving young people. However, these almost always referred to abstract, rather than specific instances. This suggests that prostitution involving young people at this time was not considered to be a significant social problem by city officials, police, and residents' groups intent on eliminating prostitution from urban streets.

At the same time, the Standing Committee was hearing debate on Bill C-53, a massive compilation of legislative proposals for the overhaul of sex-related and morals legislation, including rape/sexual assault, pornography, and sexual offences involving young people. Some organizations and officials were appearing for both (consideration of street solicitation had been added to the Bill C-53 hearings through political pressure from CROWE). Independent of these proceedings, the Badgley Committee was in the process of studying sexual abuse involving children and youths (see Chapter 6). Finally, the Juvenile Delinquents Act was in the process of being replaced by the Young Offenders Act. Given that prostitution involving young people was paid little heed in public discussions and the media of the day, probably these simultaneous proceedings were to some extent responsible for the attention it received, albeit limited, during the Standing Committee hearings on street solicitation. The dominant agenda, however, shaped by procriminalization advocates, focused on prostitutes as disruptive adults deserving of punitive state action.

Street solicitation was an activity occurring on relatively few streets in perhaps a half-dozen Canadian cities. However, through public and media attention it became identified as a national social problem. Feminist organizations questioned the necessity of using a federal criminal law to tackle a geographically specific, localized activity. They also charged that the legislation reflected a moral and discriminatory bias in punishing the most disadvantaged women – those who worked the streets – while doing nothing to address the social and economic problems that underlay prostitution. As Eleanor McDonald of the Elizabeth Fry Society stated, 'We always fall back on more police powers, more jails, more punitive powers, and all you get is more jails, more people with criminal records.'[13]

The House of Commons Standing Committee on Justice and Legal Affairs delivered its report in May 1982. It recommended that:

- Section 195.1 be amended to specify that both the prostitute and the customer be liable for prosecution for soliciting.
- The definition of a public place be broadened to include motor vehicles and private places on public view.
- A new statute be created making it an offence to offer or accept an offer to engage in prostitution in a public place, thereby removing the requirement for proof of pressing and persistent conduct.
- A new statute be created making it a criminal offence to engage in prostitution with a person under eighteen, whether or not the prostitute was known to be under eighteen.
- Once these recommendations were made law, they would be reviewed within three years, requiring the monitoring of their operation from the date of their proclamation.

The committee also noted its limited scope, which was to address only street solicitation. As its report stated: 'constrained as it is by its terms of reference, the committee has not attempted to deal with prostitution at large. It is a very contentious issue, involving broad social and economic issues. It warrants complete review in the near future.'[14]

Rather than accepting the report as a whole, in June 1983 MacGuigan proposed to amend the Criminal Code to bring only two of the recommendations into effect. Those who obtained the services of a prostitute would now be liable for prosecution, and a motor vehicle would be considered a public place.[15] These two measures would have limited impact, however, because the requirement of proof of pressing and persistent solicitation remained unchanged. At the same time that the Justice Minister tabled the bill, he announced the appointment of the Special Committee on Pornography and Prostitution (the Fraser Committee), that, as part of its mandate, was to further attempt to find a basis of consensus on street solicitation, as well as to address the wider issue of prostitution itself. The soliciting legislation was not the only prostitution-related statute causing problems for the courts, however. Procuring and bawdy-house provisions were broad enough to be interpreted in different ways by the courts, largely because they had been drafted in the late nineteenth and early twentieth centuries, when judicial support for a common moral standard was presumed to be in place. As we have seen, this confusion was compounded by the structure of the Canadian legal system itself, given the division of legislative authority between the central (federal) and subcentral (provincial and municipal) levels of government. In practice, this system has allowed for differing interpretations of legislation by the respective judiciaries of the provinces. As a result, the legal control of prostitution-related activities has become a complex and contradictory affair. Even though prostitution legislation is properly the domain of the federal government, the breadth for interpretation of the legislation leaves a lot up to individual judges in their respective judicial realms. Prior to 1982, there were three main areas of contradiction in prostitution-related legislation; first, what constitutes a bawdy-house; second, whether male customers could solicit; and third, whether men could be legally defined as prostitutes.

First, Section 193 of the Criminal Code – keeping a common bawdy-house – is sufficiently vague to have resulted in different interpretations as to what constitutes a bawdy-house, although in *The Queen. v. Patterson* (1972), the Supreme Court of Canada ruled that proof must be made of 'frequent or habitual use' of a premise for the purpose of prostitution.[16]

Second, S.195.1 did not specify whether customers or prospective customers could be charged with soliciting. In 1978 the Chief Justice of Ontario ruled in *R. v. DiPaola* that a customer could indeed be convicted of soliciting for the purpose of prostitution.[17] In the same year however, the British Columbia Court of Appeal in *R. v. Dudak* overturned the defendant's conviction by stating that only the person who potentially will receive or actually receives payment can be charged with soliciting, and moreover, that the client does not prostitute himself; he is merely satisfying a desire.[18]

Interpretations also differed as to whether a male could be considered a prostitute. In *R. v. Patterson* (1972), the Ontario County Court acquitted a man of soliciting because of his sex, as dictionary definitions defined a prostitute as a female person. In the following year the Supreme Court of British Columbia found a man guilty of the charge in *R. v. Obey*. The offence, it stated, was soliciting in a public place; it was irrelevant whether or not an act of prostitution actually took place.[19]

One of these uncertainties was resolved when Bill C-127 was proclaimed in January 1983, which specified that either sex could be a prostitute. It also made other ambiguous aspects of prostitution-related legislation more specific by stating that any person, rather than only women, who is not a common prostitute or person of known immoral character was to be protected under procuring legislation. As part of the move to gender neutrality in law initiated by the Royal Commission on the Status of Women, the bill further clarified that any person, rather than only men, could be charged with living on the avails of prostitution, a subsection of the procuring statute.[20]

MacGuigan's compromise solution was considered unsatisfactory from both sides of the debate. The Tory justice critic referred to it as a 'green light for hookers' while BC Attorney General Brian Smith stated, 'We are going to declare war on these people and drive them off the streets.'[21] On the other hand, it was clearly not a plan that the decriminalization forces could accept.[22]

A 'National' Problem Emerges

At the same time, residents' groups in Montreal, Toronto, and Halifax began to emulate the practices of CROWE as they complained that prostitutes had moved beyond their traditional areas of business and into their residential neighbourhoods. In Toronto, the major area for street soliciting, known as 'the track,' was a downtown, heavily residential area bordered by Bloor, Yonge, Carlton, and Sherbourne Streets. According to a 1981 city census, 80 per cent of the residents were between the ages of twenty and fifty-four, and were primarily employed in the professions.[23] One woman revealed a great deal about developing tensions in this area when she stated, 'I feel like prostitution is here to stay but I just wish it wasn't in my area where I own a very expensive house.'[24] A March 1985 *Globe and Mail* article entitled 'The Other Side of the Track' described the attractions of the area for upscale consumers, as well as the problems that the urban middle class was encountering as they went about their dining and shopping. For example, restaurant owners were considering laying trespassing charges against prostitutes who entered their premises.[25]

Media reporting once again played a substantial part in helping to construct a 'prostitution crisis,' as the *Toronto Star* called its three-part series in December 1984. Part One of the series began with the sensationalist claim that, according to a Metro police officer, prostitution had 'run wild' in the downtown area, and there were now several *thousand* prostitutes on downtown streets, at least two thousand of whom were under the age of eighteen.[26] Again, police raised the spectre of organized crime controlling much of the trade, lumping it together with drug trafficking and other forms of criminal activity. The mayor of Toronto, Art Eggleton, was of course anxious to maintain the city's image as 'Toronto the Good': 'symbolically, I don't want Toronto known as the city of red lights ... We have an image as a *good* city and we don't want to see it tarnished.'[27]

Toronto police and city officials were developing alternative measures to the soliciting legislation to deal with prostitution on city streets. According to a *Toronto Star* report, Metro police stated that they had laid 650 soliciting charges in 1980 but could not get convictions from the courts. By 1983 soliciting arrests were down to 51, because police claimed they had given up trying to enforce the legislation. Prostitutes' rights activists and civil libertarians challenged that the police deliberately refrained from pursuing other legislative strategies in order to heat up tensions and force the government to enact new legislation that would restore their power of arrest. However, in mid-September 1984, Metro Toronto police 'unleashed' a twenty-nine-member task force into the track 'in an attempt to harass both prostitutes and customers off the streets.'[28] Police stated that they had attempted to charge women with loitering, but the Ontario Court of Appeal had eliminated this approach. In May 1983 the court had found that prostitutes were not loitering as they were there for a specific purpose. In his decision the judge reasoned that if this law were used against prostitutes, it could be used against anyone standing on public streets, including a person waiting to meet a friend, or politicians shaking hands.[29]

The city also attempted to limit the flow of traffic in the track caused by customers and onlookers, including carloads of young men who seemingly regarded prostitutes as a tourist attraction and the deserving targets of insults hurled from car windows. However, changing street directions with no-turn and one-way signs meant that prostitutes merely shifted streets, and residents had to pass through a frustrating maze of one-way streets to get to and from their homes.[30] In Toronto and Vancouver, many women residents asserted that it was not prostitutes who were so much the problem as customers who were sexually harassing women residents. The shift of prostitutes onto the streets had also shifted the site of negotiation, as well as official regulation, from business entities to the body of the prostitute.

In Ottawa, by 1983, police began to claim that prostitution was increasing, and area residents began to complain of finding condoms on their lawns. Suddenly, something had to be done about prostitution.[31] In Halifax, an official claimed that street solicitation was harming tourism, while the primarily young professionals residing in the city's renovated waterfront area made complaints similar to those heard in Toronto and Vancouver. In November 1984 the Nova Scotia government posted a public notice naming forty-seven Halifax women as prostitutes. Eighty copies of the notice were placed on utility poles in the downtown core, and the list was also published in a city newspaper. The notice advised the women that they were named as defendants by the Attorney General's Office in an interlocutory injunction. The injunction attempted to ban them from creating a public nuisance in the downtown area. The police constable who provided the women's names for the injunction swore an affidavit attesting that most of the women had told him they were prostitutes, and also claimed that he could identify women in the business because they had 'a distinct way of dressing and have a certain method of bending at the waist to make eye contact with passing motorists, particularly lone males.' The injunction against the women named would prevent them and others from causing a nuisance through 'conduct apparently for the purpose of prostitution ... trespassing, loitering, littering, fighting, screaming, swearing, assaulting, harassing, impeding, or obstructing.' A lawyer representing one of the women stated, 'If they can get an injunction for this, they can get one for picketing, peace demonstrations or whatever they want.'[32] While the overall constitutionality of the injunction was certainly in question, it was eventually rejected by a provincial court justice who reviewed the proposal and determined that alternative, less sweeping remedies were available. One of the women publicly identified as a prostitute by the Halifax injunction wrote a letter to a city newspaper about the effects that this public exposure had on her life: the humiliation of her family, loss of her job, and potential eviction from her home. She said that over half of the women identified were single mothers on social assistance, and that while this kind of tactic would scare some of the women away, the rest would have to take the risks and continue working the streets through economic necessity.[33]

Halifax's injunction was similar to one obtained in British Columbia earlier that year. In July 1984 BC Attorney General Brian Smith won a court injunction to ban prostitutes from the West End. It identified street boundaries defining a no-business zone, and named thirty people as public nuisances, seeking damages against them, and ordering them to stay out of the area. As in Halifax some months later, their names were made public in newspapers and on lamp posts. West End residents also took matters into their own hands by starting a vigilante program called 'Shame the Johns,' which attempted to scare customers of prostitutes out of the area through public humiliation. Among other tactics, they threatened to harass men who patronized juvenile prostitutes by writing letters to their homes, following them home, and exposing them in their workplaces.[34]

Niagara Falls residents and politicians asserted that prostitutes, mainly from the United States, were tarnishing its 'Honeymoon Capital' and family image. The potential impact on tourism was stated as a prime concern, although there was no proof that tourism had yet been affected. The relation between this concern and the media's apparent willingness to report any alleged problem was (perhaps inadvertently) revealed by a spokesperson for the Niagara Falls Visitor and Convention Bureau, who said to a *Toronto Star* reporter: 'The media call me up and say, "Hey, I understand you've got a prostitution problem," but tour operators don't call me up to tell me they're hesitant about booking a tour because of our prostitutes.'[35]

Niagara Falls' main solicitation district was two kilometres from the hotel area of the city, but police claimed that some of the bolder women were moving into the tourist area itself. The city had two prostitution areas, one populated by local women and the other, by Americans. Politicians and police reported that one could find up to one hundred prostitutes on the streets on a summer weekend evening, the majority of whom were from the United States but who preferred to work in Canada to evade tougher New York State legislation and the higher incidence of violence in Buffalo.[36] Here again, prostitutes were blamed for an alleged increase in other criminal activity. For example, a September 1985 article in the *Toronto Star* referred both to the murder the previous month of a prostitute in Niagara Falls, and to the assault and robbery of a man four days later. The article did not state whether a prostitute was involved in the latter event. The assault was used to claim that the women were bringing with them drug, weapon-related, and robbery offences. In this article, which linked the murder to these other offences, the victim appeared responsible, not only for her own death, but also for tarnishing the city's image and encouraging other criminal activity. According to this article, prostitutes plied their trade 'in a sleazy downtown district that is getting sleazier each day.'[37]

Petitions were circulated in Niagara Falls demanding that the federal government impose stricter legislation, as reports were made of women flashing, disrobing, and having sexual intercourse in the street. As one woman stated, 'They're not just morally bad, they're wicked ... and they've got the nerve of the devil.' Stated another, 'Even in the daytime you're afraid to walk the street for fear they'll grab your handbag.'[38] Certainly, deteriorating economic conditions can exacerbate the fear of crime, thus encouraging the perception of a 'factual' linkage of spurious events. In addition, a Canadian Centre for Justice Statistics study of crime between 1978 and 1981 revealed that the overall crime rate was indeed increasing. Criminologist Ian Taylor noted that only murder, soliciting for the purpose of prostitution, and illegal gambling rates did not increase in this period, while crimes against property were up 34 per cent. These figures do not necessarily indicate a change in the incidence of an activity, but may, as with soliciting arrests, reflect a change in legislative or policing strategies.[39] Regardless of its real or imagined character, public belief that an increase in crime has occurred, and a general deterioration of economic and social conditions provide fertile conditions for seeking convenient answers. For residents in affected areas, the fear of crime may be exacerbated by the visible presence of prostitution. This fear was clear in CROWE's statement to the House of Commons Standing Committee on Justice and Legal Affairs. It was in evidence in Toronto's report on 'places of amusement' discussed in Chapter 2, which anticipated a 'psychological crisis' if the problem of prostitution was not addressed. These fears were perhaps intensified by the shifting and uncertain character of sexual and moral terrain.

Police, city officials, and residents stated that only a clear federal law would solve the problem of street solicitation. In the midst of this, during the latter part of 1983 and early 1984, the Fraser Committee travelled across the country holding public hearings in Canadian cities. It heard from dozens of organizations, individuals, and officials both for and against criminalization, keeping prostitution a front-page issue.[40]

Making the Problem: Beyond the Law

This chapter began with the statement that street solicitation was commonly perceived as a problem created by judicial decisions that determined the shape of the law, and requiring, therefore, a legislative solution. As I indicated, however, this approach neglects to consider economic shifts, the role of policing, media reporting, and the constitution of social class as elements of the trouble-making process. The procriminalization forces clearly blamed the change in the interpretation of soliciting legislation following the *Hutt* decision, for the perceived increase in street solicitation in major Canadian cities. While the interpretation of the soliciting section of the Criminal Code indeed became more specific and therefore less restrictive to prostitutes in the late 1970s, this explanation remains insufficient. First, it does not account for other developments, including the economic recession and a resulting contraction in the female labour market that drove prostitutes onto the streets to conduct their business. While Vancouver's West End residents were enjoying a relatively high standard of living in the early 1980s, one out of five people in British Columbia were living on welfare or unemployment insurance, a figure that did not include many of the 'hidden unemployed' – those who had either given up the job search or for some reason did not qualify for unemployment insurance or welfare benefits.[41] As the Alliance for the Safety of Prostitutes (ASP), a Vancouver prostitutes' rights organization, stated: 'We find more and more women out there, some who haven't been on the streets for years, turning to prostitution out of economic necessity. Women who were earning a wage but lost their job, have run out of UIC benefits and now are on welfare ... One woman who receives $420 monthly has to pay $380 in rent ... so she supplements her income by prostitution.'[42] There was a notable absence of concern among the procriminalization forces as to who the prostitutes were and how they came to be on the streets. Although they advocated an improvement in the general quality of life, they ignored the bases of social inequality that continue to prevent this goal from being realized. This inconsistency goes unrecognized because prostitution is regarded as a threat to the quality of life, rather than a reflection of it. Second, holding reduced policing responsible for the increase in street solicitation overlooks changes in public perception. Street prostitution came to be seen as a problem during this period when it infringed on areas whose class character afforded residents the privilege of public protest, media attention, and government response.[43]

Vancouver criminologist John Lowman has tracked street solicitation's emergence as a social problem in Vancouver in the late 1970s and early 1980s. Prior to 1975, Vancouver had two 'notorious' cabaret clubs, each frequented by from fifty to one hundred prostitutes per night. In 1975 one of these clubs was closed by police after a lengthy investigation. The other was destroyed by fire under suspicious circumstances during a similar police investigation. As a result of these closures, prostitutes were displaced onto the streets. This occurred *prior* to the changes in interpretation of the street solicitation legislation. Prostitutes shifted into both previously established areas of street solicitation, and more problematically, created two new 'track' locations in the West End of the city. Residents and business groups in the middle-class residential area of the West End quickly responded to this influx by pressuring police and city council for a 'clean-up'; a public outcry which Lowman found had *not* occurred when street solicitation had been confined to the 'less salubrious' areas of the downtown core.[44] Prostitution, then, was not a new problem to Vancouver, but only new to certain areas whose residents had some political clout. The media too played a significant role in manufacturing prostitution as a 'new' social problem in the later period, although it was only new to particular areas.

In 1978 four Calgary massage parlours which employed from twenty-five to forty women at any given time had been raided and closed. Bank accounts and safety deposit boxes were frozen pending investigation, and some women had no choice but to go on welfare. Again a pattern of displacement resulted, including relocation to other indoor businesses, and a dispersion of the women into other major Canadian cities.[45] (One of the women who worked in these parlours was later murdered while working the streets in Vancouver.) Following this, in 1978 the city of Calgary strengthened its bylaws regulating massage parlours and the increasingly popular escort services, and raised licence fees to exorbitant rates. This attempt to curb the operation and proliferation of such businesses, despite their relative invisibility, cut further the available options for women to work indoors, out of public view.[46] While prostitution decreased in Calgary once the city's boom years were over, the chairperson of the Calgary Police Commission, Brian Scott, claimed that Calgary's street solicitation problem returned full force after the Supreme Court ruled in 1981 that the city's bylaw was unconstitutional. However, if there was indeed an increase in street solicitation, it could be attributed to the city's crackdown on massage parlours and escort services, not to mention the province's economic recession and its impact on women.

In Toronto, the clean-up of indoor businesses in 1977 resulted in many prostitutes moving their trade to the streets of a primarily residential area east of Yonge Street, despite the prohibitive interpretation of the soliciting legislation then in place. However, prostitutes had been conducting their business in this area for many years. Once a neighbourhood of stately Victorian homes, the middle and upper classes had relocated to the north and west reaches of the city during Toronto's rapid industrialization in the first decades of the twentieth century. These inner-city dwellings were then converted to multiple family units and rooming houses for the working class and poor. However, as Jon Caulfield comments in his book *City Form and Everyday Life*, by the 1970s Toronto was beginning to undergo significant urban restructuring, which entailed both a process of deindustrialization (thereby making the working class 'irrelevant') and middle-class resettlement of the inner city. It was only when middle-class professionals were again attracted to the area, now known as Cabbagetown, that tensions began to heat up.[47] The gentrifiers may be regarded as reclaiming this area for the middle class after decades of absence, as Caulfield comments, but for this new urban professional middle class, the issue was not simply one of their pre-existing class privilege; the elimination of prostitutes, as with the gentrification of downtown neighbourhoods, was part of the process of the *constitution* of class in the postmodern city. This constitution merged respectability, consumption, good taste, and image as a particular 'moral repertoire'; a repertoire that was part of the establishment of the middle class as a class *for* itself[48] in Toronto's new 'corporate economy and culture.'[49]

The move of prostitutes onto the streets of Vancouver, Toronto, and Calgary is therefore what Lowman referred to in the Vancouver events as a 'derivative problem.' Court decisions respecting the interpretation of legislation were of secondary importance in the increasing numbers working the streets in some Canadian cities. These eventual decisions merely meant that attempts to curb the derivative problem were rendered ineffective. In Toronto and Halifax, prostitution also came to be seen as a problem as a result of changing urban environments with a particular class character. In Ottawa and Niagara Falls, there is some evidence that a 'problem' was created through media reporting of situations in other cities. While pockets of street solicitation already existed in these cities, they were elevated from a limited presence and concern to a major social problem. Ottawa's prostitution 'problem' emerged in the context of two developments. First, from the late 1970s the traditionally working-class francophone area of the Byward Market (lowertown) began to go through a process of transformation as it was gentrified by the middle class. Second, extensive media coverage of events in other cities turned the attention of reporters and residents to the market area, where street solicitation occurred on a relatively small scale.

In summary, the federal state had a double purpose in the regulation of prostitution. It was confronted with the practical task of providing the legislative tools for clearing the streets of what was for some a nuisance and others a moral affront. But as well, the government had the underlying purpose of buttressing state legitimacy in the moral regulatory field. The imperative of doing so was perhaps made more critical at a time when its economic regulatory function, based since the 1930s on the Keynsian mixed economy, was in crisis as a 'new' global economy and politic began to supplant it.[50] Certainly, however, the federal state was in the process of overhauling virtually all of its sex- and morals-related legislation, the key motivator for which was the pressure of feminist organizations for more comprehensive rape, assault, pornography, sexual abuse, and incest legislation. The 1980s were a high point in the reformulation of protective legislation concerning women and children, to a degree not seen since the pre–World War 1 period. The issue of prostitution was, however, the odd case.

Where further state protective legislation against male violence was being advocated in other areas, feminist organizations demanded that street solicitation be decriminalized in order to, in effect, protect prostitutes from the punitive powers of the state. As well, prostitutes' rights organizations appeared, created by sex workers who argued that the women and men of the trade were practising a legitimate profession. Most notably, Peggy Miller formed the Canadian Organization for the Rights of Prostitutes (CORP), an organization for sex workers only, after she was charged under the bawdy-house statute for entertaining customers in her home.[51] In Vancouver, the Alliance for the Safety of Prostitutes (ASP) was formed by women inside and outside of the sex trade, and chapters soon followed in Calgary and, briefly, in Toronto. At the same time, a contradictory position was being more loudly voiced both from within the state apparatus – local-level officials and police – and from some residents, who asserted that they required protection from prostitutes. Therefore, there was no clear regulatory approach, such as that which the Jaques murder had provided an impetus for in Toronto in 1977. The Special Committee on Pornography and Prostitution (the Fraser Committee) was appointed by the federal government to provide a means of balancing the interests of these competing forces. In the process, the committee was to reconstruct a fragile hegemony affirming the state's ability to regulate public moral conduct.

4

The Special Committee on Pornography and Prostitution (The Fraser Committee)

'Between State and Society': The Place of Government Commissions[1]

As discussed in the previous chapter, the federal government attempted to address street solicitation by referring the issue to the House of Commons Standing Committee on Justice and Legal Affairs. However, upon completion of their work, the standing committee noted that it had been constrained by its mandate, and that a much fuller investigation of prostitution was required to explore all aspects of the problem, rather than only street solicitation. The Special Committee on Pornography and Prostitution (the Fraser Committee, named after its chairperson) was appointed in June 1983 to accomplish this end.[2] The appointment of the Fraser Committee could be said to serve a number of objectives. From a cynical vantage point, it could be regarded as a stalling tactic, that moved two controversial issues off the federal government agenda during an election year. From a pluralist perspective, it could also be regarded as a means by which the federal state attempted to consider the opinions of interested Canadians and arrive at a compromise, given the significant disagreement about both pornography and prostitution. John McLaren, who was a member of the committee, notes that the federal government had to recognize that these issues could *not* be sidetracked, given the emphasis of a broad-based women's movement on pornography and the 'significant alliance of the Association of Canadian Police Chiefs, the mayors of most large Canadian cities, and the articulate and well-organized community groups, such as the Concerned Residents of the West End in Vancouver,' which ensured that prostitution would remain on the political stage.[3]

Neither of these perspectives is necessarily precluded by the analysis developed here. However, we need to be cognizant of how government commissions have become intrinsic to 'the process of creating the idea of the state' by being used to address social problems, as Adam Ashforth contends.[4] The government is able to take a seemingly non-political approach to these issues by appointing a committee of 'experts' to evaluate the problem at hand. It thereby shores up state legitimacy by producing 'a rational and scientific administrative discourse out of the raw materials of political struggle and debate,' presumably for the common good.[5] This 'arm's length' approach to tackling problems lends the appearance of neutrality, reinforcing the idea of a democratic, pluralist state that is responsive to its public. However, these commissions are a contemporary example of hegemony in action.

The work of the Fraser Committee provides a case in point. First, its definitional and regulatory work was limited by its mandate; a mandate predisposed to legal solutions to the problem of prostitution. Therefore, while the federal government was able to present an image of neutrality and non-interference into the work of the committee, the mandate that it had established broadly guaranteed a particular kind of outcome. Second, fulfilling its mandate required the committee to reassess private/public distinctions in legislation. While the law is largely used to regulate the public domain, the state, which operates in part through law, may shift the definitional boundaries of public and private. Through the work of government commissions, we can recognize the culturally and historically relative character of what is understood to be public and private space, and how much disagreement there is about what belongs in each category. As Annette Kuhn argues:

What is as stake in the public/private distinction, and in definitional struggles across the various social discourses which concretely construct such a distinction, is, I would argue, nothing less than the regulation of the social order. The law may be regarded as the privileged site of expression of the code public/private, in that it constantly constructs distinctions between public and private as bases for its peculiarly authoritative discourse of regulation. In general, in dividing the public from the private, legal discourses set out the terms for regulation of the former: they regulate the social order, in other words. In the moment in which legal discourse constructs a public domain, it draws the contents of that domain into the ambit of regulation and control.[6]

Third, the Fraser Committee provides an example of the 'juridification of social relations' through the specification of its mandate. Alan Hunt defines this as 'a two-fold process whereby wider areas of social life become subject to legal regulation and control and social relations themselves come to be treated and regarded in legalistic terms.'[7] As people's places in secular societies increasingly come to be understood through the discourse of legal rights and obligations, so too do we look to the law for solutions to our everyday troubles.

Fourth, the research and report of the Fraser Committee provides an example that highlights the importance of textual forms in the organization and mediation of social relations, from its production of knowledge about a piece of social organization (in this instance prostitution), to how this knowledge has been used to reorganize prostitutes' work relations. As Beng-Huat Chua notes, in modern societies, democracy itself is a textual accomplishment. These textual processes are what 'democracy is made of, and made [it] accountable in everyday life.'[8] The Fraser Committee (like the other government committees discussed in this text) is hegemony in action, as it both fulfilled democratic convention and attempted to organize consent for restructuring the coercive aspects of state power.

Finally, the committee's hegemonic role in making democracy meant that it had to address the demands of the women's movement, since it was feminists who had put pornography on the political agenda and who were claiming prostitution as a feminist issue. The appointment of feminists to the Fraser Committee ensured that this constituency would be recognized and accommodated.[9] The composition of the committee therefore indicated a hegemonic shift in state processes to account for what Heather Jon Maroney refers to as the 'male/female axis,' a process which had been initiated within state work by the Royal Commission on the Status of Women.[10] As I noted in Chapter 2, feminists demanded inclusion in the determination of private/public boundaries in law as they affected women. This demonstrates a deeper tension that the committee had to address when attempting to reconstitute the private/public distinction. The Fraser Committee was required to defend the integrity of 'the rule of law,' while redeploying it in a manner that could accommodate the 'male/female axis' described by Maroney. At the same time, however, commissions are to remain objective in the gathering and assessment of evidence in order to maintain the integrity and legitimacy of the process.[11]

The Organization of the Committee's Work

The Fraser Committee's mandate as described in its terms of reference was:

1) to consider the problems of access to pornography, its effects and what is considered to be pornographic in Canada;

2) to consider prostitution in Canada with particular reference to loitering and street soliciting for prostitution, the operation of bawdy houses, living off [sic] the avails of prostitution, the exploitation of prostitutes and the law relating to these matters;

3) to ascertain public views on ways and means to deal with these problems by inviting written submissions from concerned groups and citizens and by conducting public meetings in major centres across the country;

4) to consider, without travelling outside Canada, the experience and attempts to deal with these problems in other countries including the U.S., E.E.C. and selected Commonwealth countries such as Australia and New Zealand;

5) to consider alternatives, report its findings and recommend solutions to the problems associated with pornography and prostitution in Canada, as soon as possible, but not later than 31 December 1984.[12]

In order to accomplish the tasks set out by their mandate the Fraser Committee travelled across the country, stopping at twenty-two centres, and hearing hundreds of presentations from individuals and organizations. To supplement the presentations and briefs, the Department of Justice commissioned sixteen separate research projects on pornography and prostitution, including five regional studies of prostitution and a national survey of public attitudes toward the activity.

The committee sought to establish what harms were created by prostitution and what role the law ought to take in preventing any such harms. They first identified the 'nuisance' effects as the primary source of harm caused by street solicitation. They then reconsidered the private/public organization of prostitution-related law, seeking to prevent the nuisance effects by allowing for the possibility of alternative indoor places of work. At the same time, they broadened the definition of 'public space' and strengthened the power of criminal law within it.

Prior to the cross-country hearings, in November 1983 the committee released an 'Issues Paper' for broad public distribution. The paper provided an expository of its mandate, structuring its course of action and setting the terms for the debate about prostitution (and of course pornography). Among other considerations, it presented the philosophical debate respecting the role of the law in the regulation of morality; the allocation of 'rights' in a democratic society; the existing and potential legal and social strategies for dealing with prostitution; and a selective outline of some of the legislative history of prostitution in Canada. As well, it set out a number of questions that the committee considered critical to its work. For example, it queried the relationship between prostitution and organized crime, possible links between prostitution and sexually transmitted diseases, and the impact of street solicitation on neighbourhoods, to be able to understand potential areas of public harm caused by prostitution. This process helped to focus and order the various responses.

Although the mandate did not limit the committee to considering solely methods of legal reform, the description of some of the work relations of prostitution as a series of legal categories (soliciting, bawdy-houses, procuring) in Point 2 identified the direction for the committee's work. In addition, a significant but generally unrecognized goal of the committee's work was to consider the constitutionality of any potential legislation on pornography and prostitution. Any proposals were required to be able to withstand constitutional challenges under the newly operational Charter of Rights and Freedoms, and to be consistent with the division of legislative powers between the levels of the state and their respective judicial realms. Part One of the committee's report, which sets out its principles and goals, discusses these issues at length. Finally, although the members of the committee expressed an interest in the 'larger picture' of the place of prostitution in society, not only did the issues paper establish a legislative focus, but the alliance of police, city mayors, and residents' groups had determined that inadequate regulation of street solicitation was the key problem to be confronted. It was the perceived inadequacy of the soliciting legislation that had led to the inclusion of prostitution on the committee's agenda in the first place. Notably, the committee stated that any studies commissioned of necessity had to focus on street solicitation – the most problematic aspect of prostitution – because of limitations on time and funds.[13] However, the Bureau of Municipal Research estimated that street prostitution constituted only about 20 per cent of all prostitution occurring in Toronto, and this dropped to about 5 per cent in the winter months.[14] At the same time, escort services and other indoor methods of business were flourishing. The 1985 Toronto 'Yellow Pages' featured 143 escort service advertisements that were far from discreet about the nature of the services offered, although police continued to raid and lay charges under the bawdy-house statute where they could.

The Fraser Committee's final report was released in April 1985, having taken almost two years and 1.6 million dollars to complete. It set out a number of 'essential principles' congruent with the liberal political and legal philosophy that the committee had adopted as a guide in its work:

1 Equality between women and men.

2 Responsibility – Adults must accept responsibility for their actions.
3 Individual Liberty, since 'The basic idea that adults are responsible for their conduct carries with it the corollary that the law should permit them a zone free from regulation, in which they are responsible only to themselves.'
4 Human Dignity.
5 Appreciation of Sexuality – of voluntary sexual expression, with the belief that people benefit from sexual relationships when they are characterized by mutuality and respect.[15]

The Fraser Report commented on the difficulty of balancing the principles of individual liberty and social equality. For example, individuals might affirm the right to consume pornography, but some feminist organizations asserted that it caused harm to women generally. As well the report stated:

It is the feminist position on the rights question which provides a significant challenge to orthodox liberal theorists. According to feminists, the liberal tends to characterize the rights issue in terms of the infringement by the state on the rights of an individual. Little or no attention is paid to the fact that rights issues often develop out of what is, at base, a conflict in the exercise of rights by two individuals. True, the immediate agent of one side may be the state, but that does not alter the fact that a clash of rights between individuals is involved. If that is correct, then the legal system is not only called upon to protect rights, but also to choose which right is entitled to greater protection.[16]

This tension between competing rights was also revealed in their consideration of the right of adult prostitutes to work the streets of Canadian cities versus the nuisance affects attributed to them by residents' organizations.

Nevertheless, the Fraser Committee asserted that they wanted to use criminal legislation as sparingly as was reasonable, while being specific and clear about what conduct was to be prohibited. These strategies 'stem from the desire to leave to responsible adults as much freedom of choice and as much capacity to govern their own conduct as is consistent with protection of basic values' and 'our hope that the criminal law will, if properly fashioned, interfere with freedom of expression only to the degree necessary to safeguard other basic values.'[17]

The mandate, the philosophical framework, and the essential principles formed the basis for the work of the committee. They provide a way of 'reading' the committees' recommendations on prostitution.

The Recommendations

The Fraser Committee attempted to consider social as opposed to legal methods of dealing with prostitution, yet its primary focus remained on the Criminal Code, as its mandate reveals. Ultimately, the federal government was interested in being provided with a means out of its quandary about how to regulate prostitution through the use of legislation. Its 'social' recommendations do, however, acknowledge social inequalities created by systemic barriers faced by women, as well as young people.

The committee began on the premise that gender inequality and sexual exploitation are embedded in the Canadian social structure. It recommended that all levels of government make a moral and financial commitment both to removing inequalities based on gender, and to creating social programs to assist women and young people in need. Funding for community groups established for the assistance of prostitutes, 'both practising and reformed,' was advocated.[18] These local initiatives could include former prostitutes as workers, given their sensitivity to the needs of other prostitutes, as well as those who were still working in the business.

The committee also recognized the need to change the education and socialization of young people, to develop more responsible attitudes towards sexuality, and a greater awareness of sexual abuse and the risks associated with prostitution. To achieve this, the Fraser Report recommended the development of a national curriculum on sexuality and 'life education' for use in schools. It was noted that working out these recommendations would 'in some cases require considerable social adjustment,' particularly regarding the equality principle. Re-education and reshaping attitudes to affirm equality are long-range tasks that legislation alone cannot address. The committee qualified, 'We cannot delay legislation, however, until this process has been completed.'[19]

In the course of its work, the Fraser Committee realized that fulfilling their mandate – establishing a public consensus on prostitution – was impossible. It was left with the strategy of attempting to reach an effective compromise solution, one that would balance the interests of the pro- and anticriminalization forces. Although the committee stated that it favoured social over legal initiatives to address prostitution and believed that the role of the law should be minimized as much as possible,[20] it also stated that persons living in areas affected by street solicitation experienced real harms and interference with personal rights as a result of the activity. At the same time, it recognized that prostitution per se is not illegal in Canada, but that prostitutes were allowed no place to practise their profession. Its compromise was to state that 'the prostitution related activities of both prostitutes and customers should be removed from the Criminal Code, except insofar as they contravene non prostitution related Code provisions, and do not create a definable nuisance or nuisances.'[21]

They were receptive to the assertion by prostitutes (and a small number of feminist organizations) that 'procuring and living on the avails of prostitution' legislation presumed that anyone who lives with or is habitually in the company of a prostitute must be a pimp. Prostitutes and some advocates of decriminalization who appeared before the commission stressed that the relevant legislation attempted to determine whom a prostitute could live with and assumed that any personal relations she had were necessarily exploitive. This had the effect of regulating prostitutes' lives far beyond their working relations. In view of this concern the committee stated that 'adults who engage in prostitution can and should be counted on to take responsibility for themselves' except where coercion is involved.[22]

The Fraser Committee proposed to limit 'procuring and living on avails' statutes to those who used coercion or threatening behaviour to achieve their aims in the exploitation of adult prostitutes. The procuring statute stated:

195. (1) Every one who
(a) procures, attempts to procure or solicits a person to have illicit sexual intercourse with another person, whether in or out of Canada,
(b) inveigles or entices a person who is not a prostitute or a person of known immoral character to a bawdy house or house of assignation for the purpose of illicit sexual intercourse or prostitution,
(c) knowingly conceals a person in a common bawdy house or house of assignation,
(d) procures or attempts to procure a person to become, whether in or out of Canada, a prostitute,
(e) procures or attempts to procure a person to leave the usual place of abode of that person in Canada, if that place is not a common bawdy house, with intent that the person may become an inmate or frequenter of a common bawdy house, whether in or out of Canada,
(f) on the arrival of a person in Canada, directs or causes that person to be directed or takes or causes that person to be taken, to a common bawdy house or house of assignation,
(g) procures a person to enter or leave Canada, for the purpose of prostitution,
(h) for the purposes of gain, exercises control, direction or influence over the movements of a person in such a manner as to show that he is aiding, abetting or compelling that person to engage in or carry on prostitution with any person or generally,

(i) applies or administers to a person or causes that person to take any drug, intoxicating liquor, matter or thing with intent to stupefy or overpower that person in order to have illicit sexual intercourse with that person, or
(j) lives wholly or in part on the avails of prostitution of another person, is guilty of an indictable offence as is liable to imprisonment for ten years.

(2) Evidence that a person lives with or is habitually in the company of prostitutes, or lives in a common bawdy house or house of assignation is, in the absence of evidence to the contrary, proof that the person lives on the avails of prostitution.

(3) No person shall be convicted of an offence under subsection (1), other than an offence under paragraph (j) of that subsection, upon the evidence of only one witness unless the evidence of that witness is corroborated in a material particular by evidence that implicates the accused.

(4) No proceedings for an offence under this section shall be commenced more than one year after the time when the offence is alleged to have been committed.[23]

To replace procuring legislation, they recommended that 'everyone who:

(a) by force, threat of force or by other coercive or threatening behaviour induces a person of 18 years or older to continue engaging in prostitution with another person or generally,
(b) by force, threat of force or by other coercive or threatening behaviour compels a person of 18 years or older to continue engaging in prostitution with another person or generally is guilty of an indictable offence and liable to imprisonment for 14 years.[24]

To replace the living on the avails statute (S.195(2)):

Everyone who by force, threat of force or other coercive or threatening behaviour induces a person of 18 years or older to support him financially in whole or in part by acts of prostitution is guilty of an indictable offence and liable to imprisonment for 14 years.[25]

The committee recommended repealing Section 195.1 – soliciting for the purpose of prostitution – and shifting street solicitation to a more general nuisance category through a revision of S.171(1) of the Code, rather than singling it out for special consideration as then existed in legislation. The proposed statute would cover disorderly conduct, indecent exhibition, loitering, soliciting, and other similar areas. However, the proposal addressing street solicitation was broad enough to encompass virtually every attempt at street solicitation, and continued to identify prostitution specifically as the source of the offence, rather than the related nuisance activities such as noise making and littering. Subsection (d) would read:

Everyone who:

stands, stops, wanders about in or drives through a public place for purposes of offering to engage in prostitution or of employing the services of a prostitute or prostitutes and on more than one occasion.

i) beckons to, stops or attempts to stop pedestrians or attempts to engage them in conversation,

ii) stops or attempts to stop motor vehicles,

iii) impedes the free flow of pedestrian or vehicular traffic, or of ingress to or egress from premises adjacent to a public place.[26]

In addition, although the maximum fine for most summary offences is $500, the Fraser Committee recommended that a maximum of $1,500 be allowed under this provision, to give the courts more leverage in setting penalties for repeat offenders.

To bolster their efforts to attack the nuisance aspects of street solicitation, the committee decided to expand the category of 'public place' to encompass 'any place to which the public have access as of right or invitation, express or implied, doorways and hallways of buildings adjacent to public places and to vehicles situated in public places.'[27] This was a direct response to police complaints about the difficulty in enforcing soliciting legislation since the *Hutt* decision had determined that the interior of a motor vehicle was not a public place. Therefore the Fraser Committee supported not only a considerable expansion of the regulation of public space, but a broadening of the *definition* of public space itself.

In making this recommendation, the committee stated, 'It is our belief that it is preferable for prostitution to take place in private than in public.'[28] The committee attempted to foster the conditions that would force the transition to the 'private' by recommending a corresponding liberalization of legislation governing bawdy-houses. They suggested that it be made permissible for two persons over eighteen years of age to use their residence for the purpose of prostitution, because working from their homes would provide prostitutes with 'a less exploitive alternative to hotels, motels and other premises.'[29] In addition, they recommended that small licensed and regulated prostitution establishments[30] in non-residential areas be permitted to operate according to schemes established by the relevant province or territory. The operation of any other form of prostitution establishment would remain a criminal offence.[31]

The committee was aware of the ways in which bawdy-house legislation had been used to criminalize the activities of gay men in bars and bath houses, and were careful to recommend a formulation which would prevent this application. The suggested statute was to refer to places resorted to for the purposes of prostitution and drop the inclusion of places resorted to for the purpose of 'acts of indecency.'[32]

Two distinct rationales for the liberalization of bawdy-house legislation were expressed. First, the committee stated, 'if prostitution is an inevitable part of life, at least in the short run, then it should operate in the least offensive setting.'[33] But also, 'the adult prostitute is accorded by our proposed regime, some leeway to conduct his or her business in privacy and dignity.'[34] The committee's recognition of the contradictory standpoints of procriminalization advocates and prostitutes themselves was expressed in those statements. They were able to 'resolve' the contradiction by accommodating both positions through the private/public distinction.

The private/public regulatory strategy suggested by the committee contained contradictory gains and losses for prostitutes. The report promised more interference by the state in public sex work, through a more punitive means of regulation than had existed since the *Hutt* decision. At the same time, certain contractual arrangements between individuals in private, through the reform of bawdy-house legislation, were approved. The Fraser Committee believed that a firm demarcation of public and private sex through the law would correct the uncertain legal status of prostitutes, given that as the legislation stood, the laws might sometimes be enforced in public places as on the streets, and sometimes in private places as in massage parlours. This renegotiation of the private/public code was also used to address the demands from prostitutes themselves for human dignity and increased liberty in their work. The participation of prostitutes' rights organizations in the public hearings, while marginal with respect to the overall level of invited participation in the process, nevertheless gave prostitutes a human face. It was certainly new to have prostitutes speak for themselves in this context, rather than merely having others, supposedly representing their best interests, speak on their behalf. This participation contributed to both the committees' understanding of the work relations of and societal reaction to prostitution, and did have some influence on their decision-making process. Both the empowering and punitive aspects of the committee's recommendations concerning street solicitation and bawdy-houses were influenced by the recognition of prostitutes as 'responsible adults.' If the state was to allow them more liberty in private spaces, then prostitutes would be required to significantly curb their activities in public spaces or be subject to punishment.

However, the prostitution establishment recommendations also made room for the increased regulation of prostitutes' lives, depending on how vigorously the police enforced the proposed legislation, and how much control the provinces, territories, and municipalities might exert on prostitution establishments. While not the expressed intent of the committee, such proposals could be interpreted as permitting the legalization of certain forms of prostitution. For example, while pairs of women could work from their homes, others could be confined to red-light districts if municipal zoning regulations limited prostitution establishments to particular areas of a city, under rigid police supervision. This partial legalization was far different from the decriminalization advocated by activist prostitutes, who wanted their work recognized as a business like any other. Full decriminalization would allow prostitutes to work from their homes or from other establishments regulated and licensed through the same mechanisms as other businesses.[35] They also argued that there would be no need for specific 'procuring and living on the avails of prostitution' legislation, since where coercion was involved other criminal code sanctions could be applied, such as charges of assault, sexual assault, intimidation, unlawful confinement, and extortion. They suggested that it might also prove easier to attain convictions using these other provisions, were police committed to enforcing them. Certainly, the existing procuring legislation was of little use to that end, except in cases of extreme exploitation, as the Fraser Committee itself noted.

In arguing for full decriminalization, activist prostitutes were adamant that other criminal code legislation and municipal bylaws not specifically directed at prostitutes could be used to address complaints developing from any nuisance affects. However, they also noted that policing practices must be addressed so that prostitutes were not singled out for harassment by police. In its report, the Fraser Committee did not address policing practices. However, as discussed in Chapter 2, policing strategies contributed to the problematization of prostitution, even when a punitive Criminal Code provision was in place. It has been suggested by a Montreal defence lawyer that the city's police routinely lie to secure solicitation convictions.[36] However, the Fraser Committee was precluded by its mandate from making recommendations about the policing of prostitutes. It could only address the structure of the law, not its enforcement.

One member of the committee, Andre Ruffo, dissented from the recommendations on adult prostitution because she recognized a contradiction between the view that prostitutes are responsible adults and the rest of the committee's proposals for further regulation. Ruffo believed that prostitutes should be treated like any other persons who are engaged in a business. Singling them out through legislation contributed to their exploitation, while denying them the same right to equality, dignity, and liberty as other people in Canadian society. Although the report acknowledged that Ruffo broke ranks, and provided her explanation for doing so, it is the rest of the committee's views that stand in the report.[37]

In preparing their final report, the committee drew heavily upon the Badgley Committee's findings on prostitution involving young people. While most of the Fraser Committee's recommendations were formulated around a distinction between acceptable forms of private and public sexual behaviour, they also distinguished between the sex-related conduct of adults and youth. While the committee believed that young people should be accorded the same rights as adults regarding equality, responsibility, and dignity, it, like the Badgley Committee, asserted that the family and the state must impose limitations on their liberty to protect them from harms resulting from youth and inexperience. The Fraser Committee's recommendations on prostitution involving young persons is heavily imbued with information from the Badgley Report, drawing on the same data and opinions, and often even using the same wording in the text. It may appear appropriate for the Fraser Committee to have deferred to the more intensive study of the subject provided in the Badgley Report, which devoted more than 138 pages to the study of prostitution involving young persons. In doing so, however, the Fraser Committee fell prey to the same errors and omissions made in the Badgley Report, which will be discussed in Chapter 6. This deference would ultimately strengthen the impact of the official discourse of the Badgley Report, given that its recommendations were supported by a separate government committee as establishing 'factual' knowledge about prostitution involving young people. An important opportunity to provide an independent analysis was lost.

The only major break the Fraser Committee made from the stringent recommendations advanced in the Badgley Report was in their decision not to promote the criminalization of the activities of young prostitutes themselves. While the Badgley Committee would have made it an offence to offer, provide, or agree to offer or provide sexual services, in order to gain a legal foothold for the retention and 'treatment' of young prostitutes, the Fraser Committee maintained that there was no evidence to support the idea that such measures would necessarily lead to effective treatment.

The Limits of the Fraser Report

The Fraser Report represents the most significant attempt yet made in Canada to develop a comprehensive analysis of and strategy for the regulation of prostitution. On reading the report, one is struck by the sincerity and commitment of the committee members to democratic process. However, although it had the power to recommend particular reforms, it did not have the power to oversee their enactment. As Ashforth comments, 'Although government inquiries typically engage in fact-gathering and argument in order to produce policy-oriented recommendations, their labours rarely produce policy results commensurate with the effort and expense of inquiry. Nor are they usually accorded the time and resources to fully investigate the matters with which they are charged, a failing much commented on by participants and observers.'[38]

Although it is clear that the committee members were concerned about the relation between gender inequality and prostitution, their efforts were constrained. While feminism provided a philosophical basis for the committee's work, general feminist support for decriminalization made them an interest group among many in the prostitution debate. Yet there are more unsettling concerns about the Fraser Committee's relationship to feminism. As Zillah Eisenstein comments, the potential force of feminism as a transformative power can be constrained by the state's partial accommodation of its least radical proponents, liberal feminists.[39] Although liberalism and feminism can have conflicting approaches toward equality issues (individualist vs. collectivist), it is liberal feminists whose politics are most consistent with the general philosophy that forms the basis for law. In the Fraser Report, there is no mention of terms such as 'patriarchy' and 'female subordination,' and feminist concerns become reduced to problems stemming from 'society' and 'female disadvantage.' This is the language through which the state takes up, diverts, contains, and neutralizes grass-roots feminist activism.[40] The committee was aware of and discussed different approaches to feminism (marxist and radical feminism), but did not draw on these perspectives in their work. For example, regardless of the level of one's commitment to socialism as a political project, a socialist feminist analysis provides an invaluable tool for elaborating the class and race relations embedded in the organization of prostitution. Significantly, the concerns of the numerous socialist feminists who presented extensive discussions and briefs arguing against the censorship of pornography were reduced to 'a footnote' in the report, as McLaren acknowledges.[41]

It is important to also note that while numerous feminist organizations presented briefs supporting the decriminalization of prostitution, their resources were clearly being spent disproportionably on the other issue being addressed by the Fraser Committee: pornography. A much more problematic and divisive issue for Canadian feminists, the most controversial issue in the feminist 'sex debates' of the 1980s concerned the implications of pornography for gender equality, and the advisability of state censorship as a strategy for the elimination of pornography.[42] Enormous resources (not to mention political infighting) were devoted to the pornography debate; resources, it might be argued, that could have been more fruitfully devoted to other issues of importance for women. It is possible that this disproportionate attention to pornography also reflected a general feminist ambivalence toward prostitutes and prostitution. Although there is a growing awareness that prostitution provides often lucrative work for women, as I discussed in an earlier chapter, feminists, including those with a class analysis, have historically been uncomfortable with conceptualizing prostitution as anything other than 'female sexual slavery.'[43] As long as prostitutes could tidily be slotted into a category as victims of patriarchal oppression, whom feminists could speak on behalf of, prostitution remained an issue on which there was near unanimous agreement in the women's movement. However, by the 1980s activist prostitutes had entered the debate and upset the apple-cart.

5

A New Legal Strategy for the Policing of Prostitutes

As I noted in Chapter 3, the focus on street solicitation intensified throughout the Fraser Committee deliberations. As the committee travelled from city to city its proceedings, which were duly reported in the media, sustained prostitution as a page-one social problem. When the report was released in February 1985, its compromise solution to the problem of street solicitation was immediately controversial. Committee member John McLaren notes that the earliest reactions to the report focused on its most contentious aspects, particularly the possibility of considering licensed brothels.[1] Some newspapers (for example, the *Toronto Star*) presented the proposal as one to establish 'red light districts' in Canadian cities.[2] Again, the establishment of such districts was not a recommendation of the committee, although it certainly opened up the possibility of creating them through municipal zoning strategies and selective law enforcement practices. McLaren stated that the major criticisms of the recommendations on prostitution came from the procriminalization advocates: 'There was little or no effort to understand the Committee's desire to conceive of prostitution as a broader social problem requiring a more comprehensive and integrated socio-legal approach.' And: 'The official police response was the typically cautious one of focusing solely on enforcement, and depreciating any suggestion that the application of the criminal law and its sanctions be limited in any way.'[3]

The Fraser Committee's recommendations could not withstand the powerful alliance of police, local-level politicians, and residents' organizations. Furthermore, the Fraser Committee's recommendations were out of step with a growing political conservativism in Canada. The committee had attempted, however problematically, to reconfigure private/public distinctions to address the public nuisance aspects of street prostitution while creating greater freedom for the trade in private spaces. The conservative government was not held to such strategies. The committee itself had been appointed and its mandate determined by a Liberal government that had since fallen from grace.

On 2 May 1985, Tory Justice Minister John Crosbie tabled a bill to amend S.195.1 in such a way as to make it clear that soliciting in a public place for the purpose of prostitution need not be 'pressing and persistent' to constitute an offence, and that the definition of a public place included the interior of a motor vehicle. The scope of the proposed bill was so broad that any single attempt by a prostitute to solicit a client in a public space, no matter how quiet and unobtrusive she or he might be, presented sufficient justification for the police to make an arrest. The maximum penalty set for the offence was two thousand dollars and six months in jail. Bill C-49 specified that:

195.1 (1) Every person who in a public place or in any place open to public view
(a) stops or attempts to stop any motor vehicle,
(b) impedes the free flow of pedestrian or vehicular traffic or ingress to or egress from premises adjacent to that place, or
(c) stops or attempts to stop any person or in any manner communicates or attempts to communicate with any person for the purpose of engaging in prostitution or of obtaining the sexual services of a prostitute is guilty of an offence punishable on summary conviction.

(2) In this section, 'public place' includes any place to which the public have access as of right or by invitation, express or implied, and any motor vehicle located in a public place or in any place open to public view.[4]

Although this is strikingly similar to the soliciting statute recommended by the Fraser Committee, the Tory bill more firmly demarcates 'communication' for the purpose of prostitution as the offence, and eliminates the need to prove that the act of solicitation took place on more than one occasion, as the Fraser Committee recommended. Bill C-49 was clearly formulated to address the concerns of police, local states, and residents' organizations. This move deftly circumvented the definition of soliciting imposed by the *Hutt* decision: that it must be pressing and persistent to constitute an offence. As such, the legislation has proven to be much easier for police to enforce. The bill also made it clear that street solicitation is not only one of a number of public nuisance activities: it was marked as a distinct offence by its retention as a separate statute. The Tory government was able to co-opt the Fraser Committee's proposal on street prostitution by introducing its most punitive elements, including its significant expansion of the definition of 'public place.' However, Bill C-49 was more punitive not only because of its content but because no private space was opened up where prostitution could legally take place.

The Tory strategy did not include an attempt to liberalize bawdy-house legislation in order to open up an unregulated space for prostitutes to work, as the Fraser Committee had recommended. The anticipated effectiveness of the Fraser Committee formula was dependent upon the negotiation of the private/public distinction in law, as Chapter 4 demonstrated.[5] A few weeks prior to the introduction of the bill, Crosbie had stated that the government was not about to rush into the introduction of legislation on soliciting or other areas, such as pornography, in order to 'ensure that we take a balanced approach and act with concern and compassion.'[6]

Bill C-49 was welcomed by the procriminalization forces. More powerful than the more abstract conception of prostitutes' rights being advanced by those who opposed the bill was the position advanced by the alliance of police, city officials, and residents' organizations. For example, the following letter (dated 10 October 1985) was sent to the Standing Committee on Justice and Legal Affairs by Toronto's Ward Seven residents: 'The prostitution problem in Toronto has reached *epidemic proportions* ... the police have been totally *emasculated* by the current lack of *legal muscle* ... Ours is a mixed neighbourhood, consisting of expensive renovated homes interspersed with a few older rooming houses. Our taxes are the highest in Metro and still rising ... *Our wives and daughters* are continuously afraid to walk these streets alone after dark ... it is patently unfair for taxpayers to be *held hostage* in this manner while our elected representatives leisurely discuss the philosophical question of possible impingement upon the personal freedoms of these *poor creatures* ... consider our freedoms also, *gentlemen*. Pass Bill C-49 and give us back our streets. [my emphases]'[7]

As this letter demonstrates succinctly, one powerful tool that was used to exert pressure on the federal government was the protection of property rights, which in this letter can be interpreted to include women. The assertion of the need to protect women residents in this conversation between men directly contradicted the position being advanced by feminists and other decriminalization advocates by asserting that harm was being caused to one population of women (residents) by another group of women (prostitutes), whose rights feminists were attempting to defend. The residents' position, however, corresponded nicely with the feminist procensorship position on pornography. Censorship advocates asserted a legal protectionist stance toward a general community of women who were allegedly caused harm by the consumption of pornography,[8] while (often the same) feminists stated that harm was caused to prostitutes by state criminalization of street solicitation. In comparison to the degree of organizing of pro- and anticensorship feminists on pornography, the development of a defence of prostitutes' rights by feminists was quite limited. It was the anti-pornography discourse that was to have greater resonance as it was more easily accommodated by a traditionalist framework for the protection of women. Given the limitations of feminist activism in regard to prostitution, and the powerful protectionist stance being advanced about the relation of women to commercialized sex, the introduction of Bill C-49 cannot be attributed to the moralism of a conservative government alone.

Bill C-49 was passed by Parliament (by a vote of 111 to 35 because of the large Conservative majority) on 20 November 1985, and became law one month later as Section 195.1 of the Criminal Code, after final consideration by the Senate. In the *Toronto Star* Crosbie was reported as referring to the bill as an interim measure, designed to satisfy residents. NDP Justice Critic Svend Robinson reportedly referred to it as 'a legal sledgehammer' that would be used against the poorest of prostitutes. In response to Robinson's remark, Conservative MP Ron Stewart revealed what may have been the rationale of many who supported the bill (particularly given how few of them represented ridings with a visible prostitution presence) when he shouted across the House that women became prostitutes because 'they're too lazy to work.'[9]

The Policing of Prostitutes 1: The Standpoint of Prostitutes

The day after the legislation was introduced, Justice Minister Crosbie apparently stated that he expected the legislation to act as a deterrent, and therefore he expected few arrests.[10] Instead, however, the legislation gave police a mandate to act by providing a legal tool that would be effective for making arrests and for successful prosecution in the courts. In Toronto alone, between 1 January (the day that the legislation came into effect) and 15 October 1986, 980 charges were laid against women for communicating for the purpose of prostitution. An additional 553 charges were laid against men, but this figure includes both hustlers and customers since police statistics do not distinguish between the two. At a public forum in Toronto titled 'What's Happening on the Streets,' sponsored by the Elizabeth Fry Society, a representative of the Metropolitan Toronto Police morality squad defended the unequal number of arrests. He said that there were more male officers than females to use as undercover police, and moreover, since male customers charged had fewer previous charges against them (if any) they were more likely to have their cases dismissed. The police representative perhaps assumed that feminists' version of equality included having equal numbers of men and women arrested. Valerie Scott of CORP referred to this approach as 'equal oppression.'[11] In the year following the passage of Bill C-49, Vancouver police laid 755 charges for communication. In Canada overall, 1,225 charges were laid in 1985; by 1986, the total of charges laid had increased to 7,426 (see Appendix A).

Despite the rate of arrests, one Vancouver police inspector was reported as stating that street solicitation was even more widespread in the city than before the law was passed.[12] However, Toronto and Halifax police apparently stated that the numbers of prostitutes on the streets had been substantially reduced (not coincidentally, the winter months in these cities are less conducive to working outdoors than in Vancouver).[13] Police related through the media that the law was having a deterrent effect; many prostitutes had left the street as a result of the new law. In January 1986, Halifax police said that the number on the streets had been reduced from thirty to between five and ten.[14] In the fall of 1986 at the Elizabeth Fry Society forum on the impact of Bill C-49, Toronto's morality squad representative said that adult prostitutes had been reduced to 40 per cent of their previous number, and while he claimed that many had gone into straight jobs, he said that some had also moved to work as dancers, call girls, and bawdy-house employees. He stated that the number of young prostitutes had been reduced by 80 per cent, so that there were fewer eleven- to thirteen-year-old youths working the streets; the average age of women being arrested since Bill C-49 was passed into law was nineteen. He claimed that young girls had returned to their homes and schools, as the legislation had given parents a means of regaining custody of their children. As we shall see in the following chapters, this claim was later contradicted. The police were to assert that they had no means of holding young people, and supported the Badgley Committee's recommendation for further criminalization of young people themselves.[15] As well, I will later in this chapter demonstrate that any deterrent effect of the law was of a relatively short duration, until prostitutes adjusted to working under much more punitive conditions. Finally, it is worth recalling that the determination of 'deterrence' is dependent upon information that police themselves provide to the media. High arrest rates, bolstered by assertions that the law is having a deterrent effect, are strong messages to the public that police are doing their job.

The effects of Bill C-49 on prostitutes working the streets were manifold. Many of the women and men had not started working until after the 1978 *Hutt* decision, and so had never experienced the full impact of criminal law. Police began to use mass arrest tactics for their 'street sweeps.' Valerie Scott of CORP stated that Toronto police would go so far as to dispense with the formalities of the arrest procedure, lining the women up, and loading them in the paddy wagon, a method that police refer to as 'old style arrest.'[16] In the year following the passage of Bill C-49, approximately 80 per cent of those arrested in Toronto were convicted. The Metropolitan Toronto Police Department's Morality Squad representative claimed that this was because arrests were made only in the instance of 'concrete communication'; that a 'wink and a nod' were not sufficient grounds, contrary to the claims of women's groups who were organizing street-corner protests against the bill in numerous Canadian cities.[17] In Toronto, dozens of feminist opponents of the bill gathered at a busy corner of the track to mock and challenge the law by feigning communication.[18]

In Vancouver, a police memorandum was circulated urging jail authorities to detain prostitutes and customers overnight. Vancouver defence lawyer Tony Serka, who had been instrumental in winning the *Hutt* decision in 1978, reportedly handled about 100 communication cases in 1986, and claimed to have an acquittal rate of 35 to 40 per cent. He sought many of the dismissals on the grounds that this procedure brought the criminal justice system into disrepute.[19] Unless a crime is of a serious nature, or unless detention is required to gather evidence, establish a person's identity, or prevent the crime from continuing, the Criminal Code states that persons should be immediately released once a charge has been laid and a promise to appear in court has been obtained.

However, entrapment is not illegal in Canada and, once in court, the word of a police officer is almost always accepted over that of a prostitute. The police officer records in writing his or her alleged conversation, and has a greater degree of credibility before the law.[20] While many prostitutes claim that they are fairly astute at detecting undercover police, this can be difficult if police are themselves engaging in illegal acts in order to secure arrests. For example, in September 1986, the BC feminist news journal *Kinesis* reported that one undercover police officer had driven around town soliciting prostitutes with an open can of beer in his car, and managed to arrest sixteen women in one night.[21] In September 1989 a bawdy-house trial in Edmonton revealed that city police had paid men, including a policeman's brother, to have sex with prostitutes in order to gather evidence for prosecution under the bawdy-house legislation.[22] Tony Serka was quoted as stating that 'A lot of police are being employed working on the problem who are not doing anything but manufacturing criminals ... and it is making the courts unbelievably busy.'[23]

He suggested that although at least half of his clients have children whom they are trying to support, they are being treated more harshly than if they were thieves.[24] Single mothers risked losing their children to social service agencies like the Children's Aid.[25] In Vancouver, a group of prostitutes and feminists, the Alliance for the Safety of Prostitutes (ASP), began to pick up the children of women who were arrested, taking them to safe houses or family members before social workers could remove them from their homes, particularly where the arrested woman was on welfare and supplemented her income through prostitution. A study by the Social Planning and Research Council of British Columbia indicated that welfare rates needed to be increased by 30 to 60 per cent to meet basic needs like food and housing. Prostitutes note the irony in being categorized as 'unfit mothers' because they work in prostitution in order to adequately feed and care for their children.[26]

Valerie Scott noted that the law also put women in greater physical danger, as more women began to work individually, fearing that working in the safer buddy system made them more visible and therefore more vulnerable to the police. Through the buddy system, women pair up and take note of the licence plate numbers of car dates, so that the customer is made aware that someone else knows whom the woman is with.[27] CORP in Toronto and ASP's successor in Vancouver, Prostitutes and Other Women for Equal Rights (POWER) stated that after the law came into effect, women working in prostitution found that they could not be as selective since there were fewer customers. The women found it necessary to make their transactions quickly in order to avoid detection by police, thus rendering it more likely for the transactions to be on the customer's terms, and at his price: it was becoming a buyer's market. Valerie Scott asserted that prostitutes were now more frequently abused by customers and others on the streets, because the law symbolically conveyed the message that prostitutes were no good: 'Whores are once again forced into invisibility and are vulnerable to all the exploitation and abuse that comes with oppression ... One of the places we are going as a result of this bill is to the hospital.'[28]

Said Scott, 'the power is back in the boys' club.'[29] Once arrested for communicating (and many were being arrested repeatedly), they have to go back on the streets to be able to pay the fine. However, in Toronto, tight curfew and bail conditions were imposed upon prostitutes arrested under the communicating section. For example, some women were restricted from going out-of-doors after 9:00 P.M., and were not to be seen in areas of the city where street solicitation commonly occurred, even in cases where this was their own neighbourhood. The violation of a curfew results in a charge of 'failure to comply' (with bail conditions), the penalty for which can be greater than the original charge since the Crown can treat it as an indictable offence, rather than the less serious summary offence of soliciting.

Male prostitutes (hustlers) also faced mass arrests and, according to CORP, experienced rough treatment at the hands of police. Scott compared the sentencing practices of one Toronto judge to 'gay bashing.' She said that he routinely imposed the maximum penalty for first offences by these young men who provided sexual services to other men.[30] In the early morning of 5 June 1987, twenty-three hustlers in Toronto were arrested in a street sweep of 'Boytown,' the male prostitution stroll in the Bay and Grosvenor area. It was the first round-up of male prostitutes in the city. (It is worth noting for our later discussion that all but one of those arrested were reported to have been carrying condoms at the time, suggesting that they were practising 'safer sex' with their customers.)[31] Gary Kinsman wrote in the lesbian and gay newspaper *Rites* that police had stated that the arrests were in response to muggings of gay men. Only one of those arrested was implicated in a robbery, however. Danny Cockerline, a gay male prostitute and a spokesperson for CORP, believed that the arrests demonstrated that police were now scapegoating prostitutes for robberies and other crimes. Cockerline questioned why it was necessary to conduct a mass arrest of hustlers under the communication law, when police could proceed against any one suspect on a robbery-related charge. This kind of practice suggested that the linking of prostitution to more serious crimes provided a rationale for more intensive law enforcement in an area of the city where there had been few complaints about a prostitution presence. Toronto hustlers (a category that does not include male to female transgendered people, who have a separate stroll) work in a downtown business district, making it more difficult to justify arrests for the reasons the law was introduced to address. Kinsman speculated that the linkage of young men identified as gay to the robbery of other gay men could conveniently stifle any protest from the gay community about the policing of homosexual activity. This was a not unrealistic consideration, given the Metropolitan Toronto police's history of conflict with the gay community.[32]

The Policing of Prostitutes 2: Escort Services

Once Bill C-49 was in place as a tool for controlling street prostitution, the police began to draw attention to the absence of an effective legal tool for charging the participants in escort services. Some, though limited, media attention was directed towards escort services, which had replaced massage parlours as the primary mode of indoor prostitution after the crackdown on parlours in the late 1970s. Part of the motivation for this attention undoubtedly came from the movement for the censorship of pornography, a movement that encompassed both antipornography feminists and traditionalist moral conservatives. Attention initially focused on the sexually suggestive ads placed by escort services in the Yellow Pages directory. In 1986 the Toronto Yellow Pages advertised 146 escort services; Edmonton, by contrast, had 18. However, the number of prostitutes this actually represents is difficult to determine, as the size of the services varies, with many being run by one or two women, and some having multiple listings under different names in order to maximize their share of the market.

Police once again were the key source of news about the 'problem' of escort services. Toronto Police Sergeant Brier asserted that police needed more staff, money, and patrol units to intensify their investigations, as it took two or three weeks to investigate a small agency and about three months for a large one. Escorts do not take clients to their homes (which would make them liable to bawdy-house charges), do not provide details of the service and the price on the phone, and usually work alone. They use answering services and pagers to make appointments, and frequently change the name of their service, making it difficult for police to investigate and lay charges.[33]

After 1985, police in Toronto and Vancouver appeared to be once again attempting to make a connection between escort services and organized crime, although the Fraser Committee could find no link between the two. At the same time that Bill C-49 was being introduced, Victoria police began a closer surveillance of escort services which the city's mayor considered tainted with the same 'criminal elements' as street prostitution.[34] In 1987, Toronto daily newspapers began to report a conspicuously greater number of arrests under bawdy-house and living-on-avails legislation than they had previously. This evidence of a mounting campaign by Toronto police against indoor businesses was confirmed in November 1987, by Police Chief Jack Marks. Marks' rationale for an intensified policing of escort services was that this was where the pimps and the connections to drug trafficking were located.[35] Some police and media accounts reported that as a result of Bill C-49, a number of street prostitutes were moving into the escort services, bringing pimps and drugs with them and 'upsetting the delicate balance of the prostitution hierarchy,'[36] although reportings of arrests have yet to reveal police raids on combined drug and prostitution rings. Ironically, attempts to eliminate any means by which prostitutes may conduct their business in public or in private may increase the dangers to prostitutes, thus encouraging third-party control where prostitutes may feel too vulnerable to police to work independently.

The pressure on escort services had an effect. Toronto's three daily newspapers stopped accepting advertisements for escort services, and companies like Bell Telephone's Tele-Direct service (which produces the Yellow Pages) and credit card companies experienced pressure to do the same. However, credit card companies found it difficult to prevent escort services from using the credit card system, as the services usually pose as travel agencies and limo services on the chits. Advertisements in the 1987 Toronto Yellow Pages changed from fairly blatant, sexually suggestive pictures of women in lingerie to more discreet pictures of wine glasses, cityscapes, and even nature scenes, while some eliminated the graphics altogether. The free Toronto entertainment weekly *NOW* continued to publish pages of explicit ads offering a potpourri of sexual services in its business personals section. In August 1990 morality police laid fourteen charges against *NOW* for violating the communicating law. This application of the law to a newspaper that permitted advertisements of services was an attempt to find new avenues to pursue the indoor sex trade. Were this method successful, it would prove less time-consuming and costly than pursuing the services themselves under the bawdy-house legislation on a case-by-case basis. *NOW*'s lawyers were confident that police actions confirmed that the potential interpretation of the communicating legislation was too broad, and that ultimately a successful challenge to the viability of the legislation at the Supreme Court level could be launched. As well, *NOW*'s broad base of community supporters denounced the charges, and the Toronto press was virtually unanimous in agreeing that police had overstepped their bounds in attempting to limit their freedom to publish. The Ontario Attorney General's office wisely withdrew the charges.[37]

According to police, therefore, the operation of escort services is already constituted as criminal activity, and an effective law is required to address this. As both McLaren and Cohen[38] have noted, police are not concerned with wider issues concerning the allocation of rights; for example, the right of prostitutes to a place of work that is not criminalized. By their actions, it appears the police regard their job as activating the legislation that structures their work by enforcing law as broadly as possible.

The Policing of Prostitutes 3: The Public Health Rationale[39]

By the mid-1980s the emergence of HIV (Human Immunodeficiency Virus), the virus believed to cause AIDS (Acquired Immune Deficiency

Syndrome), was transforming our social and sexual landscape, particularly in the gay community, which was suffering the greatest casualties in the North American context. This prevalence coalesced with pervasive homophobia and resistance to a flourishing yet fragile movement for lesbian and gay human rights to create the idea of the 'Gay Plague.'[40] However, it was not so much gay men (who were generally believed to infect only one another) as prostitutes who were targeted as potentially transmitting HIV to the heterosexual population.

The existence of AIDS provided a further rationale and renewed the campaign for state control of prostitution. The stereotype of prostitutes as carriers of sexually transmitted diseases is an old one. Women who work in the sex trade have long been commonly regarded as both morally and hygienically dirty. Historically, 'sanitary policing' has been one of the most common forms of social control.[41] Now, as in the past, emphasis is placed upon prostitutes as infectors, rather than infectees. 'The public' appears to be unconcerned about the potential illness and death of prostitutes themselves (unless they are young enough to be conceptualized as 'innocent victims'), but rather fears they will transmit the virus to their male customers, who will then infect guiltless women and children. In the 1980s, prostitutes joined gay men as scapegoats for the transmission of HIV. CORP's spokesperson, Valerie Scott, referred to media accounts that were dramatizing events and mobilizing public fears as 'hate propaganda.'[42] The media of course not only simply create their own propaganda, but also publicize the misinformation of others. Journalists are not always critical enough to point out the myths others are perpetuating, and thereby relate misinformation to the public.

For example, in June 1985, a Toronto newspaper ran a medical column written by a physician who claimed that prostitutes are a 'health problem.' Rather than produce medical evidence to substantiate his assertion, he stated that he rolled up the windows of his car when driving through an area of the city frequented by prostitutes. They looked sleazy enough, he said, to give a person an STD by a mere glance. He recommended that the streets be cleared of prostitutes so that people could drive with their car windows down.[43] The connections with the sanitary policing of gay men were also clear. In March 1987, Winnipeg's chief of police stated that law enforcement officers should have the power to pick up suspected 'AIDS carriers' and have them forcibly tested. Police, he said, need to be provided with the means to protect themselves from acquiring the disease from people they arrest.[44] The police chief, who was clearly a candidate for an information session on HIV transmission, was in a position to make a public call for a broad expansion of police powers, through which every gay man, prostitute, or even non-prostitute woman considered to be sexually promiscuous could be arbitrarily picked up, detained, and tested, without proof of a crime having been committed.

In July 1986, a Toronto newspaper gave front-page coverage (dominated by a large picture of an angry-looking young woman) to the case of a young female prostitute, alleged to be HIV positive, who had escaped police custody in Ottawa. Her escape sparked a nationwide search, particularly intense in British Columbia, where Vancouver newspapers warned that she may have come to the city to take advantage of the Expo '86 tourist trade.[45] The young woman was later arrested in Montreal and sentenced to three months in jail for soliciting. When interviewed, she apparently insisted that she had always used condoms with her customers. Given that Vancouver was cleaning its streets of prostitutes and the homeless (many of whom were made homeless as their rental lodgings were converted to more lucrative accommodations for the tourist trade) for the hosting of Expo, speculation about the woman's presence may have been opportune.

In January 1987, a Toronto woman claimed to have AIDS when she was arrested for a prostitution-related offence, hoping that the police would leave her alone (she later stated that she had not even been tested for HIV). Police put on their rubber gloves and took her into custody anyway. A full-fledged media debacle ensued. When the woman showed up for her court appearance, she was chased through the building and cornered by a crowd of reporters. The scene of her cowering in a corner surrounded by reporters was later displayed on the evening news.

Also in January 1987, the city of Scarborough's medical health officer said that people should avoid prostitutes 'like the plague.'[46] In July 1987, Toronto provincial court judge William Ross refused to sentence convicted prostitutes and their clients until they had been tested for HIV and venereal disease. They were ordered to report back to him within a specified period with their test results, or face arrest warrants. Toronto lawyer Peter Maloney stated that the judge was acting beyond his jurisdiction, and that the issue of forced testing was one of public policy, to be decided by Parliament. Bernard Dickens, a professor in law and medicine at the University of Toronto, concurred that the judge did not have the power to order the tests.[47]

In June 1988, Toronto Police Commission chairperson June Rowlands advocated that the names of persons convicted on prostitution-related offences be published by the media. The threat of AIDS was stated as a reason for using this as a method to control prostitution.[48] However, in a 1987 interview, Metro Police morality squad staff inspector Jim Clark had stated that virtually all of the prostitutes charged by Toronto police were carrying condoms when they were arrested.[49]

Despite these scenarios, research available during this period failed to show a link between prostitution and HIV transmission. In June 1988, Vancouver's medical health officer Dr. John Blatherwick said that only three of the city's prostitutes had tested HIV positive.[50] As of November 1987, of the thirty-six women in Toronto who had tested HIV positive, five were prostitutes. However, four of the five also admitted to being intravenous drug users, a high-risk category as a result of the sharing and reusing of infected needles.[51] Finally, a study of 109 prostitutes in Calgary, Edmonton, and Vancouver, conducted by the federal government over a two-year period (January 1985–87), found that none had been exposed to the virus, although researchers had expected that 3 per cent would have antibodies in their blood.[52] Since HIV can be transmitted through sexual contact, we can also look at studies of prostitution and STDs for information on transmission patterns. A 1984 study of prostitution and STDs, commissioned by the Department of Justice for the Fraser Committee, concluded that prostitutes do not make a significant contribution to the spread of STDs, and 'in focusing upon the prostitute we try to find an easy solution to a complex problem.'[53] Appendix B discusses the scientific research concerning prostitution and HIV at greater length.

Prostitutes who do contract a venereal disease (or become pregnant) are far more likely to acquire it from a lover. (How many heterosexual non-prostitute women use condoms regularly with their lovers for STD prevention?) Similarly, it appears that prostitutes who do contract the virus are most likely to have contracted it through intravenous drug use. In either case, their regular use of condoms with customers means that prostitutes who do become infected are unlikely to pass it on to them. Danny Cockerline of CORP stated that most people who acquire STDs or AIDS are 'getting it for free.'[54] Prostitute activists challenged the widespread misinformation about their profession, a demanding task given the common belief that prostitution spreads sexually transmitted diseases. They insisted that information about HIV and STDs should be available to prostitutes, provided by peers in a language and context reflecting the experiences of their profession. In Toronto, this resulted in the creation of the Prostitutes' Safe Sex Project (PSSP). They asserted that by blaming prostitutes for the transmission of HIV among the heterosexual population, 'squares' forget that they are working women and men who attempt to maintain as much control over their working conditions, including hygiene, as possible.

Those outside of the business ignore the fact that prostitutes don't want to contract an STD or HIV. The perception that promiscuity spreads disease emphasizes the number of sexual contacts rather than the type of sexual act and the safety precautions used. Alexandra Highcrest (a prostitute, then a journalist, and member of CORP) issued a statement in 1990 worth quoting at some length:

Most of us can blow a safe onto a cock so smoothly, so easily, that half the time the cock's owner doesn't even know that his manhood's been sheathed in latex. We can talk frankly about sex, all kinds of sex, openly and honestly without getting red in the face, and the majority of the things we talk about, we've done. Over the years we've had hundreds of sexual encounters; collectively we've had thousands. We make a few bucks doing this but it's not necessarily our only source of income ...

Back in '86 whores were getting all kinds of bad press. We were blamed for spreading AIDS to the heterosexual community, despite the fact that not a single Canadian has gotten AIDS from a prostitute[55] ... Cops used this false blame as an excuse to harass and bust us, claiming that they had to stop the spread of HIV/AIDS. Mainstream social agencies jumped into the fray saying, 'We can save these prostitutes and halt the spread of the disease if you give us more money.' Enough already! We are quite capable of 'saving' ourselves and we are fed up with bad press and bad laws. Prostitutes were, and are, safe sex professionals and it's time that pros got credit for being what they are, front line workers in the struggle against AIDS.

The sex trade industry is, for many, a transient occupation. New people enter the business, older pros leave. When PSSP meets a new pro, we quickly bring him or her up to speed in regards to safe sex practices. And safe sex doesn't just mean preventing the transmission of STDs. For a prostitute it also entails working without getting busted, harassed, ripped off, or assaulted. These are some of the possible realities of our work.[56]

Valerie Scott of CORP commented that 'the Safe Sex Project encourages prostitutes to take pride in their work as safe-sex educators,' because prostitutes pass on this information to their customers.[57] Danny Cockerline stated that 'prostitutes are part of the solution, not part of the problem,' and that:

When we first started doing the project our approach was to find out what people knew about safe sex and offer them condoms. What we found was that a lot of people were really insulted because they knew about condoms and safe sex already. Even offering them a condom was an insult to them because they would say, 'Well, I've got my own condoms.' So we started a new approach where we would give them material like pamphlets to give to their customers. The whole approach was that this is material to educate your customer and it is not therefore an insult to you. That has been very successful ... it encourages them to feel good about the fact that they are practising safe sex and promoting it with their customers.[58]

Therefore, by developing a positive focus on education and prevention, rather than searching for villains and creating scapegoats, we can stem the rate of transmission.

The Policing of Prostitutes 4:
Addressing the Demand for Sexual Services

By the fall of 1987 it appeared that the new communication legislation was no longer effective in Toronto. On 5 November 1987 the Metropolitan Toronto Police Commission held a public meeting to hear citizens' views on street prostitution in city neighbourhoods. Alderperson Barbara Hall conveyed that residents of her ward found that a huge increase in the number of arrests had made no difference in the number of women and men who worked the streets. Her constituents were no longer calling for tougher legislation, because Bill C-49 had made no difference. Residents of her ward wanted to switch tactics to more stringent policing in their neighbourhoods, because frequent foot patrols deterred prostitutes from working in the area.[59] However, in May 1988 the South of Carleton Ratepayers' Association went to Ottawa, accompanied by Metro Police Superintendent John Getty and Staff Inspector Jim Clark. They demanded tougher legislation making solicitation an indictable offence, which would allow police to fingerprint and photograph both prostitutes and customers who were arrested.[60]

After pressure from residents' groups, the city implemented changes in street directions to deter cruising customers. This resulted in a confusing array of one-way streets and no turn signs, and only succeeded in making prostitutes shift from street to street. Toronto residents' organizations, charging that police had lost control of the streets, began to take matters into their own hands, just as CROWE in Vancouver had done a few years earlier. The South of Carleton Ratepayers' Association staged a series of vigilante actions as media events to pressure politicians to take further action. In early November 1987, a Toronto television station showed scenes of men wearing balaclavas over their heads to conceal their identities, surrounding and shouting at a lone prostitute.[61] In the same month two street outreach workers trying to assist a young prostitute reported being confronted by residents in balaclavas, who were undeterred by the workers' explanation of their role on the street.[62] Cabbagetown residents also staged street demonstrations on weekends, blocking traffic, taking photos, and recording the licence plate numbers of prostitutes' customers.

Police Chief Jack Marks and the Association of Canadian Police Chiefs called upon the federal government to enact still tougher legislation, giving the police the power to arrest a suspected prostitute for soliciting simply because she or he was on the street, and ensuring automatic jail sentences for repeat offenders. No actual solicitation would be required, and the police would not have to prove that communication for the purpose of prostitution had taken place. Prostitution would therefore once again be a 'status offence,' just as it was before 1971, when legislation regulating street prostitution as a form of vagrancy was repealed.[63] The possibility of establishing red-light districts in the city was also raised, by, among others, Toronto City Councillor Chris Korwin-Kuczynski, whose ward includes Parkdale. He believed that prostitutes would then 'pay taxes and be forced to have regular checkups.'[64] However, this proposal remained unpopular. Politicians at all levels believed that it gave the message that the state endorsed prostitution, while prostitute activists thought such areas actually increased the level of danger and outside control facing sex workers, based on the experiences of those working in red-light districts in Boston and Amsterdam.

Switching strategies Toronto police decided to focus their law enforcement efforts on customers instead of prostitutes. The fear of being arrested was sufficient to keep many men away, and therefore this new approach was well publicized to ensure potential customers were aware of the risk they would be taking. Media representatives were invited to ride in patrol cars to observe stake-outs and arrests made by undercover police, and then to duly report about them. Police also anticipated that clients, realizing too late that a woman they had just propositioned was a police officer, would be so jarred by the experience that they would not dare solicit a street prostitute again. Customers, they reported, were primarily suburban middle-class men, including prominent businessmen and men with baby seats in their cars. The prospect of a criminal record and possible publicity made them easy to intimidate. As one officer stated, if the demand for a prostitute's services were cut off, the supply was sure to dwindle.[65]

A mid-November 1987 street sweep, conducted over a three-night period, resulted in 442 customers being charged under Section 195.1.[66] In mid-December, 110 men were charged in a single night in the track and Parkdale areas; the same number as had been charged during a street sweep in late October. During the latter operation, thirty policewomen posed as prostitutes, aided by sixty male back-up officers who moved in to make the arrest once the undercover officers signalled that an offer of money in exchange for sex had been made by the customer.[67] In 1986, Metro police had laid 1,178 charges against prostitutes and customers. In the first eleven months of 1987, they had laid 2,649 charges under Section 195.1, and attributed most of this increase to an intensified focus on the buyers of the services. According to Chief Jack Marks, arrests of customers had increased by 300 per cent during 1987 over the previous year, while there was an over 30 per cent increase in the arrests of prostitutes.[68]

Morality Staff Inspector James Clark advocated that the courts hand out heavier fines to male clients, most of whom would plead guilty to get the process over with as quickly and quietly as possible.[69] Some judges appeared to be complying. One judge gave six men $500 fines for first offences. Defence lawyers often advised those charged to give $200 donations to the chaplain's office at the court, prior to their court appearance, in the hope that the judge would give them an absolute discharge. However, in a much publicized ruling, Judge Lorenzo Dicecco sentenced twenty-four men arrested in the mid-November sweep to clean the streets of the track area. They were ordered to do from ten to seventy hours of 'community work' for the South of Carleton Ratepayers' Association. The men were ordered to clean the sidewalks (in response to residents' statements about condoms littering the streets), or give donations of between $150 and $200 to the association.[70]

The Policing of Prostitutes 5: Questioning the Regulatory Rationale

Residents' organizations undoubtably had legitimate grievances about the disruption to their lives caused by street solicitation. Some residents complained of sexual acts between prostitutes and clients taking place in their yards, people urinating on their lawns, and fights breaking out on the street. The volume of noise experienced varies by the location of the stroll (and the other activities occurring in that area), as well as by who is working the corner or street. Many prostitutes work the same corner for a number of years, and may even establish a rapport with people living in the area. Others may be more transient and obtrusive. Prostitute activists suggest that those who work the streets are more likely to cooperate with residents when treated with dignity, rather than disdain. That stated, the economic context for the making of the problem of street solicitation cannot be ignored.

Residents' organizations claimed to speak for everyone in their neighbourhoods, and were publicly portrayed in this manner. Yet there was also evidence that not everyone agreed with them. Some residents openly sympathized with the prostitutes, particularly young women and those who appeared to be controlled by pimps. Others said that the residents' organizations' actions were unwarranted or excessive. For example, a man attending a residents' meeting was reported in the *Toronto Star* as stating: 'The problem started when all the people with money started moving in and wanting to change it [the neighbourhood] into a little Rosedale ... This is a mixed neighbourhood, it will never be a Rosedale. I live with the noise. It's not as bad as it's been described. I feel it's the rich people who are spearheading these changes.'[71]

In 1988 articles began to appear in the Toronto press that questioned the rationale of residents' organizations' opposition to street solicitation. Although residents frequently complained about the potential impact of the street trade on their property values, urban redevelopment, the gentrification of neighbourhoods, and a spiral of real estate speculation were pushing property values out of reach of the majority of the population. 'The Future of Toronto' emerged as a 'news theme' that challenged the interests of the affluent, including those expressed by residents' organizations.[72] Furthermore, Parkdale, a working-class area of Toronto long known for its boarding houses and group homes, was undergoing a metamorphosis similar to Cabbagetown as the affluent purchased and renovated homes. The Parkdale Business Improvement Association began to take on the task of neighbourhood improvement, including the clearing of prostitutes and other 'undesirables' from the area's streets. At a Police Commission Neighbourhoods Committee meeting in November 1987, the representative of the Parkdale Business Improvement Association commented that prostitutes were 'self-centred and selfish,' and claimed that people in the community found prostitution 'reprehensible.' Therefore, 'their rights end where our rights begin.'[73] Approximately one month after the Police Commission meeting, the Parkdale Business Improvement Association was again receiving media coverage for its efforts to stop the sale of 'bitters' (an inexpensive digestive aid containing alcohol) from corner stores, as part of its plan for cleaning up the area.[74] A similar process was anticipated in the commercial area of the Lakeshore Road motel strip, an area well-known for street solicitation. Real estate speculators bought virtually all of the property along that strip, anticipating its redevelopment.[75] Owners of the few remaining privately owned motels on the strip blamed speculation for the area's being allowed to deteriorate.[76]

The increasing polarization of the affluent and the poor, partially through the 'pushing out' of the upper working and lower middle class, was dubbed the 'Manhattanization of Toronto.' As the *Globe and Mail* stated, 'even the city's work force is being Manhattanized as middle-income jobs in the manufacturing sector are lost, replaced by higher-level office jobs and lower-level clerical, secretarial, and service occupations.'[77] As Jon Caulfield has written, in this emerging corporate economy (which was fully in place by the 1990s), property values reflected both a user demand and the interests of investment capital. Property represented more than home ownership, but an investment opportunity. This resulted in an intensification of land use (for example, through dividing up homes once again into apartments), as property values no longer reflected what people could afford. And of course, Toronto experienced an extraordinary growth in the number of homeless people living on its streets. Certainly, as Caulfield states, there had been 'a revolution in the "urban meanings" of city places for people.'[78]

New accounts expressing concern about the kinds of transformations that were taking place in Toronto questioned the power of neighbourhood lobby groups to influence political decisions about the type of housing to be allowed in a particular area. These groups allowed homeowners to 'increasingly [make] decisions on who should live near them.'[79] For example, in 1987 *Globe and Mail* columnist Michael Valpy reported that the 'main fire' of the South of Carleton group was a realtor who had lived in the area for three years. She admitted being aware that her house was in a solicitation area before she purchased it, 'but I said to myself, it's not like buying beside a glue factory. It's a moveable problem.'[80] The most critical, yet not entirely unsympathetic, article on the role of affluent residents in the battle against street solicitation was delivered in the November 1988 issue of *Toronto Life*, a magazine whose target readers are the city's affluent: 'The palpable anger on downtown streets is a sobering reminder that a beastly hangover awaits a city that has grown intoxicated with its own prosperity. Meanwhile, the merrymaking continues. Parkdale has begun to take on a nattier look, and developers are poised to have their way with the Lakeshore strip. Quickly vanishing is the reality of a mixed downtown neighbourhood where citizens of varying social and economic backgrounds live peaceably together. In the process, the precious sense of community that once made Toronto the envy of every North American metropolis is being squandered.'[81]

Some media criticism was levelled against the Metropolitan Toronto Police Force about the amount of money the city was spending on the policing of prostitutes. A September 1988 *Toronto Star* editorial chastised Toronto police for continually demanding more money and staff for a series of urban problems, including (in succession) prostitution, traffic control, and the 'war on drugs.'[82] As well, *Toronto Life* noted in November 1988 that: 'Since Bill C-49's turn of the legal screws, the Metropolitan Toronto Police have laid approximately 8,000 charges against prostitutes, johns, and pimps. Last year they hired an additional ninety constables to increase patrols in the various tracks (Cabbagetown, the Lakeshore strip, and Parkdale), resulting in the number of charges laid increasing by 150 per cent over the previous year. The police would like to get on to more pressing matters. In 1988 alone, the city will have spent $6.3 million to keep prostitutes out of work. Despite more patrols, dramatically higher conviction rates, and the ongoing, massive sweeps (something no other Canadian city had tried before), the police acknowledge that unless there is a raging blizzard the hookers will be out on the street corners tomorrow.'[83]

Policing is a critical ingredient in the determination of how public space is used and who has access to it. The policing of street prostitutes demonstrates how middle-class urban neighbourhoods are considered what Shearing and Stenning refer to as 'mass private property.'[84] At the same time, this process separates 'the scum from the public.' According to Shearing: 'What distinguishes the scum from the public is that the scum are structurally in conflict with, and are the enemies of, the public. The scum are ... "in essence" troublemakers, while the public are "in essence" their victims. In distinguishing between the scum and the public as two classes opposed to each other as enemies, the police culture makes available to the police a social theory that they can use in the context of their work to define situations and to construct a course of action in response to them. This theory enables the police to transcend the situated features of encounters by relating them to a broader social context which identifies the "real trouble-makers" and "real victims."'[85] Media reports from the period clearly demonstrate that prostitutes were identified as 'scum,' despite a coterminous and contradictory expression of sympathy for women believed to be controlled by pimps. Prostitutes, including prostitutes' rights activists, come up against negative attitudes continually. For example, at the 1987 Police Commission's Neighbourhoods Committee meeting (referred to earlier) Valerie Scott was treated with derision by politicians and commissioners. In the same year, her presentation of NAC's policy on prostitution at their annual MP lobby day on Parliament Hill was greeted with similar disdain by some Tory politicians. Non-prostitute women who queried MPs were spared such treatment.[86]

Prostitution charges provide relatively simple arrests. Strong arrest and conviction statistics provide the image that police are successful in their efforts to tackle crime; they represent 'enforcement by statistics or by computer.'[87] Prostitution-related police work is also generally liked by police because it is proactive work.[88] However, as Stanley Cohen reminds us, while proactive work is intended to *prevent* crime, it also *creates* criminals through methods such as entrapment, when police act as 'agents provocateurs.'[89]

The power of the 'rule of law' does not exist *a priori*. It is constructed through the activities of policing, of taking care of one's property rights, and of interpreting the character of rights and freedoms through the judicial process. Policing is particularly important for prostitutes because they deal with police continually as the front line of the state. Policing policy and the police themselves put the law into practice; laws are given shape and substance through policing activities. Police regard law enforcement – making arrests – as the key to solving the problem of street-level prostitution. They are generally successful in gaining support for their campaigns against 'social problems' like prostitution and drug abuse, and as Richard Ericson notes, 'the police are increasing their political potency, both symbolically and in practice.'[90]

Through this 'politicization of the police,' the police gain not only support for their work but for the expansion and maintenance of police bureaucratic forms. This has necessitated more affiliation with the news media for public relations purposes. In Toronto, this has resulted in the expansion of police public affairs, oriented towards the media, and the encouragement of media involvement in police crime prevention campaigns. Furthermore, the media rely on the police, not always uncritically, as their primary source of news about crime. Because police experience daily the 'war against crime,' 'the discourse of crime and crime control is the prerogative of the police, and all non-police accounts of it are treated as less significant.'[91] Not surprisingly, the *Canadian Newspaper Coverage of Pornography and Prostitution, 1978–1983*, the report commissioned for the Fraser Committee, found that police were by far the most frequent source of news about prostitution over the period studied.[92]

Although the emergence of activist prostitute organizations like CORP in Toronto, ASP in Vancouver, and ASP's successor, POWER (Prostitutes and Other Women for Equal Rights) compelled the mainstream media to marginally increase their inclusion of the standpoint of prostitutes in their accounts, the dominant profile of prostitutes remained one of the drug addicted, usually young, prostitute beaten and abused by her pimp. Again, this victim profile managed to coexist with a presentation of prostitutes as selfish, foul-mouthed intruders in accounts of the residents' and hookers' battle for the streets. Patterns of sexual abuse, violence in the home, and addictions were presented through interviews with social workers and other professionals as characteristic of most prostitutes' lives, although again these almost always focused on prostitutes in their teens. Somehow, once prostitutes were considered to be adults, and therefore responsible for their own actions, these 'histories' became irrelevant. Moreover, the structural conditions that may have precipitated the entry of women and young people into prostitution were almost entirely absent from these accounts. The roles of systemic racism, homophobia, gender inequality, not to mention the limited opportunities for working-class women within the Canadian class structure, remained predictably unacknowledged. Thus these important features of the Canadian social structure escaped being constituted as social problems requiring public and state response.

Race (not racism) *was* an issue for the popular *Toronto Sun* columnist Barbara Amiel, however. As she asserted in a 1985 column, 'What is the point ... of all these stories on prostitution in Toronto when no one is mentioning what everyone who covers the story or walks down Jarvis St. sees – the predominance of young black West Indian boys among the pimps and boyfriends?' And: 'In Canada ... Blacks and minority groups have become sacred cows ... One must deny the evidence of one's senses and try to blame whites or goldfish.'[93] Amiel's assertion of fact is based on the claim that she *saw* that most pimps were Black. Her 'senses' had proved what most people already 'knew' from Hollywood movies: that pimps are Black (and wear gold chains around their necks, have floppy hats, and drive cadillacs bought with the money earned by their stable of 'hos'). So entrenched is this image in popular culture that it has become synonymous with pimping. Indeed it has become such a cultural icon of Black masculinity that Amiel herself has not escaped its potency, leading her to assume that any Black male in the vicinity of a stroll must be a pimp or exploitive boyfriend (which in turn confirms her pre-existing stereotype). Having established this 'fact' she is then able to claim that there is something about the culture of these young men, 'the unstructured family life of some West-Indian people' and the absence of environments 'with emphasis on anglo-Canadian values of thrift, application, and commitment,' that makes them seek their livelihood through pimping.[94]

Of course some pimps are Black, just as some pimps are white. But Black pimps tend to be more visible *because* they are Black: they fit the stereotype. Moreover, when Black men are the 'players,' they tend to be more prevalent at the bottom end of the money-making hierarchy, just as systemic racism locates Black men in general at the bottom of the economic system. Positions of greatest, although often invisible, economic power in the sex trade (such as club owners, escort service owners, etc.), tend to be occupied by white men, just as they are in Canadian society as a whole.

For Amiel, then, pimping was a problem of race, rather than a problem of masculinity and class. Amiel's journalism was not problem *naming* as she claims; it was problem *making*, particularly given the popularity of her columns and the *Toronto Sun* tabloid itself. This Toronto daily has received an ongoing barrage of criticism for its role in mobilizing race-based fears of the Black criminal and unsuitable immigrant. These images were to have increasing political potency as the Canadian economy was 'restructured' to harmonize with global competition, unemployment rates climbed, and cuts in immigration levels implemented. Paul Gilroy comments that by linking prostitution and Black men through the image of the pimp, there is a joining of two 'problems' and, 'the idea that blacks comprise a problem, or more accurately a series of problems [pimps, criminals, immigrants] is today expressed at the core of racist reasoning.'[95] We need, he states, to ask Black scholar and activist W.E.B. DuBois' question, 'How does it feel to be a problem?'[96]

Contradictions in the Courts on the Disposition of Legal Rights

The 'rule of law' is, of course, activated not only through policing, but through the judicial system. However, the courts have not been unified on the matter of street solicitation or other prostitution-related legislation, as was demonstrated in Chapter 3. There has been significant variation in interpretation of the legislation.

Judges in British Columbia initially appeared reluctant to convict prostitutes under the new legislation, resulting in 'a flood of dismissals,' according to the *Globe and Mail*. The reasons for doing so varied. One judge rejected slang terms as evidence of communication, where the terms did not explicitly refer to sexual acts (such as 'one on one'). Another ruled that 'revving' a car engine did not constitute communication for the purpose of prostitution.[97] In Ontario, a judge dismissed a case where the alleged communication had taken place in a hotel room since such premises did not fall within the scope of the legislation's definition of a public place. Other members of the judiciary raised concrete questions about how the law should be interpreted and enforced. Some provincial court judges ruled that negotiating for a prostitute's services is not sufficient grounds for arrest, but that there must be some impeding of traffic; for example, through stopping a vehicle or person.[98] The statute was therefore interpreted unevenly by judicial agents and courts at the local level, as well as by the provinces.

In the year following the introduction of Bill C-49, women and men charged under the law would simply plead guilty to the charges, pay their fines, and go back to work, rather than take on the expense of a lawyer to argue their case. However, after repeated arrests and convictions, many found that they faced hefty fines and jail terms for further repeat offences. Some chose to plead not guilty, rather than add yet another conviction to their record. CORP encouraged Toronto prostitutes to plead not guilty, with the intent of creating a backlog in the courts.[99] This not only caused congestion in the courts, but provided defence lawyers with opportunities to challenge the constitutional validity of the law under the Charter of Rights and Freedoms at the provincial and Supreme Court levels.

'Rights' are not pre-existing in the Charter, beyond a broadly defined statement of principles. They have to be *created* through the interpretive procedures of the judiciary.[100] The Charter itself is of relatively recent origin and is in the process of being created through judicial decisions that act as a powerful symbolic mechanism. However, according to Christie Jefferson of the Women's Legal, Education, and Action Fund (LEAF), for the legal profession the Charter challenge was not about whether prostitutes were being deprived of their rights and freedoms, but about the implications of such a sweeping law for the principle of legal rights generally. The Charter is a contract between individual citizens and the state, in which the state agrees to allow certain liberties. This can allow for some real gains; for example, the repeal of the abortion law. However, the Charter cannot guarantee that these rights will be respected or maintained. Again using abortion as an example, it cannot guarantee that women will actually have access to abortion procedures, or that Parliament will not introduce a new law.

Further, access to the legal system is limited by factors such as one's ability to pay for that access. So far, the equality rights guaranteed under Section 15 have favoured the already advantaged by defending established interests.[101] The cases have comprised primarily those of corporations (given the same rights as persons), male claimants, and what were referred to as some extraordinary women claimants. (Significantly, the Supreme Court did not invoke Section 15 in overturning the abortion law.) For example, Jefferson reveals that 'of the 601 court decisions involving Section 15, only forty-four involved sex equality and only seven were initiated on behalf of women.'[102]

In her provincial court ruling in the case of *Regina. v. Jennifer Smith*, Judge J.T. Bernhard provided an instructive detailed analysis about the process entailed in determining the validity of constitutional arguments. I will closely follow her arguments here. As she conveyed, when defence lawyers challenge the constitutional validity of the legislation, they do not tackle the statute in its entirety, but impugn particular phrases or sections. This has the effect of bringing the entire statute into question. The phrase that defence lawyers have most frequently targeted as a violation of the rights and freedoms guaranteed by the Charter is contained in Section 195.1 (1) (c): 'or in any manner communicates or attempts to communicate with any person.' This phrase is, in effect, the heart of the statute, since it is communicating, either for the purpose of prostitution or for obtaining the sexual services of a prostitute in a public place that the statute is designed to penalize. Defence lawyers' tactics for challenging this particular phrase and other parts of the legislation vary, but the most common strategies involve invoking one or more sections of the Charter, typically:

Section 2. Everyone has the following fundamental freedoms: (b) freedom of thought, belief, opinion and expression, including freedom of the press and other media of communication; (d) freedom of association.

Section 7. Everyone has the right to life, liberty, and security of the person and the right not to be deprived thereof except in accordance with the principles of fundamental justice.

Section 15. (1) Every individual is equal before the law and has the right to the equal protection and equal benefit of the law without discrimination and, in particular, without discrimination based on race, national or ethnic origin, colour, religion, sex, age or mental or physical disability.[103]

This strategy is in many ways experimental, both because the legislation itself is of relatively recent origin, and because the Charter was proclaimed only in 1982. As a result, there are few test cases and precedents on which to base legal arguments. As well, defence lawyers must experiment with different kinds of arguments (some of which will be demonstrated below), and hope that their cases are tried before a judge who will be sympathetic to their reasoning. When they do achieve a ruling in their favour by a lower court judge, the decision is not binding, and instead may proceed to an appeal before a provincial higher court, where it may be upheld or overturned. Should the decision be upheld, the legislation is declared 'of no force or effect' in the respective province, while other provinces are not bound by the decision. The Supreme Court of Canada may then 'grant leave' to hear the case, and either uphold or invalidate the legislation. If the Supreme Court rules that the legislation in question is unconstitutional, it is effectively struck down in Canada, and it is up to the federal government to redraft the legislation.

When judges evaluate the impugned legislation, they attempt to determine the nature, legitimacy, and extent of the infringement upon the Charter of Rights and Freedoms. They question the importance and seriousness of the infringement, the costs to the community, and whether there are less drastic means available to control or regulate the activities which the legislation is designed to prevent or penalize. They begin from the recognition that rights and freedoms are not absolute, and may be limited where the exercising of these rights would undermine 'collective goals' that are of fundamental importance to society.

To justify a violation of the Charter, they determine whether the objective (in this case, the objective of Section 195.1 of the Criminal Code) is of sufficient importance to override a constitutionally protected right or freedom. Once they determine that the objective is significant enough to warrant such an override, they must still demonstrate that the means chosen to do so are reasonably and demonstrably justified in a free and democratic society. To do this, they subject the impugned legislation to a three-stage 'proportionality test.' First, the means of achieving the objective (here, the control of the street trade) must not be arbitrary, unfair, or based on irrational considerations: the legislation must be internally rational. Second, even if it is a rational means of achieving the objective in question, it should impair the right of the freedom in question as little as possible. Third, there must be proportionality between the effects of the measures taken (that limit a right or freedom), and the objective identified as being of sufficient importance to override the Charter.[104]

Although there have been numerous successful challenges to the legislation at the provincial court level, only in Nova Scotia was one upheld upon appeal. As a result of the Nova Scotia decision, Section 195.1 could not be enforced in that province, although it continued to be applied elsewhere, pending the decision of the Supreme Court of Canada. The Supreme Court 'granted leave' to simultaneously hear the Nova Scotia decision and cases from Manitoba and Alberta, whose Courts of Appeal upheld the legislation against constitutional arguments.[105] The Supreme Court of Canada began its deliberations in November 1988. Its 1990 decision to uphold the law will be discussed in the final chapter.

6

The Report of the Committee on Sexual Offences Against Children and Youths (The Badgley Report)[1]

The battle between residents and prostitutes over the streets gave scant attention to the participation of young people in the trade. But even as attempts to clear prostitutes from the streets were being made, a 'new' crisis had emerged: the exploitation of children and young people on the streets of Canadian cities. The work of the Badgley Committee (named after its chairperson, social scientist Robin Badgley) was to have a significant impact upon how prostitution involving young people came to be understood as a national social problem in the 1980s. It was critical to the *making* of the urban phenomenon of the 'street kid' (the contemporary version of the 'waifs and strays' of Victorian cities being transformed by industrialization) and its synergistic relative, the 'child' prostitute.[2] Its role in not only identifying a problem but simultaneously proposing the resolution to the problem contributed significantly to the Badgley Committee's successes in having a substantial number of its recommendations acted upon.

As I commented in Chapter 3, the emergence of the women's liberation movement in the 1960s made non-consensual sexual relations involving women and children a public political issue. The Canadian state was confronted with the demand to restructure its punitive and protective mechanisms through the reform of legal and social policy. As part of the procedure for accomplishing this respecting young people, the Special Committee on Sexual Offences Against Children and Youths was jointly appointed by the Minister of Justice and Attorney General of Canada, and the Minister of National Health and Welfare in February 1981. Its report was released in August 1984. It took three years to produce, at a cost of two million dollars. The ten-member committee was composed primarily of persons from the legal and medical communities, whose expertise lay in sociology, law, medicine, nursing, and social welfare.[3] The Badgley Committee's purpose, as set out in its terms of reference, was to 'enquire into the incidence and prevalence in Canada of sexual offences against children and youths and to recommend improvements in laws for the protection of young persons from sexual abuse and exploitation.'[4]

The committee's work was prescribed such that sexual activity involving young people was understood as a problem *requiring* a protection-oriented legislative solution, a supposition that marginalized social and economic considerations. They were directed to collect as much information as possible on the incidence and prevalence of child/youth sexual abuse in Canada by organizing a coherence into pre-existing but generally disparate sources of data, such as police, hospital, and social service records. They were to produce new data where possible, initiating the commission of the National Population Survey and the National Juvenile Prostitution Survey. Finally, the undertaking of this work was intended to instill 'open public acknowledgement' of the problem.[5]

As Gary Kinsman and I discussed in our earlier work together, the Badgley Committee fulfilled its mandate regarding young people involved in prostitution in three key ways. First, the committee brought about a shift in the perception of juvenile prostitution from one of a marginal social problem constituted by individual and isolated case histories in police and social service records, to a reconceptualization of it as a central manifestation of the *sexual abuse of children*. Second, through the committee's work the activities of young people in prostitution were drawn more explicitly into the legal ambit via proposals for an expansion in the regulation of the young people involved, as well as their procurers and customers. Finally, the committee's work was undertaken in a way that had the effect of marginalizing or silencing the experiences and opinions of young people who found a source of income in prostitution.

In its mandate and throughout the report, young people are identified as requiring protection from any and all sexual activity, including a range of diverse and not necessarily related activities like the production of pornography, incest, sexual violence, pornography, and consensual activity with other young people. Sexual matters were thereby organized into a coherent unity, blurring important differences among them. (Is it appropriate, for example, to ignore distinctions between what may be peer sexual play and incest?) The ability to give legal consent to sexual activity was determined through a differentiation between the legal status of adults and young people; a separation that made any sexual activity involving young people coercive by definition. The categorization of all sexual activity involving young people as dangerous was rooted in contemporary views of childhood as a period of sexual innocence. This might be forgiven, as the focus of the committee's work was to document the often horrific acts that can be perpetuated against young people. However there is certainly a need to discuss the positive aspects of developing sexuality and consensual play between peers. The committee's work required the development of a system of classification of acts and prohibitions; of what cannot be done to or between young people, by whom, at what ages, with a view to the physical and emotional harms, such as pregnancy and sexually transmitted diseases, that might be incurred. The resulting juridical-scientific taxonomy of childhood and youth sexual relations was to provide a blueprint for professionals working with young people in medicine, social work, the judicial system, and policing.[6] My comments here refer to 'young people' instead of 'children and youth' for its brevity and inclusiveness. Unfortunately, the Badgley Committee favoured references to children alone (collapsing the appropriate distinctions that should be made between the two categories), a reductionism that was to spill over into later media accounts as a moral panic was generated about 'child prostitution.' The committee was thus able to treat eighteen-year-old youths as if they had the same capacities and incapacities as twelve-year-old children, while setting the terms for public perceptions and legal policy.

As a result of the women's movement's ongoing attempts to 'break the silence' about sexual abuse and violence in the traditional family, the committee recognized that it would have to expand legal 'protection' in the private sphere as well as the public, broadening the judicial system's powers of inspection in the interests of young people. As Kuhn explains: 'The vulnerable are defined as persons who can be particularly easily exploited or corrupted. Consequently, where the law aims to protect such persons, it reenters a field of morality defined in other circumstances as private. Young people are seen to require special protection because the state of adulthood is considered a necessary precondition of the exercise of free choice and informed consent. since in law minors are not considered capable of consent, the realm of the private becomes more tightly circumscribed for them than it is for adults.'[7]

Age distinctions are therefore critical to establishing who is an offender and who is a victim requiring the law's protection. The committee proposed a shifting of age distinctions in law so that young persons receive *absolute* sexual protection under the age of sixteen, instead of fourteen, as the law then specified. However, the committee recommended that the buggery (anal sex) statute of the Criminal Code, which they recognized was commonly used against male same-sex sexual activity involving a person or persons under twenty-one years of age, be applied only to those under eighteen years of age. The committee made this decision because they believed sexual orientation to be well established by age eighteen. However, they refused to lower the acceptable age for participation in anal sex to sixteen, the age at which most consensual heterosexual sex was believed permissable, 'in the absence of persuasive evidence that such a reduction would pose no risk to developing sexual behaviour.'[8] Clearly the committee regarded heterosexuality as normative, while pathologizing homosexuality. (Imagine the reverse, where sexual activities between males and females were not permitted until such time as their sexual orientation was clearly established!)

The increasingly specific legal focus on the sexual activity of young persons expands state intervention where the needs of young people cannot be met in the context of familial relations. They must be drawn into the purview of the law through the acquisition of a 'legal personality' that is 'intended roughly to correspond to the level of intellectual, maturational, and emotional development displayed generally by children of that age, and is of necessity, coloured by each society's contemporary social views of childhood.'[9]

The legal personality, then, determines the ability to consent to sexual activity. The Badgley Committee reconceptualized the legal personality of the child as something that could exist separate from the family, an approach rejecting the idea that the nuclear family should be held together at any cost. Moreover, young people were considered to possess a legal personality distinct from that of adults, and redefining it was of course key to the committee's work. The intent of this was first, to address the difference in legal principles entailed in the abuse of young people, and second, to develop a legal framework which could more appropriately account for the complexities of sexual abuse involving young persons. As the Badgley Committee stated 'it is both confusing and counter-productive to lump very different sorts of inappropriate behaviours with children together into a few vague legal categories such as "gross indecency," "sexual assault" or "sexual exploitation."'[10]

The Recommendations for Criminal Code Reform

Youths working as prostitutes, the committee informed us, are the 'cast-offs of Canadian society.'[11] In the pages of the report, they are runaways, school drop-outs, and delinquents, who are surrounded by disease, violence, and exploitation in their daily lives. Working as prostitutes entangles young people in a criminal life, as they commit 'a variety of offences which are integrally associated with their work on the street. In this regard, the charges that had been brought against them for soliciting were almost incidental in comparison to the far larger number of charges that had been laid against them for other types of offences.'[12] From the perspective of the Badgley Committee, young people's work in prostitution appeared to lead them into other forms of criminal activity. However, as we shall see in the following chapter, the exchange of sexual services is but one (and not necessarily the dominant) of numerous survival strategies that young people may engage in. For the Badgley Committee, however, the work they did providing sexual services created their identity, that of the 'juvenile prostitute.'

From this perspective young people involved in prostitution were seen as 'young offenders' who brought harm 'upon themselves' in the regulatory frame of the report, and at the same time, as victims of sexual abuse perpetrated by their customers.[13] Since young people were considered unable to legitimately consent to sexual activity, the committee defined the customers of juvenile prostitutes as sexual abusers, who exploited the vulnerable. Customers could not be 'considered any less culpable because they agree to pay for the sexual act with a young person than if they were to threaten or coerce sexually a child or youth without payment.'[14]

Prostitution involving young people, however, was not recognized in legislation as a distinct classification separate from adult prostitution when the Badgley Committee was conducting its investigation. Nor could young prostitutes be prosecuted as juvenile delinquents, as the Juvenile Delinquents Act had been repealed and replaced with the Young Offenders Act, phased into law between 1980 and 1986. As a result, the only legal method left available for detaining and 'treating' young prostitutes was through the use of provincial child welfare legislation. Furthermore, under then current legislation prostitutes over fourteen years were able to consent to many (hetero)sexual acts, making it difficult to prosecute the users of their services for sexual offences. Therefore, the committee believed that distinct legislation regulating juvenile prostitution was required to distinguish between the sexually autonomous status of adulthood and the sexual vulnerability of children and youths. From this standpoint, the committee decided to recommend that a range of new social and particularly legal provisions be implemented to address the problem of juvenile prostitution as a form of sexual abuse.

The Badgley Committee did not ignore or deny the need for social, as opposed to legal, reforms to address juvenile prostitution. Suggestions for social reforms, however, were general and vague, subordinated to proposals for the expansion of criminal law by the committee's mandate. For example, the committee asserted that social, rather than legal initiatives are most important in curbing juvenile prostitution. For this reason, it recommended the implementation of a 'rational program of public education and health promotion' through the schools and educational television to function as a deterrent to young persons.[15] It believed that the development of new social service programs would assist those already entrenched in 'the life,' since existing social programs were clearly inadequate for reaching, protecting, and assisting juvenile prostitutes.[16] However, the committee also believed that a major limitation to the effectiveness of social service initiatives was that they lacked a means of holding youths in the care of social workers so that they could receive treatment. Further, 'the only effective means of doing this [was] through the criminal process.'[17] It therefore recommended the creation of a separate Criminal Code provision pertaining to persons under eighteen years of age. This provision would specify that:

1 Every young person who offers, provides, attempts, or agrees to offer or provide for money or other consideration to engage in a sexual act with another person is guilty of a summary conviction offence.
2 For the purpose of this section, 'young person' means a person who is under 18 years of age.[18]

This measure for the 'protection' of young prostitutes was advanced in contradiction to the committee's statement that 'there is no desire on the part of the committee to affix a criminal label to any juvenile prostitute,' and its acknowledgement that criminalization would not serve as a deterrent to young persons entering prostitution.[19] As the committee itself stated: 'Many of these juvenile prostitutes have also been at one time or another in conflict with the law. These encounters have not served to deter them from continuing their work as prostitutes. The prospects of their being charged or convicted of soliciting or other offences are seen as risks associated with the job.'[20]

The Badgley Committee's proposal to criminalize the activities of young people earning money through prostitution was intended to address the most contentious aspects of the pre–Bill C-49 soliciting legislation that was still in place by eliminating the need to prove that the prostitute had engaged in 'pressing and persistent' behaviour, or that the act of solicitation occurred in a public place. Instead they recommended criminalizing any attempt to engage in prostitution by a person under eighteen. The inadequacy of Section 195.1 in attaining convictions due to a lack of evidence of pressing and persistent behaviour was pointed to as a further rationale for adopting a separate section for juveniles, since young people had revealed in their interviews that they rarely needed to engage in this behaviour to obtain an adequate supply of customers. The requisite for determination of pressing and persistent behaviour in a public place was founded on the belief that street solicitation was a criminal offence only when it created a problem of public order: it was the public nuisance aspects of prostitution which constituted the offence; not soliciting per se. The committee, however, asserted that these concerns 'are clearly irrelevant to society's more compelling interest in deterring and punishing the exploitation of young persons by way of prostitution.'[21]

At the time that the Badgley Committee was undertaking its review, Section 195.1 of the Criminal Code did not specify whether or not customers or prospective customers of prostitutes could be charged with soliciting. As a result, interpretations of the provision varied by province.[22] The committee therefore recommended that the Criminal Code be amended to include a separate offence applying specifically to those persons who use or attempt to use the services of a juvenile prostitute,[23] and that special police units be established to investigate and lay charges against customers and pimps. No defence would be allowed on the basis that the customer or potential customer believed that the prostitute was over eighteen. Similarly, the committee recommended the extension and strengthening of existing procuring legislation to make arrests and convictions easier to obtain. A further means of deterrence would be the promotion of a national-provincial public media campaign for the publication of names of those persons convicted of soliciting juvenile prostitutes. As the committee stated, 'the prospect of public exposure and humiliation and the resultant loss of reputation, family, friends and even, in some instances, of business, would suffice in many instances to dissuade these persons from availing themselves of young prostitutes.'[24]

Respecting procuring, the proposed amendments would recognize that persons could be procured not only for sexual intercourse, but 'any sexual act,' and that a person could be determined a pimp who was in the company of a single prostitute, rather than more than one. Finally, the evidence of one person could be used in legal procedures against alleged procurers. Corroboration would no longer be necessary, making convictions easier to obtain.[25]

The National Juvenile Prostitution Survey and the Silencing of Young Prostitutes

Probably the most remarked upon feature of the Badgley Report is the massive amount of data that it organized, presented, and broadly interpreted. The National Juvenile Prostitution Survey (consisting of 244 questions) was the most extensive attempt to collect data on the activities of young prostitutes conducted in Canada, involving 229 young people identified as prostitutes in eight Canadian cities. The sample included 84 males and 145 females. The criteria for participation in the study were quite broad; that 'the boy or girl be no older than 20, and [had] to have performed at least one sexual act in exchange for money, food, shelter, drugs, alcohol, or some other valuable consideration.' The focus was almost exclusively on young people involved 'at the street level.'[26] The committee asserted that the survey was designed to enable young people to 'relate their experiences, air their views, and tell their own stories.'[27] Indeed, the survey did ask young people about their perceptions of street life, the obstacles to getting off the street, and their ideas about how new services might be designed to meet their needs. However, the survey was structured to assist the revision of Criminal Code statutes, focusing on 'salient legal issues, such as the methods by which these youths approached and negotiated with their clients.'[28] The survey was designed with the aid of a police officer, who suggested the kind of questions it would be relevant to ask.[29] Finally, the way the findings were presented in the final report served to silence young respondents, reflecting as it did the legal organization of the committee's mandate. No critique was provided of the social institutions (such as the family, homophobia, sexism, racism, structural poverty) that caused or exacerbated young people's troubles.

The questions contained in the Juvenile Prostitution Survey cannot be separated from ideologies about prostitution, as the survey was designed to address what police and other 'experts' regarded as most important. It was therefore organized such that participants' own voices were silenced, and their experiences reconstructed to fit the interpretive schema of the questionnaire's designers. As a result, rather than primary narratives being presented in the report, the voices of young people are heard through the documentary organization of police work as we are informed of these youths' case histories and criminal records. We find the voice of the official reporting that, for example, 'Marc sees himself as straight'[30] and 'Pat says that her work as a prostitute has numbed her senses and left her feeling passive towards life.'[31] Twelve brief case studies were presented (five female;

four male; three transsexual), leaving the reader only marginally better informed about young people's perspectives. Instead, these youths' lives and points of view were defined through a classification of sexual acts performed, diseases contracted, and vocabulary used.[32] They were reconstructed in an abstracted form, as statistics, files, case studies, from an adult, state-located, protectionist standpoint. Thus this massive report failed young people working in prostitution by reproducing a pattern with which they were already well too familiar. They simply were not being heard.

The only instance where young people's voices actively appeared in the discussion of juvenile prostitution was when they provided a useful moral message by advising others not to make the same mistakes, in conjunction with their perspectives on street life (virtually all limited to one or two brief sentences, likely by the survey design). When asked 'what advice they would give to the boy or girl starting out on the street,' typical responses were:

'GO HOME! You are going to be ruining your life. You'll look in the mirror every day and see a slut.'
'Don't do it; a criminal reputation blackens your reputation. You can get hurt if you're not street-wise.'
'Beat it. You won't be happy. You'll get old before your time.'
'It's a disgusting way to live.'
'There's no future.'
'I'll punch you out if you don't get off the street.'[33]

When asked what their perceptions were of street life, typical responses were:

'Horrible and disgusting, but the money is good. You risk your life.'
'A real fucked up life.'
'It's demeaning.'
'It's addictive. You always come back.'
'Freedom. It gives me a place to get away from my family.'
'It's a black hole.'
'I love my job.'
'On the street, when things are good they're really good, and when things are bad, they're really bad.'[34]

To determine the social and economic factors bearing a causal relation to young persons making money through prostitution, the National Juvenile

Prostitution Survey included questions on their social background. It was particularly concerned with early sexual experiences, young people's reasons for becoming prostitutes, and their previous contact with social services and police. However, as a result of the orientation of the committee's work to a legal mandate, its exclusive focus on sexual abuse, and the silencing of young people, the committee was unable to address its most significant findings concerning why young people resort to prostitution: economic necessity and financial gain. The survey had found that the most common reason provided by young people for engaging in prostitution was 'rapid financial gain,' with 78.6 per cent of boys and 65.5 per cent of girls listing this 'among their primary reasons.'[35] Far fewer young people stated that they had been coerced into working in prostitution than is commonly assumed to be the case. They found that 'one male and five females said they were forced to become prostitutes by a pimp while twenty-five females (17.2 per cent) said that they turned to prostitution in order to please another person who ... was likely a pimp.'[36] Therefore they found no evidence that youths were being forced into prostitution, of 'a proverbial "white slave trade."' However, the committee asserted that this finding did not discount that 'these youths may have been subject to a wide range of subtle and less dramatic forms of inducement to engage in prostitution.'[37]

The committee found that the young people who fit their criteria for inclusion in the survey came from 'all walks of life' and therefore defied stereotyping.[38] Predictably, most had experienced 'unhappy home lives.' Recollections of home life provided by survey participants were mostly unpleasant, being characterized by factors like continuous fighting and argument in the family, parental alcoholism, physical and sexual abuse, illness in the family, and strict religious upbringing. For the Badgley Committee, however, these 'unhappy home lives' reflected the failure of the individual family unit, rather than being a product of power relations which are structurally embedded within the traditional family itself.

Over three-quarters of the respondents had run away from home on at least one occasion and almost three-fifths described their action as a means of escaping family problems. A majority of them had, not surprisingly, also dropped out of school. These were the only experiences that the committee found juvenile prostitutes had in common.[39] As stated in the report, 'this combination of severing themselves from their families combined with their inexperience in other aspects of life created a condition of extreme vulnerability which fostered their transition to street life and to prostitution.'[40] No data is provided regarding the frequency of similar problems in the youth population as a whole, but they are likely quite prevalent without all those involved subsequently turning to 'a life of crime' or prostitution.

Physical abuse (other than sexual) was reported by 27.4 per cent of the male and 33.1 per cent of the female respondents. No special consideration was given to these figures, however, despite their significance. Rather, the potential importance of their findings on physical abuse could not be addressed by the committee's mandate, in which abuse was recognized specifically as a sexual problem.[41] Also, there are no means of comparing these figures with the rate of the physical abuse of young people in the population as a whole. They do not reveal whether the National Population Survey (conducted by Gallup Poll using a representative sample of 2,008 Canadians aged eighteen or over in 210 communities) queried respondents on their experiences of physical abuse as children. The lack of a comparative sample may have prevented the committee from determining any significance from this finding. The inability to make comparisons with a sample from the population as a whole was often a shortcoming in the committee's study of juvenile prostitution. An important opportunity was missed to explore the incidence and impact of violence on the lives of young people in Canada. As well, this comparison might have demonstrated just how similar young people who flee their homes and find a means of economic survival are to so many young people in their age group who don't.

Because juvenile prostitution was itself understood by the committee as a form of sexual abuse, the committee expected to be able to link it to a pattern of earlier sexual abuse. In some feminist analyses, a causal relation has been presumed to exist between early sexual abuse and the entry of women and young people into prostitution.[42] The committee sought to develop data on this theory through the National Juvenile Prostitution Survey, which queried young people's sexual histories. However, the Badgley Committee found no statistically significant difference in the occurrence of sexual abuse within the family between the findings of the National Juvenile Prostitution Survey and the National Population Survey.

What it did find was that the rate of sexual abuse in the population at large was very significant; one-half of all females and one-third of all males had been sexually abused in some way. The Badgley Committee used a very broad and controversial definition of sexual abuse, however, and its survey method has been questioned. For example, the committee's definition of sexual abuse included both 'unwanted sexual acts' and sex-related activity which young people were considered unable to legally consent to because of their age. The National Population Survey asked the following questions about 'unwanted sexual acts':[43]

Has anyone ever *exposed* the sex parts of their body to you when you didn't want this? Reply categories were: never happened to me; and circle as many as apply of penis, woman's crotch, breasts, buttocks, nude body, and other (specify).

Has anyone ever *threatened* to have sex with you when you didn't want this? Reply categories were: never happened to me, and a listing of the number of times these incidents had occurred.

Has anyone ever *touched* the sex parts of your body when you didn't want this? Reply categories were: never happened to me; and circle as many as apply of: *touched your penis, crotch, breasts, buttocks and anus; and kissed/licked your penis, crotch, breasts, and anus; and other types of touching (specify).*

Has anyone *ever tried to have sex* with you when you didn't want this, or *sexually attacked you?* Reply categories were: never happened to me; and circle as many as apply of: *tried* putting a penis in your vagina, tried putting something else (a finger or an object) in your vagina, tried putting a penis in your anus, and tried putting something else in your anus; and *forced* a penis in your vagina, forced something else in your vagina, forced a penis in your anus, and forced something else in your anus; *stimulated* or masturbated your crotch or penis; and other acts (specify).

While the studies found that the incidence of early sexual abuse in both family and non-family relations was similar for both groups, their comparison was flawed, since the population survey refers to 'unwanted sexual acts,' while the prostitution survey referred to 'use of threats or force,' and not all unwanted sexual acts involve these.

When comparing statistics for the age of first sexual experience, the juvenile prostitution survey found that 76.6 per cent of the males and 62.8 per cent of the females interviewed had their first sexual experience before the age of thirteen, compared to 5.4 per cent of the males and 1.7 per cent of the females in the National Population Survey. While these figures indicate a broad disparity between the samples, again the comparison is not valid, since the National Population Survey included persons of all ages, and there has been a tendency for people to have had their first sexual experiences at a younger age in more recent decades. It is not appropriate to compare the initial experiences of a person who was a child or teenager in the 1950s to a person who grew up in the 1980s.[44] Further, to attribute any significance to this finding, one would have to assert that the earlier a person's first sexual experience, the more likely she or he is to follow up on that experience by engaging in prostitution.

If sexual abuse bears a causal relation to young people entering prostitution, the numbers of young prostitutes should be substantially greater than they are, given that the sexual abuse of young people is pervasive, indeed systemic. The Badgley Committee recognized that it could not conclude that there was a link between early sexual abuse and entry into prostitution.[45] However, despite its findings, the similar frequency of sex abuse in prostitute and non-prostitute populations did not shift the conception of sexual abuse being organized through the report. Whether or not it caused young people to engage in prostitution, it was considered by the committee to be a condition of the work as a result of young people's contact with customers and pimps. Despite the lack of evidence linking juvenile prostitution to early experiences of sex abuse, the perception that juvenile prostitution was sexual abuse pervaded the committee's work because of its mandate.

The juvenile prostitution survey revealed that at one time or another most of the young people responding to the survey had had contact with social service or law enforcement agencies. Often their first encounter was with family and social welfare courts because of family breakdown, and resulted in many of them being placed in foster homes, group homes, or treatment centres.[46] A substantial number of the young people surveyed had therefore been shuffled through police, courts, social service agencies, and foster homes; from one form of official care to another. By the time these youths found a source of income in prostitution, therefore, their opinions of such mechanisms were already well formed; they indicated a lack of trust in social services and regarded them as 'useless.'[47] As mentioned earlier, the committee stated that it was interested in their opinions about the kind of social services they believed would serve them best, and noted some of their responses in their final report. However, these views don't appear to have been taken seriously enough to warrant their inclusion as recommendations for improvement in social service provision. Instead, the committee's recommendations were to significantly expand the power of social workers and police to hold and treat young prostitutes, without questioning what was wrong with existing social services to make them so ineffective.

The Badgley Committee concluded that social services had to play a larger preventative role through mechanisms that would 'identify the early warning signs of troubled home conditions warranting the provision of special services.'[48] Unfortunately, this did not imply that existing social services should be scrutinized and reorganized to make them more effective, but only that their power to inspect families and assume guardianship over young people should be broadened (an important but nonetheless insufficient measure).

The recommendation to criminalize the activities of young people involved in prostitution ignored the repercussions of an expansion of policing, which further criminalization would certainly entail. Moreover, the National Juvenile Prostitution Survey reported that 21.4 per cent of males and 18.6 per cent of females considered to be prostitutes had suffered beatings and other forms of abuse at the hands of police,[49] indicating that the mechanism for enforcing the committee's proposed legislation would potentially be a major barrier to achieving the stated aims of the committee: the 'protection' of young people.

The Badgley Committee was able to make the recommendations that it did because of the method by which its mandate structured its work processes. As Dorothy Smith finds, in this kind of documentary organization 'an interpretive schema is made use of in the assemblage and construction of an array of particulars as an account of what actually happened in such a way that these particulars will intend, and be interpreted by that schema. The effect is peculiarly circular for although questions of truth and falsity, accuracy and inaccuracy about the particulars may certainly be raised, the schema in itself is not called into question as a method of providing the coherence of the collection of particulars as a whole.'[50]

The recommendations implied that an inability to hold young people involved in prostitution for treatment, inadequate legal classification of age appropriateness for sexual activity, and inadequate state supervision of families were fundamentally to blame for the failure of existing social service provisions and policing practices. No critique was provided of the construction of gender relations, the institution of the family, or existing social services. The use of survey data is limited without an informed interpretive framework, and as my comments on the juvenile prostitution survey indicated, both the design of the survey and the presentation of the data were also problematic.

Although there was a clear disparity in statistical findings for females and males involved in prostitution throughout the study, no attempt was made to account for these differences in any substantive way. There was no discussion in the report about why it is virtually always males who are the sexual abusers of children and the clients of prostitutes, nor about the social and economic conditions that make prostitution such a favourable option to young women, compared with the alternatives available. Although the data found that female prostitutes are more likely to come from poor families and have more frequently experienced sexual abuse than male prostitutes, this disparity was not questioned. The report did, however, reveal that boys from middle-class and affluent homes often left because their sexual preferences were not approved of, and they found themselves more accepted in the street life. There was no recognition that the hostile environment created by homophobia and heterosexism was (and is) a major barrier to young men and women 'coming out.' These attitudes are indeed the problem. Rather, adaptation to homosexuality was presented as the individual's responsibility.

Further, the significance of the committee's findings concerning sexual abuse was made particularly powerful by the social context into which the final report was launched, the same social context that had originally motivated the appointment of the committee. The report's central concern with the protection of young people from sexual abuse was an uncontested one. The sheer scope and volume of the Badgley Report gave the incidence and prevalence of sexual abuse an empirical face, and thus presented it as something that could be measured and therefore managed. Using its extensive database as evidence, the committee was able to present concrete recommendations about how sexual abuse could be regulated through coordination of the work of the various types and levels of state power. The report was to have a far-reaching impact, as the committee's findings were activated through the media, producing a 'moral panic' about juvenile prostitution.

Previous chapters have provided indicators of the importance of textual forms and documentary processes to the organization of social relations. They have acknowledged the ways in which perceptions of prostitution are always being produced through textual forms, so that, as Smith asserts, texts do indeed organize the social relations which they are a part of.[51] Official documents like the Badgley Report occupy a privileged space in the discursive organization of prostitution, since they are oriented towards the legal practices that serve to reproduce the relations of social regulation. The Badgley Report has proven to be a powerful mechanism in restructuring our mode of knowing about prostitution involving young people, its administration, regulation, and consequently, its practice. It remains the definitive and official source of data on the sexual abuse of children and youths in Canada.

Finally, the way in which feminist concerns for legal reform were taken up by both the Fraser and Badgley Committees suggests a caution for feminist organizations intent on legal fixes. As Carol Smart comments, 'the feminist movement (broadly defined) is too easily "seduced" by law and even where it is critical of law it too often attempts to use law pragmatically in the hope that new law or more law might be better than old law.'[52] She adds that, through feminist work for law reform, 'the women's movement is tacitly accepting the significance of law in regulating the social order,' and 'while some law reforms may indeed benefit some women [and I would add, young people], it is certain that all law reforms empower law.'[53]

The committee's 'raison d'etre' was to *protect* young people from sexual harms, and yet we know in practice that the existence of prohibitive law rarely affects people's conduct. What the law really accomplishes, then, is symbolic, in establishing a society's moral code, and is punitive (and professedly 'rehabilitative'), towards those who transgress it. This reality, not to mention the ability of government commissions to incorporate and co-opt feminist initiatives, creates an ongoing dilemma for feminists and others who spend much of their time negotiating with and through state power.

7

Street Kids and Child Prostitutes: The Making of a 'New' Social Problem

The previous chapter discussed how the Badgley Committee addressed prostitution involving young people by shifting state and professional discourse about the practice from juvenile delinquency to the *sexual abuse of children*. Through the committee's work processes, juvenile prostitution was *produced as a social problem*, where prior to the release of the report, it had received little public and media attention.

Since its release in 1984, the Badgley Report has functioned as a key mechanism for the development of new standardized and coordinated definitional categories of sexual abuse, oriented to the legal process, throughout levels of government and public and private social service agencies. The social service and health care professionals, police, journalists, and so on, who continue to refer to the report as the definitive document on sexual abuse in Canada, or who are compelled to enforce its recommendations as they are made into official policy and work guidelines, accomplish the committee's regulatory proposals. At the same time, the construction of prostitution involving young people as a social problem provided a further avenue of social critique for those decrying the moral decline of Canadian society.[1]

In the period following the release of the Badgley Report, prostitution involving young people came to be considered a major social problem in Canadian cities. The work of the Badgley Committee clearly contributed to this focus, and the redefinition of youth prostitution as a form of sexual abuse of children served to obscure the economic bases for prostitution. The Badgley Report was a continual point of reference and source of data in media accounts in the period following its release. Just as the Badgley Committee's mandate structurally subordinated the economic reasons for young people entering prostitution to the all-encompassing constitution of juvenile prostitution as sexual abuse, so too did media accounts based on the Badgley Report, and the statements of police and some social workers.

The Making of a New Moral Panic in Toronto

Where previously it had been marginal to media coverage of prostitution in general, juvenile prostitution became a focus of media attention in Toronto after the release of the Badgley Report. Newspapers used the data, conceptual framework, and recommendations of the Badgley Report to address juvenile prostitution as a form of sexual abuse of children. They ran lengthy, usually front page stories with dramatic titles such as, 'Teen hooker tells sordid tale: Sex at 10'; 'The 18 month nightmare of mother whose child was trapped by a pimp'; 'Many ignorant of sexuality. Young street prostitutes vulnerable, alone in world'; 'Street kids fight their desperate existence'; '300 teen prostitutes roam streets'; and 'Young prostitutes find the life addictive.'[2]

Numerous accounts estimating the numbers of young people thought to be working as prostitutes were provided, drawing on police as a source of data, as well as on the perspectives of some social workers. Some media accounts confused the number of young people 'on the street' with the number of young prostitutes, citing the estimated number of youth on the streets and then shifting directly into a discussion of juvenile prostitution. Others moved from stating the number of runaways per year in Canada or in a specific region such as Toronto (a figure which includes both young people who return home and those who don't), to a discussion of street kids and juvenile prostitution, again correlating the issues in the minds of the readers. Still other accounts attempted to estimate the number who actually worked as prostitutes, but these figures, not to mention estimates of the total number of street youth, varied widely. For example, an October 1985 article in the *Toronto Star* stated that there were an estimated 10,000 street people in Metro Toronto, a figure which presumably included both adults and youths.[3] In July 1985, Grant Lowery of Central Toronto Youth Services was cited as estimating that as many as 12,000 young people lived on Toronto streets.[4] An April 1987 *Toronto Star* article stated that there were up to 10,000 young people on the streets,[5] while in August of 1987 the figure was cited as 10,000–20,000.[6] A February 1986 article had estimated 2,000 runaways on Toronto streets.[7]

Throughout this reporting, the 'street kid' was being created as a 'new' social problem. The typical profile provided was of a child who lacks lodgings of any kind, and never knows whether she or he will have a place to sleep that night. However, youth workers define a street kid as one who lacks *stable* housing: they have either no fixed address or only temporary housing. This can include a broad range of situations, from the young people who do indeed find shelter in Goodwill drop off boxes, to those who live in hostels or hotels, or who stay with friends for an undefined period. Young prostitutes were uniformly depicted as street kids, even though their living situations varied.

The number of street kids who were actually involved in prostitution was difficult to ascertain. In July 1985 Blanche Axton of Inner City Youth was reported as estimating that 80 per cent of young women and 50 to 60 per cent of young men on the street worked as prostitutes.[8] *Toronto Star* articles in December 1984 and June 1986 stated that there were an estimated 2,000 prostitutes under eighteen working in Metro. *Toronto Star* articles in October 1985 and July 1985 estimated that there were 1,000.[9] The October 1985 article added that 300 of them were estimated to be under eighteen, among whom the police had identified 45 as being between twelve and fifteen years old. A November 1984 *Globe and Mail* article stated that the Toronto Task Force had counted, during a one month period (17 September to 16 October 1985), 328 female prostitutes, two-thirds (231) of whom were thought to be between the ages of fourteen and twenty. The task force stated that they had also counted a total of 111 male prostitutes, three-quarters (76) of whom were thought to be between the ages of sixteen and twenty. A February 1985 *Globe and Mail* article stated that a Metro Toronto police report estimated there were 700 'streetwalkers' in Metro, 60 per cent (420) of whom were under twenty-one.[10]

There appeared to have been some wild speculation going on in the accounts that provided the high figures. Some of the confusion seems to have resulted from a lack of distinction between young people working in prostitution and those who did not. This was partially due to the indeterminacy of the identity, 'prostitute.' If only those young people who worked regularly in the trade were labelled 'prostitutes,' the numbers would of course be much smaller than if the same identity was imposed on anyone who occasionally engaged in sex for money or a place to stay at night. Media accounts rarely made a distinction between occasional and full-time prostitution. As I noted in Chapter 6, the Badgley Committee itself utilized a very broad definition that included anyone under twenty who had provided sexual services *at least once* in exchange for money or any other consideration, such as food, drugs, or a place to sleep.[11]

There were also varing definitions of what constitutes a 'young' prostitute. By including prostitutes under twenty or twenty-one years, rather than eighteen, the figure can potentially be inflated dramatically. Interestingly, however, one study based upon the broadest age range produced the most conservative figures. Conversely, if we were to think of a child prostitute as someone under sixteen, the age at which one can legally leave or be told to leave home, the number estimated would decrease substantially. However, in newspaper accounts, young prostitutes were frequently referred to as 'children,' a categorization that deepened the sense of crisis, even though the data cited included young people between the ages of sixteen and twenty-one (and in at least one case, up to twenty-five).[12] Despite this confusion, by the end of the decade the term 'street kid' was uniformly applied to young people who had fled families, foster homes, and an array of institutional settings for an uncertain, but perhaps preferable, existence in the downtown core.

Street kids, including young people working in prostitution, had developed a homogeneous identity, a phenomenon that was also found by Riccardo Lucchini in the Latin American context. As he comments, 'the image of street-children given by the medias and the political system, welfare institutions and the justice for minors doesn't take into account the diversity of personal situations and individual careers which exist in the street. These children are therefore perceived as if they would constitute a homogeneous social category constituted of perfectly interchangeable individuals ... there is a certain craze for the street-child as the medias [have] seized this problem'[13]

The street kid had become a social problem that could be managed through standardized state work processes, particularly the criminal justice system and social services provisions. However, the limits of these resolutions were predetermined by the manner of social construction – or definition – of the problem.

The identity of the 'street kid' had particular salience for young people over sixteen, for although it blurred the distinctions between them, it also allowed them more anonymity by not identifying what they actually did to survive. In addition, as measures were being implemented to address the crisis of the street kid, the identity ensured access to a range of new services, such as showers, clean clothes, basic health care, condoms, and needle exchanges, not previously available to them. Some willingly took on the label of the street kid for the advantages it offered.

More attention was also paid to male prostitution in the media than had been previously, and male prostitution was said to have increased significantly. Some accounts discussed the economic imperative for their entry into the trade. Fred Mathews of CTYS was quoted as saying 'they're mostly unemployable, with no skills and semi-literate. There's a desperate dimension. You see boys who would never have hustled before but turned to it for survival.'[14] Other accounts focused almost exclusively on the young men's presumed homosexuality as the reason for leaving their families and working in prostitution, rather than considering the possibility that their reasons may be as diverse as those of young women and girls.[15] Since homosexuality is pathologized, and for lesbians and gays one's 'identity' is considered to be synonymous with 'sexual identity,' these youths' alleged homosexuality was regarded as the source of their problems. For example, a youth worker was cited as stating that hustlers are confused about their sexual orientation, adding that 'working as a prostitute for homosexual clients confirms them in homosexuality.'[16] This marginalized the economic imperative for hustling, and further entrenched them as an outcast group. Yet hustlers generally enjoyed a much greater degree of freedom than their female counterparts, given the different gender power dynamics involved. They were less likely to be physically and emotionally abused by their male customers – some of whom regarded themselves as pals of the younger men, while the younger men regarded them as 'sugars' (sugardaddies) who could be turned to for a meal or a place to sleep on a regular basis. As well, hustlers rarely had pimps, and so had more control over their income. Transgendered prostitutes were somewhat more vulnerable since they both presented themselves as women and were at greater risk from cruising 'fag bashers.' Although the majority of hustlers were old enough to work in bars and men's saunas when the weather was inclement, in media accounts the age of hustlers was subject to distortion, so that the customers were portrayed as sexual abusers of children. A *Globe and Mail* article, covering conditions on Breadalbane Avenue, a focal point for male street prostitution in Toronto, reported that on this downtown street, 'at night ... bureaucracy gives way to pederasty.'[17] However, even the Toronto police were unable to claim knowledge of any hustlers under sixteen years of age.

A common reporting technique that was used to personalize the need for 'child saving' was the 'case study' illustrating the plight of young prostitutes. These accounts focused on the youthfulness of prostitutes, constructing profiles of girls under sixteen years of age. They typically described young girls with tough exteriors, who were nonetheless extremely vulnerable and desperate for help, and who were attempting to escape the trade, abusive pimps, and drugs. These girls were victimized by pimps and customers, but had yet to be fully corrupted. They therefore could still be saved through the quick action of social workers and police. For example:

'Christine' is 15, and has lived as a street prostitute for two years. She says she sleeps most of the day, 'parties' all night, and lives in one room of an apartment paid for by a pimp. She can't remember when she last had free time or saw a movie ... Picked up at 3 am by police, she could look like any sleepy adolescent but for dark-etched circles under her eyes and a pain in her belly from untreated venereal disease.[18]

And:

She's just 16, pretty, wears a short pink flannelette nightgown with teddybear applique and fluffy pink sippers.
Kathy's a kid.
She charges $60 for oral sex, $80 for intercourse, $100 for half-and-half and $500 for the night.
Kathy's a hooker.
And a couple of hours earlier when she arrived at Moberly House, the Isabella St. reception centre for runaways and juvenile hookers where pyjamas are a house rule, she didn't look like much of a kid.[19]

Newspaper coverage of juvenile prostitution invariably reported the vigilant control and abuse of runaway teenaged girls by pimps. The following extract draws together the fear of the city and dangers of urban life with the exploitation of innocent and vulnerable youth by pimps. 'Metro is the Mecca for runaways from all over the country and Yonge Street is the magnet that draws them into the clutches of the ever-vigilant pimp who first befriends them and then entices or forces them into prostitution.'[20]

The theme of 'sexual danger' in 'the city' is not a new one. The following text is from a 1911 tract, 'Canada's War on the White Slave Trade,' that warned against the dangers of a traffic in women and girls alleged to be occurring in Canada and other nations. 'Canada is today the Mecca of the immigrant from all lands. Its lands are wondrous wide, its grain and sand and rock are indeed golden. Here then is the slaver's golden opportunity. Men and women [!] hunt and bait and ensnare them, even as the wild things of the forest are hunted and baited and ensnared. It is easy to do.'[21] Similarly, the theme of street youth as an urban social problem has been a recurrent one since the beginnings of urbanization, although the names by which they are identified change.[22] The ability of social work professionals, police, and media to draw on these longstanding societal anxieties in the organization of a 'new' social problem made juvenile prostitution a particularly potent phenomenon.

In this, police provided the primary source of news. Toronto police added fuel to the fire by claiming that the number of pimps preying on prostitutes rose after the 1978 *Hutt* decision because the law was unenforceable. This assertion is contrary to historical evidence indicating that prostitutes are more susceptible to pimps when laws are tougher.[23] A Metro Toronto Police representative was cited in late 1984 as asserting that pimps control about 98 per cent of prostitutes.[24] In November 1987, the *Toronto Sun* ran the banner headline, 'Teen Hookers "White Slaves." Cops Report Runaways Tortured,'[25] The reference to 'white slavery' was made by a member of the Metro Police Juvenile Task Force at a seminar held the previous day. Further, Toronto Deputy Chief William McCormack was noted to have said a few days earlier that 'the real culprits behind this [juvenile prostitution] are the "white slavers" and those are the people we would like to see completely eradicated.'[26] The idea of 'white slavery' was created by late nineteenth and early twentieth century social reformers. It was a potent reference to the alleged traffic in women and girls believed to be widespread in Victorian cities. 'White slavery' was used to rally Victorian reformers toward the eradication of this evil, just as they had worked to eliminate the Black slave trade of earlier decades. Toronto police clearly remained as blithely ignorant of the racial specificity of 'white' slavery as the reformers had been.

The implications of these police statements become clearer when one recalls that pimps are stereotypically believed to be Black, sometimes immigrant men, who enslave women and girls stereotypically believed to be white. It draws upon morals discourse and anti-immigration sentiment of early in this century, when it was alleged that Chinese men (aka 'the Oriental Menace') were preying upon innocent white women and girls by luring them into prostitution. Through a process that allied race fears with contemporary discourses about women and children's victimization, the demand that Toronto's streets be cleared of prostitution acquired an additional moral imperative. This depiction reinforced race, gender, and age stereotypes, and detracted public attention from the underlying economic conditions facing young people, and indeed the city itself, as its economy was reorganized.

A 1994 *Chatelaine* magazine article, 'Pimped,' provided a blatant example of how these fears are mobilized, as it reported the story of a white girl who was exploited by a Black pimp in the 1980s. 'Marie' was a troubled teen 'on the brink of disaster. Marie's step off that brink was taken with a new boyfriend – a jobless young Black man with a fancy car – who lived a few kilometres away, in the community of North Preston.' North Preston was described as a generally impoverished, largely Black community, whose residents descended from some of Canada's earliest non-Aboriginal settlers.

In this harsh environment was spawned, during the 70s and 80s, a huge industry: pimping. Now, in almost every major city in Canada, men from North Preston and three black communities adjacent to it own the rights to most corners on the hookers' strolls – and own the mostly white teenage girls working them. Even after a nationwide crackdown in the past two years, police believe at least 50 North Preston based pimps, many related to each other, remain active in the teen prostitution network. No one knows how many thousands of Nova Scotia girls have been pimped throughout Canada and as far away as New York, Los Angeles and even, in one case, Naples, Italy. No one knows how many girls have died at the hands of pimps. Until recently, no one seemed to care.[27]

Interestingly, Marie's boyfriend – her 'step off the brink' – disappears from the narrative immediately. It is his Blackness that signifies Marie's decline, for it is not him, but another Black man, who later turns her out (into prostitution), beats her, and fathers her child. Marie eventually escapes and returns to her family, although the story explains that many were not so lucky. It is Marie's comments about her experience as a procured prostitute that open up an otherwise common narrative: 'I don't resent black men ... I do have a problem with white men. One hundred percent of the Johns were white – men who looked like my father, my brother, my cousins. They all knew what was going on, but no one tried to help. They only wanted one thing ... It was one black man who did it to me, but thousands of white men.'[28] The narrative ends by warning that the pimps of North Preston caught in the last police crackdown will have finished or are nearing the end of their sentences and, being 'unqualified for any honest work beyond flipping burgers,' will once again join the ranks of Canada's pimps. The problem will re-emerge. Vigilance must be maintained.

Important too to the making of a moral panic was police reporting of the involvement of young prostitutes in a range of crimes from drug peddling to murder. The force's representative maintained that the incidence of prostitution has grown 'ten-fold' in recent years, resulting in '10 times the number of robberies, pimps, and drug use.'[29] The following text is typical of the reporting style, which featured the police as a reliable source of news:

Prostitution has 'run wild' in Toronto, in the words of a senior Metro police officer. It has grown at such an alarming rate in the past five years that several thousand prostitutes are now working downtown streets.

Violent crimes – from drug meddling to murder – are thriving in the atmosphere of widespread prostitution, a $50 million business in Metro, police say.

Just as alarming as the growth of prostitution is the age of the prostitutes. At least 2,000 are under the age of 18. Some children start as young as 15 and even 12.

What can be done about this growing problem?[30]

Thus, these paragraphs link a series of problems as one; a general crisis of prostitution, an alleged growth of related criminal activity, and an alleged growth of juvenile prostitution (the latter would appear in these paragraphs to constitute two-thirds of a large prostitute population). The crisis scenario represented in this text could then be used to legitimate a crackdown on both adult and youth prostitution. As I have already commented, young people who find a source of income in prostitution may support themselves through a number of pursuits, both legal and illegal. However, the juxtaposition of activities in the media suggests that the existence of prostitution *causes* a growth in other criminal activity, rather than that a young person may turn tricks or pick wallets because both are a means of economic survival. This uncritical linkage is further sustained because the association of prostitution with crime is derived from its practice being criminalized (communicating, keeping a common bawdy-house), rather than from any inherent characteristic of prostitution itself. However, police continually identified 'weak laws' as encouraging the abuse of young prostitutes by pimps and customers. Young people were prevented from escaping prostitution, they claimed, because police lacked an effective legal tool for removing them from the streets.

Media accounts did not ignore the economic reasons for young people entering prostitution, including inability to find work, or to find jobs that provided a living wage. However, these factors were subordinated to the coercive power of the pimp, as the following paragraph demonstrates: 'Many juvenile prostitutes are runaways from home, the victims of sexual abuse, poorly educated, and without money or jobs. They become the victims of scheming pimps who lurk around the bus station, Union station, and the Eaton Centre – the focal point for young people flocking downtown.'[31] The authors accomplished the subordination of economic factors precipitating entrance into prostitution to the predatory pimp, while summarizing a list of conditions describing the background of young prostitutes provided by the Badgley Report.

The control of young prostitutes by pimps was thereby constructed as factual in news accounts, and alternative accounts, including those of young prostitutes themselves, were denied. For example, a July 1985 *Toronto Sun* article stated that 'most who turn up at Moberly House [a holding centre for young prostitutes picked up by police] deny they have pimps but police discount their stories.'[32] This same process was evident in the Badgley Report, which stated that, 'only about one in ten girls *was prepared to admit* that she was working for a pimp,' while approximately 38 per cent *were willing to report* that they had in the past [my emphases].'[33] The 'expert' and authoritative sources of the news – the Badgley Report, the police, and social workers, as well as the continual repetition of the pimping theme – were layered on to pre-existing stereotypes. In this way, the idea that pimps controlled virtually all prostitutes was reinforced as a truth. Moreover, a continual emphasis on very young prostitutes as victims dramatized the need for 'child saving' through state action, at the same time that this emphasis enhanced newsworthiness.[34]

The Badgley Report and the police established the initial definition of the problem of juvenile prostitution in Toronto, and this 'primary interpretation' established a structure which was extremely difficult to alter. As Hall and others note, 'the primary definition sets the limit for all subsequent discussion by framing what the problem is. This initial framework then provides the criteria by which all subsequent contributions are labelled as "relevant" to the debate, or "irrelevant" – beside the point. Contributions which stray from this framework are exposed to the charge that they are "not addressing the problem."'[35] By 1987, the control of young prostitutes by pimps and the efforts of police to crack down on the practice were the focal point of virtually all news stories on juvenile prostitution in Toronto.

State Responses to the 'Crisis'

With the release of the Badgley Report, juvenile prostitution soon became an important issue for Toronto city politicians. It was a municipal election year, and politicians quickly pointed the blame at the federal government for failing to enact tougher federal laws. As an October 1985 *Toronto Star* article reported, city politicians were 'passionate about the hundreds of street kids – "they could be yours or mine" - and the lax federal laws that prevent police or Metro social agencies from helping them.'[36] The Metro Toronto Council Executive Committee supported the Badgley Report recommendation to publish the names of customers convicted of offering money to prostitutes under eighteen years, which, in addition to a proposed two year jail term, would punish the offenders 'through humiliation and loss of reputation.' June Rowlands, then a Toronto alderperson, stated that 'we adults have virtually abandoned these children under the rubric of civil rights ... No other country in the western world allows it. It's disgraceful ... these people spouting civil rights are condemning those children to a life of tragedy.'[37] The spectre of the Emanuel Jaques murder was once again raised to reinforce the demand for more stringent legislation against prostitution. The moral panic over juvenile prostitution served as an additional impetus for the crackdown on all street prostitution. At the same time, some social workers pointed to 'the crisis' of juvenile prostitution as evidence that child welfare agencies and professionals needed to be granted more power and authority through provincial law.

The Badgley Committee's proposal to specifically criminalize the activities of juvenile prostitutes was widely condemned by social workers, however,[38] and was subsequently rejected by the federal government as too harsh a measure to be used against young people directly, since they had not yet attained the age of responsibility (eighteen years) set out by the Young Offenders Act. Legislation was, however, amended to specifically address those who purchased the services or lived on the avails of a juvenile prostitute. Bill C-15 was passed on 23 June 1987, thereby altering the existing Sections 195(2) to (4) of the Criminal Code to make those who lived on the avails of prostitution of a person under the age of eighteen liable to up to fourteen years imprisonment.[39] Toronto police moved to crack down on those who lived on the earnings of young people engaged in prostitution, aided by information provided by social service agencies that deal with runaways and young prostitutes. The courts, in turn, handed out stiffer sentences. In the year following the introduction of the new legislation police claimed that the number of young people involved in prostitution had been reduced as a result of these actions; however, subsequent media accounts dramatized high numbers involved in the trade.[40]

These measures may have made it more dangerous for those who did have bona fide pimps, because they were likely to be much more tightly controlled. At the same time, tougher prostitution legislation may have meant that young prostitutes went 'voluntarily and willingly' to men and asked them to be their pimp, as some judges residing over pimps trials were reported as finding, because young prostitutes believed that a pimp could offer them protection.[41]

While customers charged with communicating for the purpose of prostitution were caught within the scope of Bill C-49, it was thought that those who engaged the sexual services of a young person, under any conditions, deserved a harsher penalty. A provision was added to specify that 'every person who, in any place, obtains or attempts to obtain, for consideration, the sexual services of a person who is under the age of eighteen years is guilty of an indictable offence and is liable to imprisonment for a term not exceeding five years.'[42] These amendments to the Criminal Code were introduced as part of a package of legal reforms delimiting and regulating the sexual abuse of young people, all of which were a direct result of the recommendations of the Badgley Report.

The deployment of the Badgley Report's conceptual framework and recommendations (including its reconceptualization of juvenile prostitution as a form of sexual abuse, rather than juvenile delinquency), and the subsequent moral panic gave impetus to the federal and provincial governments to direct more funding towards the 'rescue,' care, and treatment of young prostitutes and 'street kids' generally. The federal government earmarked twenty million dollars over four years for addressing the sexual abuse of young people, including juvenile prostitution.[43] In Ontario, this funding was provided both to establish new services and to expand the range of already existing programs directed by private (church sponsored) organizations. Numerous programs were put into operation, providing a variety of services. Services for persons over sixteen who are not under direct state control (are not incarcerated or on probation) are generally voluntary because they cannot be held against their will. In contrast, young people under sixteen generally participate in programs involuntarily.

In early 1985, the Ministry of Community and Social Services announced the introduction of the Toronto Street Youth Project, a three-stage program of consultation, assessment, and treatment. With an initial budget allocation of 1.3 million dollars, it was directed to provide care and treatment for prostitutes and street kids considered to be 'at risk' who were under the age of sixteen.[44] Minister of Community and Social Services, John Sweeney, announced that this was to form the basis of 'a campaign to give all youngsters a childhood of innocence, free of pain, in an atmosphere of affection and support.'[45]

Phase One, the 'reception centre,' was run out of Moberly House, which provided emergency shelter and crisis counselling for up to seventy-two hours for young prostitutes and runaways. Operated by the Metro Toronto Children's Aid and Catholic Children's Aid Societies, it provided a means of holding and 'stabilizing' young people while staff workers determined the appropriate place to send them. This phase of the program was designed to provide medical examinations and counselling to assess the juvenile's needs. Those admitted were kept in pyjamas, an infantalizing process that workers asserted was necessary to break down their street veneer and make them more receptive to adult authority. It also discouraged them from 'running,' although some still managed to do so. Admissions were involuntary, and the majority were young people found loitering by the police. The youths were brought in under the authority of Ontario's Family and Child Services Act (which replaced the Child Welfare Act in October 1985), using statutes designed to provide for the protection of young people deemed to be at risk as a result of having no apparent guardian. Most of the young people had been reported missing from home, and police attempted to contact their families or guardians to investigate their home situations. The house social worker assigned the young person to a Children's Aid Worker to direct further action. Youths were not necessarily returned to their homes, since workers recognized that they ran away for a reason. During the first six months of operation, 73 per cent of the young people who were brought to Moberly House had previous involvement with child welfare services.[46]

Young people who entered Phase One either continued on to Phase Two, were returned to their families, or were placed in group homes or other kinds of care. The second phase was a thirty to ninety day live-in supervision and assessment facility, administered and staffed by a private commercial consultant group based in Kitchener, called Cassatta-Warrendale. Approximately 30 per cent moved on from stage one to stage two, and these were described as being mainly those young people who had been on the streets for a longer period of time. Their admissions included youths who were on probation, with a court order to be held for an assessment of their medical and psychological needs. While the young people were being 'stabilized,' they were prepared for their next placement, determined by Children's Aid. Not all of those who were recommended to proceed to the third phase ended up there; some were sent instead to group homes, foster homes, or their own homes, as were those whose assessments indicated that they did not require stage three treatment.

The third phase, the C.M. Hincks Treatment Centre (located at the Adult Rehabilitation Centre in Edgar, Ontario), was a non-profit long-term residential psychiatric service for adolescents, where the young person could be detained for up to two years. Hincks' aims were to inculcate a strong value system in young people. According to Fred Campbell, the ministry supervisor for the Toronto Street Youth Project, this phase was designed to address the needs of 'hard core kids in serious trouble.' The system as a whole was monitored by police, health care professionals, and the Children's Aid Society.[47]

In June 1985, the Ministry of Community and Social Services allocated funding to Anglican Houses to establish, with the assistance of the Coalition of Youth Work Professionals, a new service program for prostitutes over the age of sixteen called Street Outreach Services (SOS). For a year prior to the establishment of the program, the Downtown Churchworkers Association, with funds from Christ Church, had maintained a paid street worker to investigate the needs of young prostitutes. This provided the impetus for SOS. Participation is voluntary, and young people must determine their own goals, since efforts to assist them are futile unless the youths are willing and cooperative. Street workers stroll through areas where prostitution takes place and initiate contact with young people, attempting to establish a basis of trust, and providing information on health care, housing, employment, and youth services. A free drop in centre that provides casual counselling is also available for those who seek out services.[48] Those who express a commitment to getting off of the street enter the 'high support' phase of the program, which offers a range of support system options. Workers ensure that participants' immediate needs of shelter, food, and clothing are met, and match them with a worker who helps them to get social assistance or find employment.[49] The need to find stable housing for young people is a major concern of these youth workers, a problem which is exacerbated by Toronto's high housing prices. Cooperative housing was also maintained, although accommodation was limited to a small number of young people.[50] The agency was mandated to address the needs of young men, including a large transgendered population, working Boytown and the 'trani' (transgendered) stroll. The upper age limit for those able to access its services was eventually increased to include persons up to twenty-four years old. Workers convincingly argued that this was a necessary step given the paucity of services for older youth, and the often delayed maturation that resulted from years spent in street life. Although these are legitimate and important concerns, the reality of these service requirements further destabilizes the homogeneous characterization of the street kid being conveyed in most media accounts.[51]

Service providers at SOS (many of whom were neither schooled in nor followed a conventional social work model) made a significant effort to implement programs that realistically addressed the needs and interests of the agency's youth population. During the late 1980s and early 1990s, then controversial services like a needle exchange program and an anonymous testing site for HIV were put into place. With the assistance of staff, youth designed safe-sex information booklets, T-shirts, buttons, and even a film. The development of a peer support program provided an alternative to the top-down support model of conventional social service programs, and youth were encouraged to set their own goals. Workers emphasized that success must be measured through small steps, on a scale realistic to the culture of street life. As well, familiarity (and comfort) with issues related to sexuality, including sexual identity and sexual orientation, were regarded as critical for working with the SOS population, the majority of whom were gay, bisexual, or transgendered.

Other services for street kids in Toronto included the Beat the Street program, established by two self-described former street people to teach basic literacy skills; Inner City Youth Project, provided by Big Sisters Organization; Evergreen, provided by the Yonge Street Mission; Huntley Youth Services; Turning Point, offering shelter and counselling; and a later arrival, SHOUT Clinic, designed to provide health care services to street youth, without requiring a hospital insurance card.

Covenant House, a service of the Catholic Church, operates an 'On the Street Programme,' in which two social workers tour the downtown area in a recreational vehicle providing outreach services. Covenant House also runs an under twenty-one youth crisis centre with a curfew and a strict system of prohibitions (for example, preventing any physical contact between residents). Some youth workers have been critical of this approach, regarding it as too rigid and demanding for young people who are used to a lot of freedom.[52] Covenant House has also faced criticism from both youth and youth workers for its adherence to the principles of the Catholic Church, which are widely considered to be unrealistic in meeting the needs of street youth. For example, abortion counselling cannot be provided and condoms cannot be distributed under church policy. Nevertheless, Covenant House in Canada and the United States remains the best-known street youth service to the general public as a result of its huge and successful fundraising campaigns; its rescue and redemption mission has become the public face of street kid services.

In 1991 Native Child and Family Services of Toronto, in partnership with Central Toronto Youth Services, began the Native Youth Outreach Program, targeted toward 'Native street and curb youth' in the city ('curb kids' have a home but may be living on the street; street youth are homeless and have no alternative to the street). Their mandate was consistent with the 1985 amendment to the Child and Family Services Act, which recognized that 'Indian and Native people should be entitled to provide, wherever possible, their own child and family services and that all services to Indian and Native children and families should be provided in a manner that recognizes their culture, heritage, traditions, and the concept of the extended family.'[53]

Aboriginal street youth were described as youth who had been separated from Aboriginal culture and identity (for example, having been adopted into non-Native homes), while curb kids came from poor homes characterized by addiction patterns. Native-run agencies were regarded as offering the best hope of assisting these youth, given the racism and marginalization which they had experienced within the mainstream system and community. At a forum on Native street youth held at First Nations House in 1995, an outreach worker stated that while Canada's Aboriginal population is 3 per cent of the total population, about 10–15 per cent of street youth were believed to be Native. He suggested that the number may be higher still, given that some refuse to identify themselves as Native because of the stereotyping and stigmatization confronting Native people.[54] Native youth, however, were rarely depicted as street kids in media accounts, nor their needs and interests addressed.

Alternative Perspectives on the 'Crisis'

The organization of the moral panic surrounding juvenile prostitution emphasized sexual abuse and pimping as determinants that adults were 'allowing' to take place through inaction. The perspectives of young people themselves, which emphasized lack of job skills and employment opportunities as causal, were effectively ignored.

Fred Mathews of Central Toronto Youth Services finds that the focus on individual pathology caused by factors like sexual abuse, early sexual experience, family problems, and coercion by pimps as precipitating entrance into prostitution is a problematic one. Mathews undertook a three-year study of social service agencies and workers, police, and centrally, young prostitutes themselves. From his interviews with social workers and young prostitutes, he concluded that 'pimps are *not* the only or major factor affecting an adolescent's decision to enter prostitution'[55] Mathews developed a 'Social Effects Model' which 'views entrance into prostitution not as a problem for the adolescent but as a solution.'[56] This model takes into account the needs, skills, and values of young people that facilitate their entry into prostitution, and then work to keep them there. The model considers, first, young people's *needs*, including economic needs such as food and shelter, their desire for status through the consumption of goods and services, and their psychological needs in escaping bad family situations or in a desire for adventure. Second, it examines their *skills*, including little or no job training, a low level of education, some sexual experience, and a culturally valued youthful appearance. Third, the model recognizes the *values* of young people regarding sexuality, consumption, the law, and in their view of prostitution as an acceptable form of work.[57]

Valerie Scott of CORP also implies that young people may regard prostitution not as a problem but as a solution. As she states, 'the juvenile prostitution issue has nothing to do with prostitution. What it has to do with is young people in crisis.' Furthermore, 'CORP does not encourage children to be prostitutes ... but we do defend their right to survive if the rest of society refuses to provide adequate opportunities for these kids.' The crisis that young people find themselves in emerged prior to their working as prostitutes, and getting them out of the business alone is not going to alleviate either the original crisis, or juvenile prostitution.[58]

A focus on sexual abuse, based on distinctions between adults and youths, does not address the possibility that youths (particularly female) may become prostitutes for the same reasons as adults do. Terry Sullivan, also of Central Toronto Youth Services, suggests that only a minority of these young people are disturbed and require the assistance of programs directed to treat those problems. He favours the view that 'juvenile prostitution is the economically rational behaviour of a minority of unskilled, uneducated young people. They are striving for the "good life" in a free market economy which provides few options to them, and which equates substantial income with worthiness.'[59]

There are very few jobs for young people who lack skills and have no other means of financial support, and what jobs are available pay minimum wage. Jobs in fast food restaurants, 'McJobs,' are viable only for the young person who is being supported by family and wants to purchase extras such as clothes and entertainment, or save money for a postsecondary education. As well, the lure of a rapid and substantial income is a powerful message, and some young people get into prostitution not because of poverty and desperation, but from a desire for the immediate gratification and economic freedom provided by a disposable income.

Structuring social services according to a distinction between the perceived social and legal capabilities of adults and youths can serve to construct incapacities in youths and deny them the possibility of autonomy from their families, when it may be the organization of the family and the economy that cause them to leave home and find work as prostitutes. Youth under sixteen will do their best to avoid contact with social service agencies, who have the power to detain them against their will, preferring the freedom and dangers of the streets to another restrictive setting.[60] For them, social workers are interchangeable with police, a realistic perspective since social workers and police indeed work in concert. Thus even services they might regard as useful, such as health care, may be out of reach of those under sixteen. Programs for young people tend to follow conventional models (whose effectiveness the Badgley Committee failed to critique), providing some assistance to those who want to get out of prostitution. However, that most of the young people in these programs have already had previous contact with child welfare services, indicates serious limitations and/or shortcomings in the system. Sullivan asserts that these services are 'notoriously ineffective,' a position which is shared by Mathews and Visano.[61] According to Mathews, young people and adults working in prostitution, as well as those who have in the past, must be involved in the design of social service programs if they are to be made more effective. This entails the recognition that young people working as prostitutes may be knowledgeable about their work relations and have the capacity for decision making, a standpoint contrary to the image of the child abducted by predatory pimp.

Second, even well-designed programs and those directed specifically towards youth employment cannot fully address the social and economic conditions that provide the impetus for getting involved in prostitution in the first place, and that must inevitably be confronted once again when young people choose to leave the life. As Sullivan comments of youth employment programs: 'The principal anomaly is that these programs do not significantly affect the unemployment rate. Most youth employment programs provide employment disadvantaged youth with a structured "first job" experience. It is argued they will then be better prepared to compete for jobs. While this may be arguably true, it does not allow for the fact that for every 100 young people looking for work in this country, only 75 to 80 will find it. Training does not create jobs! Twenty to twenty-five percent of youth will continue to be unemployed for the foreseeable future regardless of what training or targeting takes place. Training merely increases the odds of winning the job "lottery."'[62] Social service provision itself will always be stressed beyond the system's ability to function effectively as long as the structural problems inherent in Canadian society and the 'traditional' family (for example, chronic unemployment, family violence, racism) continue unabated. The shift from a family-centred to a child-centred model of service delivery will be limited in its effectiveness if it is not accompanied by an attempt to account for and modify these structural determinants.

The ideology of family life as the 'haven in a heartless world' cloaks relations of exploitation and abuse, and it is no wonder that so many young people choose to flee their families. However, the sexualization of young people in the media and the perceived disintegration of the traditional family has resulted in a move to reaffirm the viability of this family model, and reassert young people's innocence and dependence. The ahistorical use of terms like the 'loss of innocence' in reference to juvenile prostitutes reinforces this process. However, the years of childhood, and particularly adolescence, have never been a period of blissful ignorance for the young. Adolescence, particularly, is a relatively modern concept, dating from the late nineteenth century.[63] While attempts are being made to shore up the traditional family unit, the perceived increase in the numbers of young people working in prostitution during the 1980s would, if accurate, pose a direct challenge to the efficacy of this family model.

The moral panic surrounding juvenile prostitution developed in accordance with the Badgley Report's emphasis on young people as victims of sexual abuse by customers and pimps in a schema that produced a focus on the need for further legislation – a focus that police in particular amplified in order to acquire the legislative means to increase their powers of arrest. In news report after report, police were cited as feeling stymied by their lack of legal tools to 'protect' young people from the abuses of the streets, and particularly, of pimps. At the same time, the moral panic spurred an increase in funding and expansion of programs for the rescue and rehabilitation of young prostitutes, thus broadening the terrain of social service professionals, and providing, as one social work professional cynically commented, increased job opportunities for middle-class social workers.[64]

While we have not yet achieved a better world for young people to live in, by 1990 media attention had ebbed, suggesting that the problem of juvenile prostitution had been largely addressed through state interventions. Following the summer of 1988, concerns about young people focused on drug use (although drug use appeared to have been much more prevalent among teenagers in the previous generation), and their apparently growing involvement in criminal activity, including violent crime, in the 1990s. However, while the numbers reported in official data may be increasing, criminologists repeatedly caution that the statistical increase may be the result of a change in crime reporting as a 'zero tolerance policy' was put into place in public institutions like the educational system. As well, in the 1980s the manufacture of public concern around juvenile crime appeared to be linked to the police demand for the review of the Young Offenders Act. The demand for this review was fuelled by a barrage of media accounts of juvenile crime invariably stating that the name of the accused cannot be revealed under the terms of this Act; a procedure that lends the appearance of placing people at further risk. Young people are now increasingly being portrayed as perpetrators of crimes rather than as victims.[65]

8

And On It Goes ...

My work has examined not only how campaigns against prostitution are organized but how prostitution itself is organized at particular moments in history. It has been possible to see how particular forms of the business of prostitution were *produced* as visible and regulatable social problems over the past two decades. As I undertook this process, the standpoint of women and men working in prostitution has been kept in mind, in order to describe the impact upon them as their work relations were continually re-organized. The preceding chapters have discussed some of the ways in which people finding a source of income through prostitution have been prevented from entering into discourses which determine their work and construct their identities. The identification of prostitution as a social problem to be simply swept from the streets by police has been increasingly challenged by these sex workers themselves in the aftermath of the Fraser Report release. Women who work in prostitution in particular have been brought into view as social subjects, rather than merely as social problems.

Activists are demanding inclusion in the relations that organize their work and construct their public identities. This *resistance* is also being utilized to develop stronger alliances with feminist and lesbian and gay rights organizations to determine how sex (and sex work) is to be regulated. For example, sex workers in Canadian and U.S. cities are working with gay men to curb the scapegoating of both groups for HIV transmission. There have been recurrent attempts in the media to link prostitutes to HIV transmission among the heterosexual population, which could potentially incite a further campaign against prostitutes as a threat to public health.[1]

After almost twenty-five years of building activism internationally, there are signs of some progress in prostitutes' efforts to gain more control over their working conditions. For example, in two countries where there is a history of toleration of prostitution already in place, Germany and Holland, prostitutes appear to be moving beyond 'toleration' and into the mainstream labour force. In Germany, they are campaigning for full legal rights, including health care, unemployment, and retirement benefits. In Holland, an estimated 30,000 prostitutes have joined the country's main trade union. In Calcutta, a prostitutes' rights organization is demanding trade union status, health care benefits, and the elimination of police abuse.[2]

In late 1989, following the completion of this study in its original form (a doctoral dissertation), a mandatory cross-country review of what had been accomplished through Bill-49 was completed and released. After two years of study, *Street Prostitution: Assessing the Impact of the Law* found that the new Section 195.1 – communication for the purpose of prostitution – was not working, despite its punitive character.[3] The report found that intensive enforcement of the law through a massive number of arrests merely spatially shifted prostitution. It also acknowledged that changes in land use in cities and communities had contributed to the problematization of prostitution.[4]

Prostitution has been relocated through regulatory and policing activities. The trade has been shifted from relatively private indoor places of business to the markedly public sphere of the streets. It has been moved from street to street within neighbourhoods and cities. Its guise changes, from massage parlours to encounter studios to escort services, in an attempt to circumvent the law. It is the subject of periodic moral panics, for example, over 'child' prostitution, or over the moral and physical degeneration of downtown cores. But clearly, the legislators, the courts, and the police cannot make prostitution disappear. All that can be done is to create new laws and patterns of enforcement that ultimately accomplish little except to make life more difficult for people working in prostitution. In what for many has been a battle of 'deviance' and social control, there have been no winners.

The standpoint of adult prostitutes raised in this text has revealed their practical consciousness about how their work is organized and their identities constructed, particularly through the coercive powers of the state. Women working in prostitution have revealed themselves as often knowledgable and savvy political subjects; more so because they come up against the state in a more direct and unpleasant way than most people experience in this country, on a daily basis. Through developing an activist voice, they are stating that they are not simply hapless dupes of patriarchal relations. They want more control over their working conditions and the same rights and responsibilities as other political subjects. The accomplishment of this end requires the decriminalization of prostitution. Moreover, it indicates that any 'solution' to the 'problem' of prostitution cannot be achieved without the participation of sex-trade workers themselves.

Criminalization cannot eliminate or necessarily decrease the sex trade, because women (and men) have to work, and will continue to find new ways to do so. It cannot adequately address the 'crisis' of youth prostitution, because prostitution is not the source of young people's problems. It does not 'protect' women and young people from violence and coercion, but instead mandates regulatory strategies that may increase their vulnerability. Criminal legislation does more than make their profession difficult for these sex-trade workers, however. As Valerie Scott made clear, it profoundly affects their everyday lives; for example, through the silencing of prostitutes in relation to the regulation of their work, in interactions with family members, in opening a bank account, or in renting an apartment. Although the criminal label is not the only force at work in the creation of 'the prostitute' as a deviant identity and outcast status, the most difficult part of the prostitute identity may be, not the use of one's body for sexual commerce but the stigma of the occupation, which criminal sanctions reinforce. Through regulatory procedures, the public identity of the prostitute is constructed. As Valerie Scott succinctly states, 'the government has told society that it's OK to treat us like shit because the government is treating us like shit.'[5] The murders of numerous women and transgendered people while working strolls in Canadian cities in recent years are therefore not simply the acts of the individuals who commit them.

Statistics Canada has reported that between 1991 and 1995, sixty-three *known* prostitutes were murdered in Canada, and most of their murders have been attributed to 'customers' (generally men who find women working the streets easy prey), although more than half of the murders have not been solved. This figure represents 5 per cent of the women killed in Canada over the same period.[6] Simon Fraser University criminologist John Lowman has been researching and writing about prostitution in British Columbia for almost two decades. He found that at least forty-eight prostitutes were killed in the province between 1988 and 1996, and that 77 per cent of Vancouver prostitutes had at least one violent customer every month. Unless British Columbia is a proportionally much more dangerous place for prostitutes to work, Lowman's research suggests that the murder of prostitutes for Canada as a whole is underreported.[7]

Although the data may prove to be a source of dispute, it remains clear that social marginalization has deadly consequences. Two recent cases grimly illustrate this point. In April 1995, Pamela George was beaten to death in Regina by two young white male university students. George was a twenty-eight-year-old Native woman and mother of two children, who reputedly worked the streets twice a month to support her family. The young men had consumed a substantial amount of alcohol and then driven around Regina looking for a prostitute to pick up, with one hiding in the back seat. A witness reported that the young men had bragged about killing Pamela George, saying that she deserved it because she was an Indian. Prior to their deliberations, the jury was instructed by the judge to keep in mind that 'Ms. George was indeed a prostitute' and that the young men were quite intoxicated (they had used excessive alcohol use as a defence) at the time that they beat George (so badly that a closed coffin was required for her service) and left her in a ditch. Social justice organizations understandably responded with outrage. The all-white jury, consisting of eight women and three men, convicted the men of the lesser charge of manslaughter, rather than first-degree murder as charged. They were each sentenced to six and one-half years imprisonment. Chief Lindsay Kaye of the Sakimay Indian Band (George's band) pointed to the verdict as evidence that Canada had two justice systems, one for white people and another for Indians. Pamela George died because she was a Native, a woman, and found a source of income through prostitution. Clearly, however, the judge and jury regarded Pamela George as the social problem, rather than the social relations that these young men represented.[8]

Two transvestite prostitutes were murdered on Homewood Avenue, part of the 'trani stroll' in downtown Toronto, on the same evening in May 1996 that a young woman was murdered in Parkdale. All three had been shot in the head with the same gun. The youngest victim was identified as a nineteen-year-old street youth. A man was charged with all three homicides shortly after.[9] Some residents of Homewood blamed the victims for inflicting their own deaths upon the horrified people living in the neighbourhood. It was people working in prostitution, not the men who preyed upon them, not the laws that stigmatized and marginalized them, and not homophobia toward gay men and lesbians and ridicule of transgendered people, that caused prostitute murders. Yet as earlier chapters have demonstrated, punitive and ineffective regulatory strategies, which some residents have participated in engineering, have exacerbated tensions on the street and put prostitutes at further risk.

Criminal legislation cannot address the causes of prostitution; it merely perpetuates unequal power relations. As long as prostitution appears to be the most favourable option available, some women and young people will continue to use it as a source of livelihood. The sex trade will continue to be a viable option for women, particularly working-class women, as long as they are faced with unequal pay and poor job prospects, unfavourable educational streaming, a high cost of living, inadequate services such as childcare, and the lack of reproductive freedom to determine when and how many children they will have. It will continue to be a viable profession for transgendered people who are refused entry into social life, including employment opportunities, owing to a very narrow, rigid, and prescribed notion of what is 'normal.'

The traditional nuclear family is often not a 'haven in a heartless world,' and sometimes the best thing that women and young people can do is to flee from it. Yet 'the family' remains such a privileged concept in state policy that the impetus and resources available to provide viable alternatives are inadequate indeed. Young people faced with the prospects of going it alone are confronted by the economic legacy of the 1970s and 1980s; what they don't have today they are unlikely to acquire tomorrow. They are not the first generation to grow up in difficult economic times, but they are the first to do so in a period when young people have been targeted as consumers in their own right.[10]

Prostitutes' rights advocates recognize that the decriminalization of prostitution is not an ideal solution. Should the federal government relinquish control of the right to regulate prostitution, the door will be open for provincial and local governments to develop their own regulatory strategies. While not criminal procedures, their effect may be as or more stringent. As well, there is nothing to prevent police from using bylaws, even those that are non-prostitution specific, against even the most unobtrusive prostitute. A reform of the law does not necessarily imply a reform of policing practices. Both are aspects of state regulation, but the state is not an organic unity, where a change in one part causes changes in the whole. Finally, prostitutes' rights advocates suggest that a program of full decriminalization is unlikely to entirely eliminate street solicitation, even though the repeal of bawdy-house legislation would expand the options for working indoors. Some women and men will continue to work the street; for the free advertising that a visible street presence provides, and for the mobility and lack of overhead costs entailed in street work. Activist prostitutes state that many of those who now work the streets would prefer the option of working indoors, and those who remain would shift out of residential areas into more advantageous locations. They assert that sex workers have a right to use public space, just as do the street vendors and restaurants that add sidewalk cafes to their premises.[11]

As I discussed in Chapter 5, by the late 1980s numerous police forces across Canada had turned their efforts toward arresting potential customers of street-level prostitutes, expecting that the fear of criminal prosecution would deter them from cruising the streets and seeking out sexual services. Although this measure proved to be largely ineffective, in January 1997 Vancouver police decided to focus their efforts almost exclusively on customers, as well as pimps. They stated that they would only charge prostitutes if they rejected assistance in leaving prostitution, or persisted in working near playgrounds, schools, parks, or in residential areas.[12] In Toronto in 1996, a 'John School' was opened as the result of the efforts of a Toronto Councillor. The purpose of the school was to 'educate' men facing an initial conviction under the communicating law about the personal and social costs of prostitution. The first 'student' of the course was a Tory MPP. Over 400 men attended the school in its first year of operation.[13] In light of the analysis presented in previous chapters, the targetting of customers through john reform schools is unlikely to decrease street solicitation in the near future.

For several years following the production of this work as a doctoral dissertation, I lived on a busy downtown stroll. It was noisy at the corner of Homewood and Carleton. But it was not the noise created by the women and transgendered people who worked the stroll, or their customers, that made me insert my ear plugs night after night. Instead, it was the crowds who poured from Maple Leaf Gardens, most boisterously on those infrequent nights when the Leafs won, or those going to and from the concert/dance hall on Sherbourne. It was sirens from ambulances heading to and from nearby hospitals, and the sound of streetcars as they passed along Carleton. The sounds, then, were the sounds of a vibrant downtown core, a place where people lived and worked and socialized. Residents' organizations would do well to remember that it is this vibrancy and the conveniences of downtown living that draw us to live in cities, rather than in the suburbs or countryside. The sounds outside my window were also the sounds of the urban poor; of anger, addiction, and hopelessness. These sounds are intensifying as the new right agenda strips the urban poor of the financial and other resources that make their lives tolerable. Finally, since I am raising my subjective experiences here, I can't not mention the sounds of the stereo in apartment 105. In this scenario, the sounds of the sex trade were almost unnoticeable; indeed, most of the time they worked quietly, desiring to attract the attention of no one but potential customers. However, residents continued to blame those working the stroll for the noise, the traffic, and the drug use in the area, as if eliminating the trade on Homewood Avenue would eliminate noise and traffic and drugs. This is a familiar theme.

Following the production of this work I found part-time work at Street Outreach Services (SOS), an agency whose primary mandate is to work with young men between the ages of sixteen and twenty-five who work in prostitution. At SOS, I developed an appreciation of the struggles of the primarily bisexual, gay, and transgendered youth who sought out the services and support that the agency offered. These were the faces behind the media stories. However, by the early 1990s the media stories about street kids and child prostitutes were yesterday's news, and instead young people were increasingly being portrayed as perpetrators rather than victims. 'Violent youth crime' was the new story. With the shift in attention of media, the public, and politicians, and the rise of a new right political agenda which conveniently blamed the welfare state for the creation of government deficits and debts, services for youth began to be dismantled. This was particularly true in Toronto, where numerous initiatives had been implemented during the 1980s. Little remains of the Toronto Street Youth Project, the Inner City Youth Project has had its funding eliminated, and SOS struggles to piece funding together to survive. Only Covenant House, the youth project least favoured by street youth themselves, remains secure, thanks to its private funding. However, the Toronto street youth population has actually grown significantly since the 1980s, if my subjective assessment of Toronto streets is an accurate indicator. How many of them engage in survival sex is, as usual, difficult to measure. However, there has been no accompanying moral panic manufactured by politicians, police, and media, whose main focus now is on youth crime and the mantra of fiscal restraint.

There is clearly no correlation between the creation of moral panics and the degree of urgency of a situation. Urgent situations can be happening without a panic resulting. Hard luck stories remain just that. For example, in the spring of 1996 a number of street youth were 'evicted' from an empty and boarded-up building on Carleton Street that they had been using for shelter. They chose to publicize their homelessness by establishing a tent city in City Hall square. The same local-level politicians who had been decrying the plight of the street kid a decade earlier had these youth arrested for their action.

In other areas of the country, by 1996–97 there was an increased emphasis on child and youth prostitution by police, local and provincial governments, and media. The city of Calgary and the province of British Columbia both pledged to tackle the involvement of persons under eighteen in prostitution. Reports produced in both Calgary and British Columbia succeed in institutionalizing the understanding that this a form of sexual abuse, a reconceptualization initiated with the Badgley Report. They recommend still tougher legal penalties for those caught obtaining the sexual services, procuring, or living on the avails of a person under eighteen. As my earlier analysis suggests, neither of these approaches addresses the reasons why young people engage in survival prostitution, nor is likely to have an impact upon their numbers. However, the *Handbook for Action Against Prostitution of Youth in Calgary* raises the criticism that social initiatives suggested in the past have been largely ignored, and provides a series of goals and recommended actions, focusing on social services, education, health, and the justice system. The handbook outlines a coordinated approach to addressing prostitution involving persons under eighteen, through the cooperation of street workers and others in social services, as well as educators, health care professionals (both physical and mental), and police and other people involved in the justice system. The handbook's authors hope that it will serve as a blueprint that will be adopted across Canada. The *Community Consultation on Prostitution in British Columbia* made the effort to survey adults and youth involved in prostitution about their needs and recommendations. The youth spoke very favourably about their contact with street workers, but wanted more flexible services and less judgemental workers in other areas of service contact. Fred Mathews of Central Toronto Youth Services, who developed the 'Social Effects Model' discussed in Chapter 7, has commented that the approaches taken in Calgary and British Columbia are promising new initiatives. However, it would be premature for me to comment on what the outcome of these reports might be.[14]

In 1990 and 1992, the Supreme Court of Canada arrived at two long-awaited legal decisions, both disappointments to prostitutes' rights activists. First, in 1990 the court upheld both the communication law and the bawdy-house law, following a constitutional challenge on the grounds that Sections 195.1 and 193 offended the right to freedom of expression, as well as the right to liberty guaranteed by the Charter of Rights and Freedoms. In a four to two ruling split along gender lines, with the two women justices dissenting from the judgement, the court determined that whatever the infringements on charter rights, there remained a greater social interest in restricting street solicitation. The majority ruling also stated that charter rights were not applicable to the operation of bawdy-houses. As they stated of the communication legislation:

First, there is a rational connection between the impugned legislation and the prevention of the social nuisance associated with the public display of the sale of sex. Second, s. 195.1(1)(c) is not unduly intrusive. Although s. 195.1(1)(c) is not confined to places where there will necessarily be many people who will be offended by street solicitation, the section is not overly broad because the objective of the provision is not restricted to the control of actual disturbances or nuisances but extends to the general curtailment of visible solicitation for the purposes of prostitution. Also, the definition of communication may be wide but the courts are capable of restricting the meaning of 'communication' in its context by reference to the purpose of the impugned legislation. Third, the effects of the legislation on freedom of expression are not so severe as to outweigh the government's pressing and substantial objective. The curtailment of street solicitation is in keeping with the interests of many in our society for whom the nuisance-related aspects of solicitation constitute serious problems. A legislative scheme aimed at street solicitation must be, in view of this Court's decision in *Westendrop*, of a criminal nature.[15]

As well, in 1993 the Supreme Court upheld the 'living on the avails of prostitution' statute in a four to three decision. The majority ruled that while the law presumes that people who live with or are habitually in the company of prostitutes are procurers, thereby infringing on people's constitutional right to be presumed innocent, this is justified in order to protect women and young people against a parasitical activity.[16]

Despite these decisions, in 1995 the City of Toronto Health Committee, comprising most of the city's councillors, voted in favour of the decriminalization of prostitution, and the investigation of alternative strategies for addressing the sex trade. Members were persuaded by the indisputable evidence that criminalization was ineffective. At least one residents' organization, the Toronto East Downtown Residents' Association, was also in favour of decriminalization. Not surprisingly, Toronto police were not. The recommendation in favour of decriminalization was conveyed to the federal Department of Justice, where it was not well received. Still, the vote represented an important shift in regulatory strategy by these forces in social problem construction.

The preceding pages, I hope, draw attention to the necessity of reshaping the way in which social and legal 'rights' are allocated. The standpoint of those who are working in prostitution demonstrates the need for a participatory rather than a regulatory process in the allocation of rights; to develop a politics of rights that transcends regulation based upon state defined public/private and adult/youth distinctions, and the present assignment of individual and property rights. This requires accounting for the origin and distribution of these rights, based on factors such as gender, class, age, and race, not to mention perceived 'moral' conduct (for example, sex-trade workers' relative degree of 'worthiness' before the law). It also necessitates changing the social conditions that give rise to rights, for example, by creating the conditions necessary for the autonomy of women and young people when they require independence from the family. Further, in this task, feminism needs to flexible enough to respond to the diversity of interests and experiences among women, in order to grasp the complexities of women's lived experience, including the experiences of prostitutes and other sex-trade workers. We might relinquish attempts to eliminate the sex trade and set ourselves to improving conditions for women within it, in order that prostitutes gain more control over their working conditions. This will not eliminate the sex trade, but it will transform it.

Prostitution Crime Rates (Canada)

Year	Total*	Bawdy-House	Procuring	Other
1987	10,457	684	530	9,243
1986	7,426			
1985	1,225	715	236	274
1984	1,024	675	189	160
1983	935	561	151	223
1982	700	299	134	267
1981	1,551	699	108	744
1980	1,504	442	153	909
1979	1,283	453	146	684
1978	1,808	555	138	1,115
1977	2,843	888	172	1,783
1976	2,841	849	135	1,857
1975	3,409	1,184	163	2,062
1974	3,249	796	196	2,257
1973	3,573	NOT PROVIDED		
1972	2,183			

* Police-reported, prostitution-related crimes (not convictions). Includes bawdy-house, pro-curing, other (soliciting/communicating).
For data from 1972 to 1985 see *Canadian Crime Statistics* (Ottawa: Statistics Canada, 1986).
For 1987 data see *Canadian Crime Statistics* (Ottawa: Statistics Canada, Canadian Centre for Justice Statistics, 1988).

Prostitutes and HIV/AIDS Transmission

It is common for heterosexual men who test HIV positive to claim heterosexual contact as their only risk factor. A Massachusetts study on HIV transmission stated that 'in recent epidemiological studies, 34% of men with AIDS and no identifiable risk factor (i.e. who were not gay or bisexual, who did not use IV drugs or receive a blood transfusion prior to blood donation screening) gave a history of sexual contact with prostitutes.'[1]

How reliable is this evidence? A study was conducted on customers of prostitutes, using a sample of 300 men in New York City. Six (2 per cent) of these men tested positive; however two had also participated in other risk behaviour, and two more did not return for further interviewing so that other possible risk factors could be determined. Further, when the New York City Health Department interviewed twenty military recruits who had claimed to have contracted the virus through contact with prostitutes, eighteen of them later admitted to other high-risk activity.[2]

The 20 September 1988 *New York Times* reported that two studies had been conducted on a total of 627 customers of female prostitutes in New York City. Only three cases were found in which 'the virus was thought to have been caught from a prostitute.' Dr. William Darrow, who oversaw epidemiological research on AIDS at the Federal Centres for Disease Control in Atlanta, stated that he knew of no proven cases of female prostitutes infecting their customers.[3]

Other information was also available which indicated that the link between prostitution and HIV transmission is much exaggerated. While half of the women in the United States who have tested positive lived in New York as of 1987, 'only 5% of the men who claim they got AIDS from a woman reside there,' according to the *Los Angeles Times*.[4] This evidence suggests that infected men from other areas may claim heterosexual contact as their only possible source of transmission because they are reluctant to admit to having had sex with other men or to IV drug use. Danny Cockerline adds that none of the studies of the customers of prostitutes attempted to determine whether men who claimed to have become infected through sexual contact with a woman in the sex trade had had sexual contact with other women. If their claims were to be given any validity, they would have had to have sexual contact *only* with prostitutes.[5]

Further, the Centre for Disease Control in Atlanta, which was involved in an ongoing multicentre study of prostitutes, found that the prevalence of exposure for prostitutes varied widely from city to city, with the highest rates being found in New York and Florida. Significantly, this paralleled the cumulative incidence of AIDS in all women in these areas. This means that the risk of prostitutes becoming HIV positive was the same as that for other women in their geographical areas. They concluded that 'the major risk factor for HIV infection in prostitutes appears to be IV drug abuse,' and that proper and consistent use of condoms greatly reduced the risk of infection. Street prostitutes in large U.S. cities are often also IV drug users (a connection that is not as evident in Canada), and the sharing of used and infected hypodermic needles has been identified as the main means of AIDS transmission through the IV drug user population.[6]

The emphasis on prostitutes as infectors, rather than infectees, ignores evidence that transmission of the virus occurs more readily from men to women than from women to men. In March 1986, researchers found small amounts of the virus in vaginal fluid, but were cautious about the findings, and stood by the assertion that female to male transmission is difficult.

The isolation of the virus from vaginal and/or cervical secretions of seropositive women was accomplished in two separate studies in Massachusetts and California. The results of these studies were published in the 8 March 1986 issue of *The Lancet*. In Massachusetts, study was based on women who were seropositive (whose sera contained antibodies to the virus, meaning that they had been exposed to HIV). The virus was found in the cervical secretions of four of fourteen women tested, and the venous blood of seven of thirteen tested. The California study isolated it in the vaginal and/or cervical secretions of four out of eight women. Women were drawn from two high-risk groups: IV drug users and women who had sexual contact with men who were infected or belonged to a high-risk group. California researchers were the most cautious about the findings, noting that they had difficulty isolating sufficient quantities of the virus, and therefore 'the vaginal canal under certain conditions could be a source of transmission.'[7]

Researchers had in earlier studies isolated extremely low levels of the virus in body fluids such as tears, urine, and saliva, but considered these 'highly unlikely to be a source of transmission.' Using data from December 1985, they reported that only twenty-eight men with AIDS in the United States (0.1 per cent of all U.S. AIDS cases) 'appeared to have been infected with the AIDS virus through contact with high risk women.' The researchers concluded that these men could have contracted the virus through 'normal vaginal intercourse.' However, the low levels found were consistent with the epidemiological evidence, indicating that 'this route of transmission is rare.' While they recognized that 'conditions in the vagina in a low state of arousal do not necessarily reflect the situation during intercourse,' a post-orgasm sample from one woman did not find a higher level of the virus than the other positive samples they received. They suggested that the virus may be passed more easily by a woman with an active venereal disease. Since it requires access to the bloodstream for transmission, the condition of the penis and urethra (whether there is broken skin) may determine the male's susceptibility.[8]

As of 26 September 1988 the CDC in Atlanta reported the number of men to have been exposed through heterosexual contact to be 1,331 persons, or 2 per cent of all cumulative cases. This includes 451 men who have had 'heterosexual contact with a person with AIDS or at risk for AIDS' and 880 men 'without other identified risks who were born in countries in which heterosexual transmission is believed to play a major role although precise means of transmission have not been fully defined.'[9] While this represents a significant increase, it must be remembered that U.S. data is collected state by state, and the degree of rigour in tracking transmission patterns varies from place to place. We must be careful to identify distinctions between men who claim to have been exposed from a women and cases where no other source of transmission can be found (this distinction is unfortunately not made in the CDC statistics). Even then, the claim of heterosexual transmission may have to be accepted for lack of other evidence. As the studies of prostitutes' customers indicated, follow-up interviews with men who claim this as the only possible route of transmission may eventually reveal other risk behaviour.[10]

APPENDIX C

Criminal Code Provisions Relating to Prostitution[a]

197. (1) In this Part,

'common bawdy-house' means a place that is
  (a) kept or occupied, or
  (b) resorted to by one or more persons
for the purpose of prostitution or the practice of acts of indecency;

'prostitute' means a person of either sex who engages in prostitution;

'public place' includes any place to which the public have access as of right or by invitation, express or implied.

210. (1) Every one who keeps a common bawdy-house is guilty of an indictable offence and liable to imprisonment for a term not exceeding two years.

(2) Every one who
  (a) is an inmate of a common bawdy-house,
  (b) is found, without lawful excuse, in a common bawdy-house, or
  (c) as owner, landlord, lessor, tenant, occupier, agent or otherwise having charge or control of any place, knowingly permits the place or any part thereof to be let or used for the purposes of a common bawdy-house,
is guilty of an offence punishable on summary conviction.

(3) Where a person is convicted of an offence under subsection (1), the court shall cause a notice of the conviction to be served on the owner, landlord or lessor of the

---

[a]Federal-Provincial-Territorial Working Group on Prostitution, *Dealing with Prostitution in Canada: A Consultation Paper* (March 1995). Note that Canadian Criminal Code statutes have been renumbered. The new numbers are provided here.

place in respect of which the person is convicted or his agent, and the notice shall contain a statement to the effect that it is being served pursuant to this section.

(4) Where a person on whom a notice is served under subsection (3) fails forthwith to exercise any right he may have to determine the tenancy or right of occupation of the person so convicted, and thereafter any person is convicted of an offence under subsection (1) in respect of the same premises, the person on whom the notice was served shall be deemed to have committed an offence under subsection (1) unless he proves that he has taken all reasonable steps to prevent the recurrrence of the offence.

211. Every one who knowingly takes, transports, directs, or offers to take, transport or direct, any other person to a common bawdy-house is guilty of an offence punishable on summary conviction.

212. (1) Every one who
(a) procures, attempts to procure or solicits a person to have illicit sexual intercourse with another person, whether in or out of Canada,
(b) inveigles or entices a person who is not a prostitute or a person of known immoral character to a common bawdy-house or house of assignation for the purpose of illicit sexual intercourse or prostitution,
(c) knowingly conceals a person in a common bawdy-house or house of assignation,
(d) procures or attempts to procure a person to become, whether in or out of Canada, a prostitute,
(e) procures or attempts to procure a person to leave the usual place of abode of that person in Canada, if that place is not a common bawdy-house, with intent that the person may become an inmate or frequenter of a common bawdy-house, whether in or out of Canada,
(f) on the arrival of a person in Canada, directs or causes that person to be directed or takes or causes that person to be taken, to a common bawdy-house or house of assignation,
(g) procures a person to enter or leave Canada, for the purpose of prostitution,
(h) for the purposes of gain, exercises control, direction or influence over the movements of a person in such manner as to show that he is aiding, abetting or compelling that person to engage in or carry on prostitution with any person or generally,
(i) applies or administers to a person or causes that person to take any drug, intoxicating liquor, matter or thing with intent to stupefy or overpower that person in order thereby to enable any person to have illicit sexual intercourse with that person, or

(j) lives wholly or in part on the avails of prostitution of another person,
is guilty of an indictable offence and liable to imprisonment for a term not exceeding ten years.

(2) Notwithstanding paragraph (1)(j), every person who lives wholly or in part on the avails of prostitution of another person who is under the age of eighteen years is guilty of an indictable offence and liable to imprisonment for a term not exceeding fourteen years.

(3) Evidence that a person lives with or is habitually in the company of a prostitute or lives in a common bawdy-house or in a house of assignation is, in the absence of evidence to the contrary, proof that the person lives on the avails of prostitution, for the purposes of paragraph (1)(j) and subsection (2).

(4) Every person who, in any place, obtains or attempts to obtain, for consideration, the sexual services of a person who is under the age of eighteen years is guilty of an indictable offence and liable to imprisonment for a term not exceeding five years.

213. (1) Every person who in a public place or in any place open to public view
    (a) stops or attempts to stop any motor vehicle,
    (b) impedes the free flow of pedestrian or vehicular traffic or ingress to or egress from premises adjacent to that place, or
    (c) stops or attempts to stop any person or in any manner communicates or attempts to communicate with any person
for the purpose of engaging in prostitution or of obtaining the sexual services of a prostitute is guilty of an offence punishable on summary conviction.

(2) In this section, 'public place' includes any place to which the public have access as of right or by invitation, express or implied, and any motor vehicle located in a public place or in any place open to public view.

Notes

1: Sexual Regulation and Sex Work

1 The names of two women whom I have interviewed for this study have been changed for the sake of anonymity. They will be referred to as 'Liz' and 'Donna.'

2 For example, see Li, *The Making of Post-War Canada.*

3 For example, see Weeks, *Sex, Politics and Society; Sexuality and Its Discontents;* and Rubin, 'Thinking Sex.'

4 For example, for information on the rise of the 'playboy ethic' and the male rebellion see Ehrenreich, *The Hearts of Men.* More discussion follows on page 25, Chapter 2.

5 Weeks, *Sex, Politics and Society,* 288.

6 Gusfield, *The Culture of Public Problems,* 3.

7 Although I agree with the necessity of examining the legal regulation of prostitution in order to understand the impact of the law on women working in prostitution, it nevertheless is not sufficient to simply understand how regulation is enacted and applied. For examples of the regulation process, see Boles and Tatro, 'Legal and Extra Legal Methods of Controlling Prostitution'; Canadian Advisory Council on the Status of Women, *Prostitution in Canada;* Vorenberg and Vorenberg, 'The Biggest Pimp of All'; Women Endorsing Decriminalization, 'Prostitution: A Non-Victim Crime?'; and Tong, *Women, Sex, and the Law.*

8 Smart and Brophy, 'Locating Law,' 17.

9 Smart, 'Legal Subjects and Sexual Objects,' 51.

10 For analyses of moral regulation see Corrigan, 'On Moral Regulation'; and Valverde and Weir, 'The Struggles of the Immoral.'

11 Hall, 'The Rediscovery of "Ideology,"' 83.

12 Ericson, Baranek, and Chan, *Negotiating Control.*

13 Ibid., 396.
14 The overall effect of the identification of prostitution as a social problem was the control of prostitutes; however, the concept of 'social control' cannot take into account the uneven character of the regulatory process, the relations between state and extrastate agencies, and intrastate tensions, in holding the social relations of prostitution in place. While this research has developed out of and owes much to sociological work concerning deviancy and social control, a recognition of the standpoint of prostitutes and the complexities of regulation mean that my work cannot be fully accommodated by these perspectives. The deviancy perspective of the Chicago school, which uses symbolic interactionism as its theoretical base, investigates the breaking of rules. It is a value-laden concept which presumes a state of normalcy against which difference and rule breakers must be judged. As a label, it can be used to suppress, contain, and stigmatize 'difference.' Since it is a static concept, it easily becomes reified and looses its sense of social construction, while assuming a social control which is not investigated. As a microsociological approach, a deviancy perspective cannot tell us who makes the rules and why. Finally, it cannot accommodate the point of view of prostitutes themselves, since this perspective is oriented to their marginalization and policing, as rule breakers.

   Radical criminologists have attempted to correct this imbalance by locating deviancy within a social control model, an approach which links micro- and macrosociology. However, there are limits to what this bridging can accomplish. First, it does not shed the value-laden character of the concept of deviancy (which prevents the entry of prostitutes into the discourse) even as it tries to explain it. Second, the concept of social control is itself problematic.

   The social control perspective does not express the complexities of hegemonic power relations at work. It reduces power to the power of the state, and the power of the state to a coercive function/alism. It does not acknowledge that state power can also have a positive character (for example, legislation against acts of violence) and can be the result of the demands of those who expect the state to provide them with some protection. Further, a social control model cannot incorporate variables such as those who are presumed to be in control being reluctant to act (as I will discuss in Chapter 3).
15 Foucault, *The History of Sexuality*.
16 The analysis of prostitution presented in this chapter refers specifically to adult women. I do occasionally discuss male prostitution in the rest of this study, but because it almost always entails the provision of sexual services by men to other men, there are different social and economic power relations at work (e.g., the marginalization of homosexual activity and the absence of gender inequality in relations between prostitute and customer). For more on male prostitution see

Visano, *This Idle Trade*. As well, most male prostitutes are not adults. Young prostitutes, both female and male, face a different set of social and economic constraints because of their age. Prostitution involving young people will be discussed at length in Chapters 6 and 7.

17 Armstrong and Armstrong, 'Beyond Sexless Class and Classless Sex.'

18 Since I conducted these interviews, a growing body of writing has emerged in which women who work in prostitution talk about their jobs and life experiences. As a result of the growth of the prostitutes' rights movement, women in the sex trade now speak for themselves, rather than through interviews with sociologists and other 'experts.' However, these interviews are still informative, so I chose to retain them, while minimizing my own interpretations of the women's beliefs and experiences. For writing by women in the sex trade see: Pheterson, *A Vindication of the Rights of Whores*; Delacoste and Alexander, *Sex Work*; Bell, *Good Girls/Bad Girls*; *Gauntlet*, 'Special Issue'; and *Social Text*, 'Special Issue on the Sex Trade.'

19 Marx, *Economic and Philosophic Manuscripts of 1844*, 94.

20 McLeod, *Women Working*, 26.

21 See Terkel, *Working*, for first-person accounts of people's experiences in a variety of forms of work, in particular Roberta Victor's 'Hooker.'

   In contrast, others have attempted to explore alternative explanations for women entering prostitution. Lombroso and Ferrero, in *The Female Offender*, initiated a process of attempting to uncover pathological reasons for prostitution and other female crime. Some feminists now attempt to link women entering prostitution to social-pathological experiences in their backgrounds, particularly incest and other sexual abuse, resulting from the patriarchal organization of society. For example, see Newman and Caplan, 'Juvenile Female Prostitution as Gender Consistent Response to Early Deprivation.' Also see Boyer and James, 'Juvenile Prostitution.' However, as Chapter 6 shows, it is difficult to clearly demonstrate a connection. For example, it appears that the rate of sexual abuse among all females is quite high, and only a small number of women who were sexually abused when young end up working as prostitutes.

22 That female prostitutes come from predominantly working-class backgrounds has been documented elsewhere. For England, see McLeod, *Women Working*. For the United States, see Barnett, 'The Political Economy of Rape and Prostitution.'

23 According to Labour Canada, *Women in the Labour Force*, in 1985 women received 59.6 per cent of men's wages, (for both full- and part-time work), 71.9 per cent of part-time workers were women, and 59.3 per cent of women in the labour force were employed in clerical, sales, and service occupations. By 1995, the wage gap between women and men had narrowed, with women earning 73.1

cents for every dollar earned by a man (jumping from 69.8 cents in 1994). How-ever, the narrowing of the gap has been attributed largely to a fall in men's wages, rather than a rise in women's, as companies downsize and Canadian workers lose ground. See Alanna Mitchell, 'Wage Gap Narrows Between Women, Men,' *Globe and Mail*, 28 January 1997, A1.

24 For example, see Pheterson, *A Vindication of the Rights of Whores*, and Dela-coste and Alexander, *Sex Work*.

25 Some writers believe that prostitution has not always – or in all societies – been organized in terms of relations of male dominance and female subordination. See Roberts, *Whores in History*.

26 Valverde, *Sex, Power, and Pleasure*, 18–19.

27 See the ICPR policy papers in Delacoste and Alexander, *Sex Work*, and Pheter-son, *A Vindication of the Rights of Whores*.

28 Ibid.

29 Beyond the collections *Sex Work* and *A Vindication of the Rights of Whores* (cited above), both of which consist primarily of writings by prostitutes, one may consult Jaget, *Prostitutes*. Numerous organizations have produced newspa-pers and letters by and for prostitutes, including *COYOTE HOWLS*, produced by COYOTE throughout the 1970s; *P.R.O.S. STREET BEAT*, produced by the English Collective of Prostitutes (issues available to me are from the late 1970s); and *Network: News from the English Collective of Prostitutes* (available issues are from the early to mid-1980s). One organization, comprising former prostitutes, reflects a different perspective. WHISPER (Women Hurt in Sys-tems of Prostitution Engaged in Revolt) identifies prostitutes as victims of male oppression. See Wynter, 'Whisper' and Cole, 'Whispering Out Loud.'

30 For example, see Margo St James' letter in *Aegis* 34, (Spring 1982), 47. See also the position advanced by CORP and St James in 'The Reclamation of Whores.'

31 Delacoste and Alexander, *Sex Work*. This statement has also been published in Pheterson, *A Vindication of the Rights of Whores*.

32 In the interviews with Liz and Donna, it was apparent that they did not believe it necessary to gloss over the unpleasant aspects of their work in order to assert prostitution as a viable occupation. Prostitutes' rights activists are not often as forthcoming when they are defending their work. When feminists want to talk about patriarchy, prostitutes' rights activists regard this as a signal that their agenda – the decriminalization of prostitution and better working conditions for women – is going to be taken up and transformed into an account of the male oppression of women. While modern prostitution's connection with women's oppression is one that activist prostitutes cannot simply wish away, neither can we dissociate prostitution from other forms of female labour.

33 See Pheterson, *A Vindication of the Rights of Whores*.

34 For a partial account of the conference proceedings see Bell, *Good Girls/Bad Girls*. For my critique of the role of sex trade workers in this conference, see Brock, 'Beyond Images.'

35 The prostitution committee remained an active subcommittee of NAC until about 1990. Prostitution is now under the preview of the subcommittee on justice.

36 Smith, *The Everyday World as Problematic*.

37 Griffith and Smith, 'Constructing Cultural Knowledge,' 89.

2: Campaigns and Moral Panics

1 Ehrenreich, *The Hearts of Men*.

2 Thanks to Mariana Valverde for a discussion of this point.

3 Cooke, 'Stripping.'

4 For a more elaborate discussion of the social and political context of the 1969 criminal code reforms, particularly governing homosexuality, see Kinsman, 'Official Discourse as Sexual Regulation.'

5 Canada, *Report of the Royal Commission on the Status of Women*.

6 Ibid., 369.

7 Ibid., 370.

8 Quebec, Commission of Inquiry into the Administration of Justice in Criminal and Penal Matters in Quebec, *Report*.

9 Canada, *Report of the Royal Commission on the Status of Women*, 371.

10 *Report of the Committee on Homosexual Offences and Prostitution*. For critiques of the report see Bland, 'Sexuality and Reproduction' and Hall, 'Reformism and the Legislation of Consent.'

11 Hall, 'Reformism and the Legislation of Consent,' 13.

12 Ibid.

13 Hall develops this notion by drawing on Foucault's work on social discipline in Foucault, *Discipline and Punish*.

14 See Kinsman, *The Regulation of Desire*.

15 Cited in Bland, 'Sexuality and Reproduction,' 108.

16 *Report of the Committee on Homosexual Offences and Prostitution*, 169.

17 See Chapter 9, 'Criminal Law and Women Offenders' in Canada, *Report of the Royal Commission on the Status of Women*.

18 On the tensions between liberalism and feminism, see Eisenstein, *The Radical Future of Liberal Feminism*.

19 Canada, *Statutes of Canada*. Statutes contained in the Criminal Code of Canada have since been renumbered. See Appendix C.

20 Canada, House of Commons, *Debates*.

21 See Ehrenreich, *Re-making Love*, and D'Emilio, *Sexual Politics, Sexual Communities*.

22 Toronto, City of, *Report of the Special Committee on Places of Amusement*.

23 I want to acknowledge the importance of Yvonne Ng's research in informing much of the discussion that follows. Ng, 'Ideology, Media and Moral Panics.' For a detailed account of Crombie's early period as mayor, see Caulfield, *The Tiny Perfect Mayor*.

24 Ng, 'Ideology, Media and Moral Panics.'

25 On Canada, see Ng, 'Ideology, Media and Moral Panics' and Kinsman, 'The Metro Toronto Police and the Gay Community.' On 'the rule of law' see National Deviancy Conference, *Capitalism and the Rule of Law*.

26 See also Stace, 'Legal Forms and Moral Phenomena.'

27 Toronto, City of, *Report of the Special Committee on Places of Amusement*, 32–3.

28 Ibid.

29 Ibid., 5.

30 Ibid.

31 Ibid., 33.

32 Ibid.

33 *Toronto Star*, 28 July 1977, cited in Stace, 'Legal Forms and Moral Phenomena.'

34 Toronto Wages for Housework Committee, 'Fact Sheet on the Yonge Street Crackdown.'

35 Ramirez, 'Hookers fight Back.'

36 'Zelda.'

37 Robert Miller, 'Mean Streets,' *Maclean's* (5 September 1977), 18.

38 Ibid.

39 See, for example, the numerous articles about the murder contained in the *Toronto Star* and the *Globe and Mail* during the first week of August 1977. Each of the 2 August and 3 August 1977 issues of the *Toronto Star* (the first report by the press that the boy had been murdered) contained at least six separate articles on pages one and two alone.

40 Stace, 'Legal Forms and Moral Phenomena.'

41 Rodrigues, *Pocket Criminal Code*.

42 The 'Fact Sheet on the Yonge Street Crackdown' and 'Metro Toronto Police Statistics Information Sheet' were produced by the Toronto Wages for Housework Committee, November 1977 (source: Canadian Women's Movement Archives, Toronto).

43 Stace, 'Legal Forms and Moral Phenomena.'

44 Miller, 'Mean Streets.'

45 Lowman, 'Geography, Crime and Social Control.'
46 Thanks to Tom Warner for making me aware of these events. Also see Hannon, 'The Anatomy of a Sex Scandal,' 10.
47 Ibid.
48 Cohen, *Folk Devils and Moral Panics*. A 'moral panic' does not necessarily always precede a campaign against prostitution, as the following chapter demonstrates.
49 Hall, *Policing the Crisis*, 165.
50 Ericson, *Reproducing Order*, 204.
51 Voumvakis and Ericson, *News Accounts of Attacks on Women*, 10.
52 Ericson, *Reproducing Order*, 195.
53 Also see 'Violent Crime Declines in Canada,' *Vancouver Sun*, 3 August 1977, 21.
54 Ng, 'Ideology, Media and Moral Panics.'
55 Hoy, cited in Lynch, 'Media Fosters Bigotry with Murder Coverage.' Thanks again to Tom Warner. See also Rick Bebout's 1995 historical essay, 'The Body Politic and Visions of Community' online at the Canadian Lesbian and Gay Archives home page <http://www.clga.ca/archives/what/papers/inven/tbp/tbpint.htm>.
56 Stace, 'Legal Forms and Moral Phenomena.'
57 See Jackson and Persky, *Flaunting It!*, Kinsman, 'The Metro Toronto Police and the Gay Community,' and McCaskell, 'The Bath House Raids and Gay Poltics.'
58 See Kinsman, 'The Metro Toronto Police and the Gay Community' and *The Regulation of Desire*.
59 Ramirez, 'Hookers Fight Back.'
60 Ibid.; and Miller, 'Mean Streets.'
61 Ericson, *Reproducing Order*, 195.
62 Miller, 'Mean Streets.'
63 Helen Bullock, 'Sex Strip Braces for Crackdown after Slaying,' *Toronto Star*, 2 August 1977, A1.
64 BEAVER later changed its name to CASH (Committee Against Street Harassment). For more about this organization, see an interview with its founder and spokesperson, Margaret Dwight-Spore, 'Speaking Up for Our Sisters: Decriminalization of Prostitution.' The prostitute's resource office, 'Maggie's' (founded by sex-trade workers in the 1980s) was named for Dwight-Spore.
65 For more on the International Wages for Housework Campaign, which was a source of considerable debate in the women's movement at this time, see Dalla Costa and James, *The Power of Women and the Subversion of Community*.
66 Engels, *The Origin of the Family, Private Property and the State*, 71.
67 Ramirez, 'Hookers Fight Back.'
68 Ibid.

69 Ibid.
70 Smart, 'Law and the Control of Women's Sexuality: The Case of the 1950's,' 50.

3: The Problem of Street Solicitation

1 I first explored these issues in my MA thesis. See Brock, 'Feminist Perspectives on Prostitution.'
2 See Taylor, *Crime, Capitalism and Community*.
3 *Tremeerar's Criminal Annotations*.
4 Some judges subsequently did not abide by this aspect of the *Hutt* decision, however, determining that the interior of a motor vehicle was indeed a public place.
5 Alberta, Provincial Court of Alberta, *Reasons for Judgement of His Honour, Judge H. G. Oliver*.
6 For a quantitative general analysis of newspaper coverage during this period see Komos, *Canadian Newspaper Coverage of Prostitution and Pornography*. This study was undertaken as part of the work of the Special Committee on Pornography and Prostitution, which will be discussed in the chapter to follow.
7 Jeff Sallot, 'Calgary Bylaw Ruled Unconstitutional,' *Globe and Mail*, 26 January 1983, reprinted in 'Prostitution,' *National Association of Women and the Law Newsletter*.
8 Denys Horgan, 'Accord Sought on Ways to Curb Street Soliciting,' *Globe and Mail*, 1 December 1983, 8.
9 Bureau of Municipal Research, 'A Canadian City Problem,' reprinted in 'Prostitution,' *National Association of Women and the Law Newsletter*.
10 Concerned Residents of the West End, 'Appendix "Just-37,"' Vancouver, British Columbia, 8 March 1982. Wilson and Kelling commented, 'If a window in a building is broken and is left unrepaired ... all of the rest of the windows will soon be broken.' Without the maintenance of public order, where disreputable (but not necessarily dangerous or criminal) people like prostitutes and panhandlers were allowed to loiture, more serious crime would soon follow. Thirty years earlier, a Stanford University Pyschologist by the name of Philip Zimbardo conducted an experiment in which he had parked a car on a street in an affluent suburb, where it sat undisturbed for a week. He then smashed one of the car's windows. The car was vandalized within hours. For more on 'broken windows,' see Fred Kaplan, 'New York Fixes Its Broken Windows,' *Globe and Mail*, 1 February 1997, D4.
11 Canada, House of Commons Standing Committee on Justice and Legal Affairs, *Order of Reference Respecting Soliciting for the Purpose of Prostitution*. See also Concerned Residents of the West End, 'Appendix "Just-37."'

12 'Prostitution Is Necessary: Vancouverites,' *Globe and Mail*, 26 January 1984.

13 Quoted in Horgan, 'Accord Sought on Ways to Curb Street Soliciting.' For further information on these points, see the following: Montreal Association of Women and the Law, *Position Paper on Soliciting* (November 1980); J. Willmont, *The Osgoode Women's Caucus Brief on Prostitution* (Toronto: 1980–81); National Association of Women and the Law, *Soliciting for the Purpose of Prostitution,* Statement to the House of Commons Standing Committee on Justice and Legal Affairs (29 May 1982); Status of Women Action Group, *Brief to the House of Commons Standing Committee on Justice and Legal Affairs Re: Decriminalization of Prostitution* (Victoria: 25 May 1982); National Action Committee on the Status of Women, *Background Paper on Prostitution, Soliciting Bawdy Houses and Related Matters.* Presented to the Standing Committee on Justice and Legal Affairs (Ottawa, 1 June 1982).

14 Canada, House of Commons Standing Committee on Justice and Legal Affairs, *Seventh Report.*

15 See Canada, Minister of Justice, *Proposed Act to Amend the Criminal Code.*

16 Canada, Special Committee on Pornography and Prostitution, *Pornography and Prostitution: Issues Paper.*

17 Rozovsky and Rozovsky, *Legal Sex.*

18 Hoegg, 'Summary of Case Law on Soliciting.'

19 Ibid.

20 Canadian Advisory Council on the Status of Women, *Prostitution in Canada.*

21 Herald Staff, 'Sex Bill "Green Light" for Prostitutes,' *Calgary Herald*, 24 June 1983, 1.

22 Ben Tierney, 'War Against Hookers Back in BC Court,' *Ottawa Citizen*, 23 June 1984, 59.

23 Lucille De Saint-Andre, 'The Other Side of the Track,' *Globe and Mail*, 28 March 1985, L1.

24 Brian MacAndrew and Sandra Contenta, 'Downtown Residents Fight Sex Invasion,' *Toronto Star*, 16 December 1984, A1.

25 Ibid.

26 Brian MacAndrew and Sandra Contenta, 'The Prostitution Crisis,' *Toronto Star*, 2, 9, 16 December 1984, 1.

27 Ibid.

28 Ibid.

29 Ibid.

30 Ibid.

31 See, for example, 'Rough Trade of the Streets,' *Ottawa Review*, 12 July 1983, 1.

32 Deborah Jones, 'N.S. Posts Names in War on Prostitutes,' *Globe and Mail*, 30 November 1984, 1.

33 Ibid.
34 See 'Vancouver Prostitutes, Customers Face Tough Legal Challenge,' *Ottawa Citizen*, 1 June 1984, 115; Tierney, 'War against Hookers Back in BC Court,' 59; Larry Still, 'Purge of Prostitutes Okayed,' *Vancouver Sun*, 4 July 1984, 1.
35 Tim Harper, 'Invasion of U.S. Prostitutes Tarnishes Niagara's Honeymoon Capital Image,' *Toronto Star*, 1 September 1985, A1.
36 This number of prostitutes was reported to be large for a city of 71,000 people. However, even if it is an accurate rather than inflated figure, it is misrepresentative because tourists swell the population figure substantially, and when the tourists are not there, neither are the prostitutes.
37 Harper, 'Invasion of U.S. Prostitutes Tarnishes Niagara's Honeymoon Capital Image,' A1.
38 Ibid.
39 Taylor, *Crime, Capitalism and Community*.
40 See Burstyn, *Women Against Censorship*.
41 Ian Mulgrew, 'One of Five in BC Lives on Welfare, U.I.,' *Globe and Mail*, 5 April 1984, 1.
42 The Alliance for the Safety of Prostitutes, quoted in the National Action Committee on the Status of Women, *Brief to the Special Committee on Pornography and Prostitution* (February 1984).
43 Lowman, 'Geography, Crime and Social Control.'
44 Ibid.
45 'Massage Parlours Raided; 25 on Prostitution Charges,' *Calgary Herald*, 11 May 1977, 1.
46 By-Law No. 135/78, 'Being a By-Law of the City of Calgary to License, Regulate and Control Body Painting Studios, Encounter Studios, Dating and Escort Services and Model Studios.' The information about the displacement of Calgary-based prostitutes was provided by Liz and Donna, whose interviews are contained in Chapter 1.
47 Caulfield, *City Form and Everyday Life*.
48 For an account of the gentrification of Cabbagetown (as the backdrop for a novel), see Garner, *The Intruders*. This same process can now be seen occurring in Parkdale, located in the southwest of Toronto, as rental housing, boarding houses, and halfway houses are replaced by the private homes of the privileged. This will be discussed further in Chapter 5. On 'moral repertoires' see Corrigan, 'On Moral Regulation,' 319.
49 Caulfield, *City Form and Everyday Life*, 60. Caulfield reminds us that this area was once called Donvale: the real Cabbagetown was a slum district which met the wrecker's ball of 1950s urban renewal schemes and was replaced by public housing. Ironically, Donvale was also slated for urban renewal in the 1960s, but

was saved by reform activists who were determined to see the existing housing preserved as affordable housing for the working class. Caulfield's analysis of Toronto's gentrification recognizes the central importance of the transformation of capital in the postindustrial city to the urban renewal process. However, he provides a more nuanced account of who the gentrifiers were than is provided in my analysis, demonstrating that a diversity of middle-class people were attracted to inner-city neighbourhoods for their offerings of anonymity, carnival, pleasure, and possibility. However, in his discussion of Donvale, our perspectives appear to be more congruent.

50 According to Ian Taylor, Stuart Hall demonstrates how the British state was experiencing a 'crisis of hegemony' on both fronts during the 1970s, thereby producing populist support for the development of 'Thatcherism.' Taylor asserts that while capitalism was in crisis in Canada, there was not a loss of faith in the bourgeois project itself, and therefore the crisis in Canada did not develop into a crisis of hegemony as it did in Britain. Hall, *Policing the Crisis*; Taylor, *Crime, Capitalism and Community*.

51 Rosie DiManno, 'Pros Aim to Stay on the Street,' *Toronto Star*, 7 February 1984.

4: The Special Committee on Pornography and Prostitution (The Fraser Committee)

1 This formulation is from Ashforth, 'Reckoning Schemes of Legitimation.'
2 It was also to address the perhaps more politically problematic issue of how the state should regulate pornography. See Lacombe, *Ideology and Public Policy*; Canada, Special Committee on Pornography and Prostitution, *Pornography and Prostitution in Canada* (hereafter referred to as The Fraser Report).
3 McLaren, 'The Fraser Committee,' 40. CROWE was a well-developed political lobby organization with legal counsel and a structure of subcommittees including one for women and one for children. Its class character was noted in the previous chapter.
4 Ashforth, 'Reckoning Schemes of Legitimation,' 4.
5 Ibid., 3.
6 Kuhn, 'Public versus Private,' 58.
7 Hunt, 'The Politics of Law and Justice,' 5.
8 See Chua, 'Democracy as a Textual Accomplishment,' 547. For a fuller discussion of textually mediated social organization, see Smith, 'The Active Text'; Smith, 'No-One Commits Suicide'; Smith, 'The Social Construction of Documentary Reality'; and Smith, 'Textually Mediated Social Organization.'
9 The Fraser Committee comprised four men and three women, including four

L.L.B.'s (one of whom was an expert on constitutional law and equality rights), a criminologist, a sociologist, and a legal historian. All four women had strong public records on women's issues. The members were Paul Fraser, John McLaren, Mary Eberts, Joan Wallace, Andree Ruffo, Susan Clark, and Jean-Paul Gilbert.

10 Maroney, 'Using Gramsci for Women.'

11 Ashforth, 'Reckoning Schemes of Legitimation.'

12 Canada, Special Committee on Pornography and Prostitution, *Pornography and Prostitution: Issues Paper*, 1.

13 Ibid., 367.

14 'Prostitution.'

15 The Fraser Report, 25.

16 Ibid., 20.

17 Ibid., 27. The committee noted that the determination of these 'basic values' was itself a source of debate.

18 Ibid., 27.

19 Ibid., 28.

20 As they stated, criminal law 'attaches too much significance to legal expedients as the effective instrumentalities of social change.' Ibid., 534.

21 Ibid., 539.

22 Ibid., 28.

23 Ibid., 413–14. As will be discussed in Chapter 7, sections (2), (3), and (4) were later repealed and replaced with similar sections that also referred specifically to those living on the avails of persons under eighteen years of age, or obtaining or attempting to obtain the services of a prostitute under eighteen.

24 The Fraser Report, 543.

25 Ibid., 545.

26 Ibid., 539.

27 Ibid.

28 Ibid., 549.

29 Ibid., 27.

30 The term 'common bawdy-house' was considered archaic and its elimination from the Criminal Code therefore recommended.

31 The Fraser Report, 538.

32 For a more detailed discussion of the use of prostitution legislation pertaining to bawdy-houses for the harassment of gay men see Russell, 'The Offence of Keeping a Common Bawdy-House in Canadian Criminal Law,' 270.

33 The Fraser Report, 534.

34 Ibid., 27.

35 For more on the limits of legalization, see Brock, 'Feminist Perspectives on

Prostitution'; Canadian Advisory Council on the Status of Women, *Prostitution in Canada*.

36 See Shaver, 'Prostitution,' 15. Further allegations of questionable policing practices will be raised in the following chapter.

37 The Fraser Report, 535. The committee does acknowledge, however, that prostitution-specific regulation may indeed need to be eliminated in the future for the reasons Ruffo suggests. The Fraser Report, 29–30.

38 Ashforth, 'Reckoning Schemes of Legitimation,' 1. On the latter point, recall that the Fraser Committee commented that they were constrained by time and money considerations so that the bulk of their resources were used to investigate street solicitation. It is also possible that these constraints limited their ability to conduct an independent study of prostitution involving young people.

39 Eisenstein, *The Radical Future of Liberal Feminism*.

40 Ibid.

41 McLaren, 'The Fraser Committee.'

42 For the contradictions in evidence in the Fraser Committee's attempts to accomodate both liberal (liberty) and feminist (equality) approaches to the regulation of pornography, see Lacombe, *Blue Politics: Pornography and the Law in the Age of Feminism*.

43 See Barry, *Female Sexual Slavery*.

5: A New Legal Strategy for the Policing of Prostitutes

1 A Gallup Poll was conducted on the matter of prostitutes working from their own homes in July 1985. It indicated a fairly even split in opinion about allowing women to work from their own homes. The nationwide sample indicated that 47 per cent were opposed to allowing prostitutes to work from their own homes, 44 per cent were in favour, and 9 per cent had no opinion. The statistics for Ontario were the same as the national average; in BC, where there has been such active campaigning against prostitutes it was a respectable 50/50, and in Quebec, 52 per cent favoured the proposal. 'People Split on Prostitutes Working in Homes: Poll,' *Toronto Star*, 11 July 1985, A3.

2 McLaren, 'The Fraser Committee.' The *Toronto Star* also commented that the Tory government should proceed with the committee's recommendations on street solicitation. It stated that the legislation being considered by the Tories was far too 'heavy-handed.' 'Editorial,' *Toronto Star*, 27 Oct. 1985, F2.

3 McLaren, 'The Fraser Committee,' 51.

4 Canada. Minister of Justice, 'Bill C-49.'

5 According to the *Toronto Star* Crosbie claimed that the provinces had unani-

mously rejected the Fraser Committee proposal that prostitutes be allowed to work in their own homes because, he thought, they did not want to have to try to control or regulate 'this kind of thing.' Apparently, however, discussions with the provinces' attorneys general, upon whom the decision for further action rested, were quite limited. Two or three responded with quiet No's, while others, according to Crosbie, transmitted through 'visual means their lack of enthusiasm.' Ontario's Attorney General, Ian Scott was reported as saying that Ontario opposed the strategy as it could not guarantee that street prostitution would be eliminated. 'Crosbie Says Provinces Refused Prostitution Plan,' *Toronto Star*, 11 June 1986, A10.

6 'Planned Revisions to Criminal Code Take Time,' *Toronto Star*, 9 November 1984, A4.

7 Thanks to Mary Ann Coffey for providing me with this letter.

8 See Brown, 'A Feminist Interest in Pornography.'

9 'MPs Approve Curb on Street Prostitution,' *Toronto Star*, 21 November 1985, A1.

10 'Police Armed with New Law on Street Sex,' *Toronto Star*, 21 December 1985, A1.

11 Sgt Richard Brier, *What's Happening on the Streets?* Also see interview with Valerie Scott in Kinsman, 'Whores Fight Back,' 9.

12 Brian Gory, 'BC Hookers Flouting New Law,' *Globe and Mail*, 27 December 1986, A4.

13 Ibid.

14 Kirk Makin, 'Prostitution Laws Accomplish Little but Confusion,' *Globe and Mail*, 31 October 1987, D2.

15 Elizabeth Fry Society, *What's Happening on the Streets?*

16 Sgt Richard Brier, *What's Happening on the Streets?*

17 Ibid.

18 See Kirk Makin, 'Anti-hooker Laws Working – For Now,' *Globe and Mail*, 18 January 1986, 1.

19 Gory, 'BC Hookers Flouting New Law.'

20 Elizabeth Fry Society, *What's Happening on the Streets?*

21 Shannon, 'Vancouver Prostitutes Fear Increasing Violence,' 3. Another example of how entrapment works was provided in the following letter to the Toronto weekly newspaper *NOW*, 15–21 June 1989, 7:

Two men in a bush, hiding, surveilling. Scary. They're going to jump me, right? Wrong. They're going to jump him. 'A john,' seen at this moment chatting with a woman on the corner. I don't stick around to see, (or alert the john) because I would be interfering with the law.

What deception! Whose reality? If the cop/whore hadn't been standing there, he wouldn't have stopped. Whose constitutional rights?
Nothing's wrong with my neighbourhood except for the cops in the bush.

This is not an unusual scenario. It is also a common way of arresting men on morals charges who are 'cruising' in public parks for consensual (and free of charge) sexual encounters with other men.

22 George Oake, 'City Pays Men to Have Sex with Prostitutes,' *Toronto Star*, 8 September 1989, A1.

23 Kirk Makin, 'Prostitution Laws Accomplish Little but Confusion,' *Toronto Star*, 31 October 1987, D2.

24 Ibid.

25 Ibid. Also see Ann Rauhala, 'Prostitutes Jailed Unfairly, Groups Say,' *Globe and Mail*, 27 March 1987, A3.

26 Linda Hossie, 'Hooker's Children Protected,' *Globe and Mail*, 29 March 1986, A8.

27 In June 1987, this method led to charges of attempted sexual assault, communicating for the purpose of prostitution, forcible confinement, and impersonating a police officer, all laid against a man who, on the pretence of being a police officer, had picked up a prostitute and demanded free sex. 'Prostitute Jots Down Licence, Spurs Arrest,' *Toronto Star*, 17 June 1987, A25.

28 Kinsman, 'Whores Fight Back!' 8.

29 Ibid.

30 Ibid.

31 Glen Wheeler, 'Sweeping Up the Sex Trade,' *NOW*, 11 June 1987, 13.

32 See Kinsman, 'Whores Fight Back!.'

33 Paula Todd, 'Prostitution: Off Street, into Yellow Pages,' *Toronto Star*, 27 April 1986, A8.

34 Paul Loong, 'Street Prostitution Law Leads Experts to Debate Future of Escort Services,' *Toronto Star*, 26 December 1985, D23.

35 Makin, 'Prostitution Laws Accomplish Little but Confusion.'

36 Todd, 'Prostitution.'

37 Police were perhaps emboldened by the recent decision of the Supreme Court of Canada to uphold the communicating law, under a constitutional challenge spearheaded by CORP (This will be discussed in Chapter 8). See Donald Grant, 'Sex Ads in Paper Bring Charges,' *Globe and Mail*, 1 September 1990, A1; 'Editorial,' *Globe and Mail*, 5 September 1990, A12; Glenn Wheeler, '*NOW* Magazine Hit by Morality Squad,' *NOW*, 6–12 September 1990, 19; Glenn Wheeler, '*NOW*, Police Chief Clash at Commission Meeting,' *NOW*, 11–17 October 1990, 17.

38 McLaren, 'The Fraser Committee,' and Cohen, *Visions of Social Control.*
39 The following discussion is reproduced, with revisions, from a previously published article: Brock, 'Prostitutes Are Scapegoats in the AIDS Panic.'
40 The lesbian and gay community developed such a spirited resistance to this ideological attack that by the mid-1990s AIDS had become a mainstream issue, with a focus on compassion for the terminally ill. However, the community was so successful in challenging the identification of HIV and AIDS as a gay male disease that the reality that gay men comprised the largest number of the afflicted and dying became invisible in mainstream fundraisers and their corporate endorsements. AIDS activists and service providers expressed concern that the suffering of gay men and the hard struggles of lesbian and gay activists to get education programs, treatment services, and medical research in place, in absence of a broader (straight) community and state response, would go unacknowledged.
41 For a discussion of 'sanitary policing,' see Weir, 'The Medicalization of Sexual Danger.'
42 Conversation with Valerie Scott, May 1988.
43 Dr. Howard Seiden, 'Prostitutes Are Health Problem,' *Toronto Star*, 13 June 1985, D3.
44 'Allow Police to Pick Up Possible AIDS Victims Winnipeg Chief Says,' *Toronto Star*, 31 March 1987, A5.
45 Pauline Comeau, 'Police Search for AIDS Hooker in Vancouver,' *Toronto Sun*, 16 July 1986, 1.
46 Deborah Wilson, 'Health Officials on AIDS: Avoid Hookers "Like the Plague,"' *Globe and Mail*, 26 January 1987, A15.
47 Glen Wheeler, 'AIDS Order Questioned,' *Toronto Star*, 4 July 1987, A3.
48 'Police May Release Names of Prostitutes, Johns,' *Toronto Star*, 1 June 1988, A6.
49 Glen Wheeler, 'AIDS Order Questioned.'
50 John Cruikshank, 'Most Heterosexuals Called Free from AIDS,' *Globe and Mail*, 14 June 1988, A12.
51 Lillian Newberg, '50% of Teen Prostitutes Carry Sexual Diseases, Study Finds,' *Toronto Star*, 5 November 1987, A23.
52 'No AIDS Found in Hooker Study,' *Globe and Mail*, 12 February 1987, A4.
53 Haug and Cini, *The Ladies (and Gentlemen) of the Night and the Spread of Sexually Transmitted Diseases.*
54 Conversation with Danny Cockerline, 25 October 1988.
55 As of 1995, there were no documented cases of prostitutes transmitting HIV to customers.
56 Statement shortened and adapted from Highcrest, 'Communicating for the Purposes of ...,' 10.
57 Conversation with Valerie Scott, 25 October 1988.

58 Conversation with Danny Cockerline, 25 October 1988.
59 Metropolitan Toronto Police Commission, *Neighbourhoods Committee Meeting*.
60 On their previous trip, the group had apparently been accompanied by Toronto Mayor Art Eggleton. Heather Bird, 'Toughen Laws on Prostitution Metro Police, Citizens Ask MPs,' *Toronto Star*, 25 May 1988, A7.
61 According to Valerie Scott of CORP, a staged-for-media vigilante action was almost foiled one evening when no prostitutes could be found working in the area. A media representative who was on hand to film the residents in action informed Scott that the residents solved this problem by gathering around a tree and yelling at it, while the scene was duly filmed to obscure the presence of the tree and absence of the prostitute. Interview with Valerie Scott, 18 November 1987.
62 Lois Sweet, 'Wrong Way to Rid Area of Prostitutes,' *Toronto Star*, 27 November 1987, B1.
63 Residents produced sweatshirts for these actions that read 'street solicitation buster,' and depicted a woman leaning into a car window conversing with a male driver. Embossed over the picture was a diagonal slash within a circle. Their intent was summarized in a placard which stated, 'put some jaws in the laws and bite them where it hurts.' Leslie Scrivener, 'Declaring War on Prostitution,' *Toronto Star*, 22 November 1987, A3. Also see Frank Jones, 'Cabbagetown Residents Right to Harass Prostitutes,' *Toronto Star*, 30 November 1987; Michael Valpy, 'Track Patrol Fights to Reclaim Streets,' *Globe and Mail*, 4 December 1987, A8; Lois Sweet, 'Wrong Way to Rid Area of Prostitutes,' *Toronto Star*, 27 November 1987, B1.
64 Cited in 'Alderman Proposes Red-Light Districts,' *Globe and Mail*, 5 February 1988, A11.
65 Makin, 'Prostitution Laws Accomplish Little but Confusion.'
66 'Police, Courts Focus on "Johns" in Fight against Prostitution,' *Toronto Star*, 13 December 1987, A1.
67 'Police Arrest, Charge 110 Men in Sweep against Prostitution,' *Toronto Star*, 23 October 1987, A7.
68 Metropolitan Toronto Police Commission, *Neighbourhoods Committee Meeting*.
69 When the communication legislation was initially introduced, convictions were more likely to be handed down to prostitutes than to customers. In a *Toronto Star* article, police allegedly claimed that this happened because prostitutes were more likely to be repeat offenders. However, it was also clear that police were more likely to arrest prostitutes than customers. For a first offence, Vancouver judges tended to give customers a conditional discharge, while prostitutes

received fines of $25 to $150, and sometimes more. Some also were sentenced to a day in jail. Customers of Toronto prostitutes were frequently given discharges for first offences as well. In November 1986, judges gave a number of men discharges provided that they donate money to charity, with amounts of up to $150 being specified. In one week in November, over seven thousand dollars was donated to charities by customers. 'Johns Escape Jail by Donating to Charity,' *Toronto Star*, 19 November 1986, A18.

70 Deborah Wilson, 'Judge Orders 24 "Johns" to Rid Streets of Condoms,' *Globe and Mail*, 11 December 1987, A18. See also Tom Spears, 'Undercover Officers Help Derail "the Johns" in Metro's Track Area,' *Toronto Star*, 13 December 1987, A8. This attempt to 'shame the johns' reportedly raised the ire of the union representing Toronto street cleaners, which had 200 members out of work at the time. The union was said to argue that these cleaners should be the first to be offered any available work, rather than the courts using a system of 'convict labour,' and that whereas this punishment would deprive some men of employment, certain bona fide charitable organizations such as the Salvation Army would benefit from the court-appointed volunteer work. Alexandra Radkewycz, 'Judge's Order Draws Cleaners' Protests,' *Globe and Mail*, 21 December 1987, A18.

71 Leslie Scrivener, 'Hookers Haunt Homes along the Track,' *Toronto Star*, 25 October 1987, A14. The division between antiprostitution residents and resident detractors cannot be reduced to class position alone, however. For example, residents of the working-class neighbourhood of Mount Pleasant in Vancouver, where many prostitutes relocated after being pressured out of the west end of the city, initially decided to live with the trade, rather than simply push it to another area. See Dan Smith, 'Vancouver Area Tries New Solution,' *Toronto Star*, 16 December 1984, A1. However, a later media report stated that residents were complaining about the presence of the trade near schoolyards and condoms found on school grounds. See Gory, 'BC Hookers Flouting New Law,' A4. In Toronto, some women residents of Regent Park, a social housing project located where the original Cabbagetown once stood, have attempted to pressure prostitutes out of the area by taking their places on the streets and intimidating inquiring customers. See 'Pssst ... Guess Who's Hookin?' *Regent Park T.O!* 2, no. 7 (June 27 1991). However, residents of working-class areas are generally cynical about the limited police response to problems in their areas.

Working-class residents of mixed neighbourhoods also participate in anti–street solicitation campaigns. They are in the unenviable position, however, of unwittingly participating in their own dislocation as their neighbourhoods are gentrified.

72 On 'news themes' see Ericson et al., *Negotiating Control*.

73 Metropolitan Toronto Police Commission, *Neighbourhoods Committee Meeting*. Also see Peter Cheney, 'Prostitution "Threatening" Streets despite Record Arrests,' *Toronto Star*, 6 November 1987, A6.

74 Peter Kuitenbrouwer, 'Bearing Down on Bitters,' *NOW*, 3–9 December 1987, 11.

75 Mike Funston, 'Etobicoke Motel Strip Study Waived,' *Toronto Star*, 10 May 1989, A9. As of 1995, the anticipated transformation had not materialized, likely owing to the Toronto area recession that followed its late 1980s real estate boom, leaving a glut of commercial and residential (condominium) real estate on the market.

76 See David MacFarlane, 'The Strip,' *Toronto Life*, July 1989, 16.

77 Sean Fine, 'Metro's Rental Crunch Leaving Its Mark on Neighbourhoods,' *Globe and Mail*, 8 June 1988, A14. For example, between 1976 and 1987 Toronto manufacturing jobs decreased by 27.2 per cent. See Table 5.1.

TABLE 5.1
Labour Force by Occupation, City of Toronto 1976–87[a]

	1976		1987		Growth rate 1976–87
	#('000)	%	#('000)	%	%
All Occupations	324.2	100.0	372.6	100.0	14.9
Managers	86.9	26.8	134.1	36.0	54.3
Clerical	68.1	21.0	62.9	16.9	(–7.6)
Sales	27.4	8.5	33.2	8.9	21.2
Service	51.9	16.0	57.8	15.5	11.4
Manufacturing	46.7	14.4	34.0	9.1	(–27.2)
Others	43.2	13.3	50.6	13.6	17.1

[a]Source: Unpublished data provided by the City of Toronto Planning and Development Department, based on the Labour Force Survey. Industrial Development Institute, 'Table 5.'

78 In Caulfield's analysis, this revolution began with post-war urban renewal plans. Caulfield, *City Form and Everyday Life*, 26. Also see J. Zarocostas, 'Toronto Ranked as Most Expensive City in Western Hemisphere, 28th in World,' *Globe and Mail*, 9 May 1990, A1. Middle-class resettlement in older inner-city neighbourhoods in Canada, the U.S., Britain, and Australia is discussed in Smith and Williams, *Gentrification of the City*.

79 Susan Pigg, 'Home-Owner Groups Flex Bigotry Muscle?' *Toronto Star*, 24 March 1988, A25.

80 Michael Valpy, 'A Classic Conflict in Red-Light Area,' *Globe and Mail*, 23

November 1987, A8. The real estate company that employed her reputedly enjoyed much of its success as a result of its role in the gentrification of Cabbagetown.

81 Wendy Dennis, 'Street Fight: In the War between the Homeowners and Hookers, Is the Real Issue Propriety or Property Values,' *Toronto Life*, November 1988, 85. A number of events began to alter the character of Vancouver as well. Urban redevelopment and a 'clean-up' of city streets during the building and run of Expo '87 was well publicized. Subsequently, Vancouver experienced an influx of financial capital as businesses based in Hong Kong invested heavily in the city to shift their capital before the 1997 return of the colony to China. The boom in the city's economy, its population growth, and the corresponding increase in physical size raised concerns (one far from noble – the discomfort with an influx of Asian immigrants expressed by some white people) for Vancouver residents about the future of the city.

82 Editorial, 'Police Must Set Their Priorities,' *Toronto Star*, 4 September 1988, B2. Ericson notes that spending on the police in Canada per 100,000 population increased by 65% between 1962 and 1977, with most of the growth occurring in patrol work. Ericson, *Reproducing Order*, 4. On the importance of police news releases to media reporting on crime (as well as the news as a police resource), see Wheeler, 'Reporting Crime,' 15. Wheeler finds that this formal account is ideological not because it is untrue but 'rather that it transforms the lived world of the "criminal" into a world seen from the point of view of the organization.'

83 Dennis, 'Street Fight,' 128. In 1984, the city of Halifax was estimated to have spent $104,398.25 per prostitution arrest, including the cost of police personnel, vehicles, patrols, booking procedures, court time, and miscellaneous costs. Crook, *Report on Prostitution in the Atlantic Provinces*. Julie Pearl's article 'The Highest Paying Customers' provides a detailed accounting of the cost of prostitution legislation enforcement in varying sizes of American cities in 1985. For example, in New York, costs were estimated at $1,961 per arrest; in Chicago, $942; and in Baltimore, $2,180.

84 This expands Shearing and Stenning's definition, which includes shopping malls, residential estates, campuses, and airports. Shearing and Stenning, 'Private Security.' Similarly, Ian Taylor asserts that 'the key significance of the crime prevention programs are their resonance for the propertied Canadian bourgeoisie and the settled, largely white, working population.' Taylor, 'Martyrdom and Surveillance,' 69.

85 Shearing, 'Subterranean Processes in the Maintenance of Power,' 283, cited in Kinsman, 'Official Discourse as Sexual Regulation,' 240. It is interesting to speculate whether consumption (particularly conspicuous consumption) and

taking care of one's property represents a 'new morality' of the urban and affluent. For similar musings, see Ehrenreich, *Fear of Falling*.

86 CORP became a NAC member group in 1985, demanding that the women's
movement be inclusive of the standpoint of prostitutes. A prostitution subcommittee was formed, comprising prostitute and non-prostitute women, to establish a dialogue between women inside and outside of the sex trade, and to assist
NAC in developing a policy on prostitution that included prostitutes in the
women's movement. In proposing a series of controversial resolutions at
NAC's annual general meetings, the committee (which I was a member of from
1987 to 1989) was faced with the difficult task of challenging the conventional
feminist perspective that prostitutes are passive victims of patriarchal oppression, held by the majority of representatives of member groups. The committee
succeeded in having NAC policy oppose any legislation which seeks to limit
choices in the business and personal lives of adult prostitutes (1986); recognize
the right of prostitutes to determine and carry out their own work priorities
(1986); condemn Section 195(2) of the Criminal Code, living on the avails of
prostitution, as placing legal judgments on women's (prostitutes') personal relationships [procuring would remain in the Code] (1987); oppose forced testing
for HIV or other STDs (1987); support the development of autonomous services for and by prostitutes (1988); challenge the racial bias in solicitation
enforcement practices (1988); and oppose the criminalization of young prostitutes' lives, while supporting tougher legislation against those who exploit them
(1986). See the 'Index of Abridged Resolutions of NAC,' produced annually.

87 Police themselves may be ambivalent about this process because it enforces a
quota system that judges their work by the number of charges laid. For example, see Gary Webb-Proctor, 'Police Say Constable in Trouble for Not Issuing
Enough Tickets,' *Globe and Mail*, 13 August 1987, A17.

88 Ericson, *Reproducing Order*; Lowman, 'Prostitution in Vancouver.'

89 Cohen, *Visions of Social Control*.

90 Ericson et al., *Negotiating Control*.

91 Ibid., 123.

92 The five most frequently cited sources (in a list of eighteen) were: police (296);
municipal councillor (197); lawyer (187); journalist (176); judge (163). Adult
prostitutes were seventh on the list (107), although the author of the report
noted that these interviews seldom asked prostitutes how they thought prostitution should be organized. Women's groups were only sourced twenty-five
times, and ranked thirteenth on the list. Komos, *Canadian Newspaper Coverage of Prostitution and Pornography, 1978–1983*, 33.

93 Barbara Amiel, 'Straight Talk on Blacks,' *Toronto Sun*, 1 October 1985, 12.

94 Ibid.

95 Gilroy, *'There Ain't No Black in the Union Jack,'* 11.
96 Ibid.
97 Brian Gory, 'BC Hookers Flouting New Law,' *Globe and Mail,* 27 December 1986, A4.
98 Ibid. For example, in July of 1985, a Toronto provincial court judge (DiCecco) gave absolute discharges to a prostitute and client arrested while having sex in a car, even though both had pleaded guilty. The judge stated: 'You are practising a lawful profession – because parliament has said it is legal – but it is the only lawful profession in Canada that cannot be legally practised in a normal place of business. I can sympathize with your quandary.' At the same time, he asked the prostitute to be sensitive to the desire of people not to see what she was doing. He added that he had ruled the previous year that being in a common bawdy-house was not an offence, and that the Crown had not appealed the decision 'because they know I am right.' Susan Craig, 'Judge Gives Prostitute and Client Nothing but Sympathy,' *Toronto Star,* 9 July 1985, A3.

DiCecco made a series of controversial rulings on prostitution, most of which were favourable to prostitutes and their clients. For example, in March 1988 he incurred the wrath of Toronto police by fining a woman twenty-five cents for soliciting because she was a single mother of two children, surviving on welfare. Damien Cox, 'Woman Fined 25 Cents for Soliciting Didn't Deserve to Go to Jail, Judge Says,' *Toronto Star,* 22 March 1988, A2.

DiCecco's controversial rulings are noteworthy because they lent the appearance that the judicial system and the legislation regulating prostitution were in disarray. In August of 1989 DiCecco resigned his judicial post amid suggestions that the Ontario Judicial Council investigate his judicial conduct.
99 According to Valerie Scott, when she and Ryan Hotchkiss postered an information sheet on the law on Toronto streets, they were arrested, strip-searched, and charged with mischief in relation to property. The charges were later withdrawn. Conversation with Valerie Scott, May 1987.
100 As Alan Hunt notes, the concept of 'rights' is itself problematic:

First, the concept of rights abstract from the socio-economic relations within which people live and act, and in lifting them outside this reality it cloaks them with property in a right which they may exercise, through the institutions and procedures of law, against other individuals. Thus 'rights' are inherently abstract. Second, 'rights' invoke the legal subject, the atomised individual as citizen; thus rights are seen, not only as abstract, but as individualised. Finally, rights either explicitly or implicitly refer to some view about the basic or fundamental character of people which provides grounds for giving priority to certain classes of claims as constituting rights; in other words the concept of rights is seen as invoking some ontological view of the character of the species, where different ontological views clash they express themselves by giving priority to different rights. The general objection then is that the idea of rights involves some reference to the essence or universal nature of people.

Therefore, 'what is needed is a struggle to transform the content of rights and the terms in which interests are identified and given priority.' Hunt, 'The Politics of Law and Justice,' 15.

101 According to Andrew Petter; cited in Jefferson, 'The Promise of Equality,' 1.
102 Jefferson, 'The Promise of Equality,' 1.
103 Canada. *The Charter of Rights and Freedoms.*
104 Judge J.T. Bernhard, 'Reasons for Judgement' in *Regina v. Jennifer Smith* (Provincial Court, Criminal Division, Judicial District of York, 10 July 1987).
105 *Regina v Skinner* (The Supreme Court of Nova Scotia, Appeal Division, 20 May 1987); Judge Robert L. Kopstein, 'Reasons for Judgement' in *Regina v Cunningham* et al. (Provincial Court of Manitoba, Criminal Division, 3 November 1986); Judge G.G. Cioni, 'Reasons for Judgement' in *Regina v Bear* et al. (Provincial Court of Alberta, 25 September 1986).

6: The Report of the Committee on Sexual Offences Against Children and Youths (The Badgley Report)

1 For a fuller discussion of the Badgley Report see Brock and Kinsman, 'Patriarchal Relations Ignored.' That article was published earlier as Brock and Kinsman, 'Patriarchy Ignored.' The discussion of prostitution involving young people in this chapter is largely derived from a portion of that article. Note that while the Badgley Report confers the identity 'prostitute' ('juvenile prostitute') on young people, I generally avoid this formulation as it implies a fixed and dominant identity that my analysis reveals may not actually exist. Instead, I prefer to use phrases such as, 'young people who find a source of income through prostitution' because providing sexual services may not be all that they do to survive.
2 See Housten, '"Waifs and Strays" of a Late Victorian City.' Recently, all young people identified as street prostitutes came to be discursively positioned under the rubric of the street kid. As well, most street kids were believed to engage in some degree of prostitution (among other activities) for their economic survival. Moreover, as the following chapter will reveal, during the moral panic which was activated following the release of the Badgley Report, professionals were far from clear about who a 'child' actually was.
3 Canada. Special Committee on Sexual Offences Against Children and Youths,

Sexual Offences Against Children, 3 (hereafter referred to as the Badgley Report). Its chairperson, Robin F. Badgley, is a professor of behavioural science in the Faculty of Medicine at the University of Toronto (cross-appointed in the Department of Sociology). Other committee members were Herbert Allard, Norma McCormick, Patricia Proudfoot, Denyse Fortin, Doris Ogilvie, Quentin Rae-Grant, Paul-Marcel Gelinas, Lucie Pepin, and Sylvia Sutherland.

4 Ibid., 3.

5 Ibid., 962.

6 The expansion of this juridical-scientific taxonomy and its influence on social relations provides one example of the ongoing development of a multiplicity of discourses about sexuality described by Foucault in his work considering the Victorian period. See Foucault, *The History of Sexuality*.

7 Kuhn, 'Public versus Private,' 64.

8 The Badgley Report, 54.

9 Ibid., 293.

10 Ibid., 335.

11 Ibid., 91.

12 Ibid., 1033.

13 Ibid., 95.

14 Ibid., 96.

15 Ibid., 92. See recommendation 41.

16 Ibid., 93. See recommendations 42 and 43.

17 Ibid., 95.

18 Ibid.

19 Ibid., 962.

20 Ibid.

21 Ibid., 96.

22 The passage of Bill C-19 through the Criminal Law Reform Act in 1985 (soon after the release of the Badgley Report) rectified this, however, by amending the then current S.195.1 to specify its applicability to customers.

23 Ibid., 96. See recommendation 46.

24 Ibid., 97. See recommendation 47 regarding customers.

25 Ibid., 94. See recommendation 44 regarding procuring.

26 Ibid., 968.

27 Ibid.

28 Ibid.

29 Ibid. The committee was assisted by an officer from the Metro Toronto police force who served as a research associate.

30 Ibid., 1000.

31 Ibid., 999.

32 Ibid., 989. In particular see Chapter 44 including the series of case studies of young people engaged in prostitution.
33 Ibid., 1034–6.
34 Ibid., 1036–7.
35 Ibid., 991. 8.3 per cent of girls and 9.5 per cent of boys indicated 'economic necessity,' that is, having no other source of income, as the primary reason, while 29.8 per cent of boys and 17.2 per cent of girls stated that they found income through prostitution as they had no other means of employment. I suggest that the distinctions between these categories are fairly flexible (for example, most would have been influenced to various degrees by lack of employment, economic necessity, and desire for fast money).
36 Ibid., 992.
37 Ibid.
38 The criteria used for determining socio-economic background were the employment and educational status of parents, and the degree to which those interviewed felt that their 'basic necessities' had been met in the context of the family. In reporting their parents' employment status, the respondents revealed that 33.6 per cent of their mothers and 59.4 per cent of their fathers were employed on a full-time basis, while 20.5 per cent of their mothers and 7.9 per cent of their fathers had maintained part-time work (employment status was not known or reported for 10.5 per cent of their mothers and 20.1 per cent of their fathers). The unemployment rate was apparently higher among the parents of females than males, but no breakdown of this was provided. However, males revealed that 23.9 per cent of their mothers and 10.9 per cent of their fathers received some form of government financial support, while the findings for females were 33.1 per cent and 31.2 per cent, respectively. Males further reported that 42.8 per cent of their mothers and 47.6 per cent of their fathers had completed high school and/or some form of post-secondary education, as compared to 35.9 per cent of the mothers and 25.5 per cent of the fathers of females.

Finally, the report revealed that when the respondents were asked if their 'basic necessities' such as food, clothing, and shelter had been provided for, three-quarters (76.4 per cent) replied that these needs had been 'completely met.' Of the remainder, 13.5 per cent 'reported that these necessities have not always been fully provided for,' while information on 10.1 per cent was 'unknown.'

However, the questions posed were sufficiently vague to allow for a variety of both responses and interpretations. The employment status of parents, for example, does not provide an indication of income level. Education level does not provide an indicator of factors like underemployment. Nor does a vague reference to 'basic necessities' give a clear picture of a family's standard of living with respect to, for example, the type of shelter and quality of food provided. In addition, comparison data was not provided from the general population.

39 The Badgley Report, 983.

40 Ibid.

41 Ibid., 984.

42 For example, see Cole, *Pornography and the Sex Crisis.*

43 The Badgley Report, 179–80.

44 On this point, see Bearchell, *The Body Politic.*

45 The Badgley Report, 179. See Wachtel, 'Some Reflections on the Badgley Report.' Also see my article, 'Talkin 'Bout a Revelation.'

46 Of those interviewed, 37.1 per cent reported such contact. Moreover, 40.5 per cent had been found delinquent by a juvenile court, which again resulted in the majority being placed in some form of extrafamilial care. In both instances females outnumbered males two to one. However, of the 229 young prostitutes interviewed, 145 were female and 84 male, and the data are not proportional to the participation rates by gender. Ibid., 1028–9.

47 Ibid., 92.

48 Ibid., 986.

49 Ibid., 1027.

50 Smith, 'The Active Text,' 25.

51 Ibid.

52 Smart, *Feminism and the Power of Law,* 160.

53 Ibid., 161.

7: Street Kids and Child Prostitutes: The Making of a 'New' Social Problem

1 For example, Sgt Luc Dussault of the Montreal police force blamed the fact that there were more single parent families and working mothers: women just did not have time to look after their children. Juvenile prostitution was a direct result of women entering the workforce en masse, thereby neglecting their children. This position sidesteps the overwhelming majority of single-parent families where young people do not run away from home and work as prostitutes, as well as those young people fleeing traditional family arrangements who do. The lack of adequate social services and daycare, the default of fathers on child support payments, and the economic status of women generally are subordinated to the concern with maintaining the 'traditional' family unit. '150,000 Runaways in Canada Last Year,' *Toronto Star,* 21 December 1985.

2 Jan Lounder, 'Teen Hooker Tells Sordid Tale: Sex at 10,' *Toronto Sun,* 23 June 1986, 28; Wendy Darroch, 'The 18 Month Nightmare of Mother Whose Child Was Trapped by a Pimp,' *Toronto Star,* 6 February 1986, 1; Linda Hossie, 'Many

Ignorant of Sexuality: Young Street Prostitutes Vulnerable, Alone in World,'
Globe and Mail, 20 November 1984, 1; Ellie Tesher, 'Street Kids Fight Their
Desperate Existence,' *Toronto Star*, 15 July 1985, A13; Ellie Tesher, '300 Teen
Prostitutes Roam Streets,' *Toronto Star*, 14 July 1985, A1; Linda Hossie, 'Young
Prostitutes Find the Life Addictive,' *Globe and Mail*, 17 November 1984, 1.

3 Tom Kerr, 'Quality of Life Tops Our Civic Election,' *Toronto Star*, 26 October
   1985, B1.

4 Ellie Tesher, 'Despair Haunts Homeless Street Kids,' *Toronto Star*, 13 July
   1985, A6.

5 Shelly Page, 'Rescuing Runaways,' *Toronto Star*, 30 April 1987, B1.

6 Kim Zarzour, 'Bringing Kids Back from the Street,' *Toronto Star*, 17 August
   1987, C1.

7 Darroch, 'The 18 Month Nightmare of Mother Whose Child Was Trapped by a
   Pimp.' A Native Youth Outreach Worker commented at a 1995 forum on street
   youth at First Nations House (when the figure of 10,000 street kids in Toronto
   was still being reported as factual) that this inflated number was derived from
   multiplying one agency's daily statistics (representing youth who access that
   service) by the number of services targeted to the street youth population.
   However, youth may access a number of services according to their needs over a
   given day; one service may provide a bed, another 'the best sandwiches,' and
   another bus tokens. Thanks to Jerry Halbot for this information from his paper,
   'Street Youth: Causes and Conditions,' Youth and Society course, Ryerson
   Polytechnical University, 1995.

8 Ellie Tesher, 'Street Kids Fight Their Desperate Existence.'

9 Brian MacAndrew and Sandra Contenta, 'Prostitution Is "Running Wild" Here,
   Metro Police Warn,' *Toronto Star*, 2 December 1984, A1; Joel Ruimy, 'Juvenile
   Prostitutes' Clients Might Face 5 Year Jail Terms,' *Toronto Star*, 11 June 1986,
   A10; Tom Kerr, 'Quality of Life Tops Our Civic Election.'

10 Sylvia Stead, 'Ontario Has Plan for Youth of Streets,' *Globe and Mail*, 5 February 1985, M1.

11 The Badgley Report.

12 Data are equally loose when it comes to estimating the number of pimps controlling street prostitution in Toronto. One article states that there are 100
   pimps (Ellie Tesher, 'Street Kids Fight Their Desperate Existence'), while
   another asserts 300 (Ellie Tesher, 'Can Crackdown Halt Selling of Sex on
   Streets?' *Toronto Star*, 26 January 1986, A6). Sgt Brier estimates that 90 per cent
   of street prostitutes, presumably including adults, are controlled by pimps.
   However, the Badgley Report's juvenile prostitution survey stated that 10 per
   cent of the young prostitutes interviewed had had pimps, while another 40 per
   cent stated that they had pimps in the past. This raises the question of who

defines what constitutes a pimp. The only thing clear from this mass of contradictory reports is that the number of people involved in one way or another in
youth prostitution is extremely difficult to measure.

13 Lucchini himself contributes to this levelling process, however, by referring
uncritically to the 'street child,' thereby blurring the range in ages of the young
people involved. Lucchini, 'Street Children,' 3.

14 Tesher, '300 Teen Prostitutes Roam Streets,' A14.

15 Hossie, 'Many Ignorant of Sexuality,' 1; Kim Zarzour, 'Bringing Kids Back
from the Streets,' C1. For an exception (which focuses on economics) see
Tesher, '300 Teen Prostitutes Roam Streets'

16 Hossie, 'Many Ignorant of Sexuality,' 1.

17 Philip Plews, 'The Hustlers,' *Globe and Mail*, 1 August 1985, A17.

18 Tesher, '300 Teen Prostitutes Roam Streets,' A14.

19 Louder, 'Teen Hooker Tells Sordid Tale,' 28.

20 Kerr, 'Quality of Life Tops Our Civic Election,' B1. The same discursive organization was later used to describe innocent youths being pulled into the vortex
of the illicit drug trade, as this paragraph demonstrates: 'the youths were swept
into an international drug smuggling ring that lures Metro-area teens from
under-age dance clubs and shopping malls to faraway, tropical islands. Using
fresh-faced Metro teens to run drugs between countries is on the rise, police
say.' See Shelley Page and Jennifer Gold, 'Metro Teens Tell Story from Trinidad
Prison,' *Toronto Star*, 18 June 1989, A22.

21 Shearer, 'Canada's War on the White Slave Trade.' On the discourse of the
social purity movement, see Strange, 'The Toronto Social Survey Commission
of 1915 and the Search for Sexual Order in the City.'

22 See, for example, Brake, *Comparative Youth Culture*; Housten 'Waifs and
Strays of a Late Victorian City'; Platt, *The Child Savers*.

23 For example see Rosen, *The Lost Sisterhood*.

24 MacAndrew and Contenta, 'The Prostitution Crisis.' In July 1985 a *Toronto
Star* reporter stated that 'only a few prostitutes manage to work without pimps.'
Tesher, '300 Teen Prostitutes Roam Streets,' A14.

25 Stuart MacCarthy, 'Teen Hookers "White Slaves." Cops Report Runaways
Tortured,' *Toronto Sun*, 4 November 1987, 1.

26 Gwyn Thomas, 'Street Workers Aided Prostitution Arrests Deputy Chief Says,'
Toronto Star, 31 October 1987, A17.

27 'Pimped,' *Chatelaine*, November 1994, 109.

28 Ibid., 113.

29 Elizabeth Fry Society, *What's Happening on the Streets?*

30 MacAndrew and Contenta, 'Prostitution Is "Running Wild" Here, Metro
Police Warn,' A1.

31 McAndrew and Contenta, 'The Prostitution Crisis.'

32 Jean Sonmor, 'Getting Kids off the Street,' *Toronto Sun*, 19 July 1985, 69.

33 The Badgley Report, 1062.

34 Hall, *Policing the Crisis.*

35 Ibid., 59.

36 Kerr, 'Quality of Life Tops Our Civic Election,' B1.

37 Ibid.

38 Mathews, *Familiar Strangers.*

39 Canada. The House of Commons, 'Bill C-15, An Act to Amend the Criminal Code and the Canada Evidence Act.'

40 For example see: Vivian Snead, 'Police Crackdown Discourages Pimps,' *Toronto Teens*, September 1987, 8; Shelley Page, 'Crackdown on Pimps Cuts Teen Prostitution, Police Say,' *Toronto Star*, 2 May 1987, F8; Gwyn Thomas, 'Street Workers Aided Prostitution Arrests Deputy Chief Says,' and 'California Man Jailed 9 Months for Being Pimp,' *Toronto Star*, 31 October 1987, A17; Wendy Darroch, 'Man, 22, Jailed 3 Years for Being Pimp to Teens,' *Toronto Star*, 30 September 1987, A31; 'Teenaged Prostitution Network Lured Runaways, Officers Say,' *Toronto Star*, 10 September 1987, A2; Peter Edwards, 'Ottawa Children for Sex Ring Alleged,' *Toronto Star*, 29 May 1987, A5; Gary Oakes, 'Pimp Jailed after Attempting to Force Runaway Girl to Become a Prostitute,' *Toronto Star*, 12 May 1987, A23.

41 'Man Jailed for Pimping, Beating Prostitute, 15,' *Toronto Star*, 16 November 1987, A14.

42 Canada. The House of Commons, 'Bill C-15, An Act to Amend the Criminal Code and the Canada Evidence Act.'

43 Mathews, *Familiar Strangers.*

44 Stead, 'Ontario Has Plan for Youth of Streets,' M1.

45 Canada, Minister of Community and Social Services, *On the Rising Incidence of Child Abuse.*

46 Yaworski, *Mandated Services to Teen Prostitutes.*

47 Sarah Jane Growe, 'Project "Last Chance" for Child Prostitutes,' *Toronto Star*, 29 July 1985, C1. Information on services has been compiled from the following sources: Newspaper: Ellie Tesher, 'Metro's Teen Tragedy,' *Toronto Star*, 13–15 July 1985; Growe, 'Project "Last Chance" for Child Prostitutes,' C1; Sonmor, 'Getting Kids off the Street,' 69; Page, 'Rescuing Runaways,' B1; Zarzour, 'Bringing Kids Back from the Street,' C1. Ministry of Community and Social Services: Canada, Minister of Community and Social Services, *On the Rising Incidence of Child Abuse*; Toronto Street Youth Project, *Report of the Toronto Street Youth Project Reception Centre, May–Nov. 1985*; Yaworski, *Mandated Services to Teen Prostitutes*; Kochendorfer, *Toronto Street Youth Project Initial*

Status Report; Doherty Social Planning Consultants, *A Study of the Services Required by Youths Admitted into Cassatta-Warrendale*; Toronto Street Youth Project Steering Committee, *Terms of Reference*; Anglican Houses, *First Overall Progress Report*; Anglican Houses, *Second Overall Progress Report*.

48 Anglican Houses, *First Overall Progress Report*; Anglican Houses, *Second Overall Progress Report*.

49 This matching of young people and workers in a high support model was ended in 1991 as a result of budget cutbacks, and replaced with a community support model, where groups of young people met with a worker or workers. While the high support model was considered to be the most effective approach, the street kid was no longer a front page issue, leaving agencies more vulnerable to the widespread cutbacks in social services.

50 Anglican House workers stated that 50–60 per cent of the young people they had contact with had at one time been wards of the Children's Aid, and that most had run away from home and would never return. They could not go back to their old lives and expect to fit in with their peer group, so required the resources and skills to live independently.

51 Much of my knowledge of SOS was gained as a part-time high support worker with the agency in the year before that program was cancelled as a result of budget constraints.

52 Linda Hossie, 'Many Ignorant of Sexuality.'

53 Banner and Mathews, *Native Child and Family Services of Toronto Youth Outreach Program Review*.

54 Thanks again to Jerry Halbot for this information from his paper 'Street Youth.'

55 Mathews, *Familiar Strangers*, 6.

56 Ibid., 8.

57 Ibid. Also see Street Outreach Services, 'Program Overview, Description of Street Youth in Prostitution, Service Statistics and Outcomes.'

58 See Kinsman, 'Whores Fight Back.'

59 Sullivan, 'Juvenile Prostitution,' 12.

60 Visano, *This Idle Trade*.

61 Sullivan, 'Juvenile Prostitution'; Mathews, *Familiar Strangers*; Visano, *This Idle Trade*.

62 Sullivan, 'Juvenile Prostitution,' 12. For more on economic conditions facing youth generally, see Cote and Allahar, *Generation on Hold*.

63 On the 'history of childhood' see Aries, *Centuries of Childhood*. On the history of family violence, see Gordon, *Heroes of Their Own Lives*.

64 See Sullivan, 'Juvenile Prostitution.'

65 This trend has also been commented on in the U.S. context by Grossberg, 'Rock and Youth.' Two books that began their gestation during the moral panic about

street youth, Marlene Webber's *Street Kids: The Tragedy of Canada's Runaways* (1991) and Evelyn Lau's *Runaway: Diary of a Street Kid* (1989) mitigated this shift somewhat. Webber provides a more comprehensive account of young people's lives on the street than did the Badgley Report or media accounts. However, the book contains numerous problems of the sort that I critiqued in my discussion of the Badgley Report. For example, she uncritically accepts the Badgley Report's formulation that prostitution involving young people is equivalent to sexual abuse. She conflates the ages of her subjects, and makes problematic references to, for example, children 'selling their bodies' which dramatizes unnecessarily. These young people's stories, as they tell them in Webber's book, are compelling enough.

Evelyn Lau is a talented young writer who fled her Vancouver family for the streets in 1986, at age 14. Lau's book began as a journal that she kept during her time on the streets (Lau had already been writing for a number of years, and had even had work published). *Runaway* conveys Lau's inner turmoil, her gritty experiences on the streets, and her conflictual relationship with social service workers.

8: And On It Goes ...

1 For a fuller discussion, see Brock, 'Prostitutes Are Scapegoats in the AIDS Panic.'
2 Prostitutes Launch Campaign,' *Globe and Mail*, 23 November 1996, A20; Philip Jackman, 'And in Other News ...,' *Globe and Mail*, 30 September 1995, D3; John Stackhouse, 'Calcutta's Prostitutes Fight for Rights,' *Globe and Mail*, 13 January 1997, A12.
3 *Street Prostitution: Assessing the Impact of the Law*. A copy of the report was obtained by the *Toronto Star* under the Freedom of Information Act, prior to its public release. See David Vienneau, 'Soliciting Law Hasn't Reduced Street Prostitution, Study Shows,' *Toronto Star*, 1 August 1989, A3. Also see Michael Valpy, 'Different Faces of Street Prostitution,' *Globe and Mail*, 2 August 1989, A8.
4 *Street Prostitution: Assessing the Impact of the Law*. Also see Chapter 4.
5 Kinsman, 'Whores Fight Back,' 8.
6 Henry Hess, 'Sex-Trade Activity Up, Statscan Finds,' *Globe and Mail*, 14 February 1997, A3.
7 Ross Howard, 'Sex Trade Industry Flourishing in B.C.,' *Globe and Mail*, 3 September 1996, A8.
8 'Judge's Remarks Create Outrage,' *Globe and Mail*, 24 December 1996, A6; David Roberts, 'Pair Guilty in Slaying of Regina Prostitute,' *Globe and Mail*, 21

December 1996, A9; David Roberts, 'Natives Scorn Killers' Sentences,' *Globe and Mail*, 31 January 1997, A1.

9 See, for example, Philip Mascoll, Bruce DeMara, and Moira Welsh, '2 Transvestites Gunned Down,' *Toronto Star*, 22 May 1996, A6.

10 Brock and Kinsman, 'Patriarchal Relations Ignored.'

11 A recent book by former Toronto prostitute and activist Alexandra Highcrest provides further arguments from the perspective of a sex trade worker. See Highcrest, *At Home on the Stroll*.

12 Robert Matas and Miro Cernetig, 'Vancouver Police Target Sex Customers,' *Globe and Mail*, 19 February 1997, A1.

13 Gary Abate, 'Johns on the Spot Sent to School,' *Globe and Mail*, 8 January 1996, A8. Several months later a program called 'Streetlight' was implemented to help get Toronto prostitutes off of the streets. Attendance at Streetlight is offered as an alternative to fines or jail terms. See 'Prostitutes to Get Help Leaving Street,' *Globe and Mail*, 1 March 1997, A3.

14 Thanks to Fred Mathews for providing me with the following reports, and for sharing his observations of them. Recommendations fo the Prostitution Policy, Service and Research Committee for the Calgary Community, *Handbook for Action Against Prostitution of Youth in Calgary* (1996). A later task force repeats the Badgley Report's conflation and ommissions by refering only to 'child' prostitution in its report. See Report by the Task Force on Children Involved in Prostitution, *Children Involved in Prostitution*, Calgary (28 January 1997). Also see British Columbia's *Community Consultation on Prostitution in British Columbia: Overview of Results* (March 1996). Unfortunately (and perhaps ominously) this report refers to all children, youth, and adults who find a source of income in prostitution as 'sexually procured.' Also see 'Label Prostitution as Abuse, Groups Say,' *Globe and Mail*, 29 February 1996, A13; Alanna Mitchell, 'Alberta to Tackle Underage Sex Trade,' *Globe and Mail*, 8 February 1997, A5; Paul Knox, 'Change Focus, Ex-Prostitute Urges,' *Globe and Mail*, 29 August 1996, A12.

15 Canada, Supreme Court of Canada, *In the Matter of the Constitutional Questions Act, Being Chapter C-180*, 5.

16 'Top Court Endorses War against Pimps,' *Toronto Star*, 22 May 1992, A15.

Appendix B: Prostitutes and HIV/AIDS Transmission

1 Vogt et al., 'Isolation of HTLV-III/LAV from Cervical Secretions of Women at Risk for AIDS,' 525.

2 Robert Scheer, 'AIDS Threat to All – How Serious?' *Los Angeles Times*, 14 August 1987, 1.

3 Bruce Lambert, 'AIDS in Prostitutes Not as Prevalent as Believed, Studies Find,' *New York Times* Science (20 September 1988), 24.

4 Scheer, 'AIDS Threat to All – How Serious?.'

5 Interview with Danny Cockerline, 25 October 1988.

6 'Antibody to Human Immunodeficiency Virus in Female Prostitutes,' 2011.

7 Vogt et al., 'Isolation of HTLV-III/LAV from Cervical Secretions of Women at Risk for AIDS'; Wofsy, 'Isolation of AIDS-Associated Retrovirus from Genital Secretions of Women with Antibodies to the Virus,' 527.

8 Wofsy, 'Isolation of AIDS-Associated Retrovirus from Genital Secretions of Women with Antibodies to the Virus,' 529.

9 Center for Disease Control, Atlanta. *AIDS Weekly Surveillance Report.*

10 Vogt et al., 'Isolation of HTLV-III/LAV from Cervical Secretions of Women at Risk for AIDS.'

References

Alberta. Provincial Court of Alberta. *Reasons for Judgements of His Honour, Judge H.G. Oliver*. In the Provincial Court of Alberta Between Her Majesty the Queen and Lenore Jacqueline Westendrop, Calgary, Alberta, 7 October 1981.

Anglican Houses. *First Overall Progress Report: Street Outreach Services, September–November 1985*. Submitted 27 November 1985.

– *Second Overall Progress Report: Street Outreach Services, September 1985– September 1986*. Submitted 31 October, 1986.

'Antibody to Human Immunodeficiency Virus in Female Prostitutes.' *Morbidity and Mortality Weekly Report* 36, no. 11, Centers for Disease Control, Atlanta (1987); reprinted in *Journal of American Medicine* 257, no. 15 (17 April 1987), 2011–13.

Aries, Philipe. *Centuries of Childhood: A Social History of Family Life*. New York: Vintage, 1965.

Armstrong, Pat, and Hugh Armstrong. 'Beyond Sexless Class and Classless Sex: Towards Feminist Marxism.' *Studies in Political Economy* 10 (Winter 1983): 7–43.

Ashforth, Adam. 'Reckoning Schemes of Legitimation: On Commissions of Inquiry as Power/Knowledge Forms.' *Journal of Historical Sociology* 3, no. 1 (March 1990): 1–22.

Banner, J., and F. Mathews. *Native Child and Family Services of Toronto Youth Outreach Program Review*. Undated (pre-1995).

Barry, Kathleen. *Female Sexual Slavery*. New York: Avon, 1979.

Barnett, Harold C. 'The Political Economy of Rape and Prostitution.' *Review of Radical Political Economics* 8, no. 1 (Spring 1976): 59–68.

Bearchell, Chris. 'Taking Advantage of Abuse.' *The Body Politic* (January 1985): 27–9.

Bell, Laurie, ed. *Good Girls/Bad Girls*. Toronto: Women's Press, 1987.

Bland, Lucy, Trisha McCabe, and Frank Mort. 'Sexuality and Reproduction: Three Official Instances.' In *Ideology and Cultural Production*, edited by Michelle Barrett, Philip Corrigan, Annette Kuhn, and Janet Wolff. London: Croom Helm, 1979.

Boles, Jacqueline, and Charlotte Tatro. 'Legal and Extra Legal Methods of Controlling Prostitution: A Cross Cultural Comparison.' *International Journal of Comparative and Applied Criminal Justice* 2 (Spring 1978): 98–110.

Boyer, Debra, and Jennifer James. 'Juvenile Prostitution.' In *The Female Offender*, edited by C. Griffiths and M. Nance. Vancouver: Simon Fraser University Research Centre, 1980.

Brake, Michael. *Comparative Youth Culture*. London: Routledge and Kegan Paul, 1985.

Brier, Sgt. Richard, Morality Bureau, Metropolitan Toronto Police Department. 'What's Happening on the Streets?' Public Forum sponsored by the Elizabeth Fry Society, Toronto, 15 October 1986.

British Columbia. *Community Consultation on Prostitution in British Columbia: Overview of Results*, March 1996.

Brock, Deborah. 'Beyond Images: Hookers and Feminists.' *Broadside* 7, no. 6 (April 1986): 8–9.

– 'Feminist Perspectives on Prostitution: Addressing the Canadian Dilemma.' Master's thesis, Carleton University, 1984.

– 'Prostitutes Are Scapegoats in the AIDS Panic.' *Resources for Feminist Research* 18, no. 2 (June 1989): 13–17.

– 'Regulating Prostitution/Policing Prostitutes: Some Canadian Examples, 1970–1989.' PhD thesis, University of Toronto, 1989.

– 'Talkin 'Bout a Revelation: Feminist Popular Discourse on Sexual Abuse.' *Canadian Women's Studies* 12: 1 (1991): 12–16. Republished in *And Still We Rise*, edited by Linda Carty. Toronto: Women's Press, 1993.

Brock, Deborah, and Gary Kinsman. 'Patriarchal Relations Ignored: An Analysis and Critique of the Badgley Report on Sexual Offenses Against Children and Youths.' In *Regulating Sex: An Anthology of Commentaries on the Findings and Recommendations of the Badgley and Fraser Reports*, edited by John Lowman, M.A. Jackson, T.S. Palys, and S. Gavigan. Vancouver: School of Criminology, Simon Fraser University, 1986.

– 'Patriarchy Ignored: A Critique of the Badgley Report.' *Canadian Criminology Forum* 8 (Winter 1987): 15–29.

Brown, Beverley. 'A Feminist Interest in Pornography: Some Modest Proposals.' *m/f* 5, no. 6 (1981): 5–18.

Bureau of Municipal Research. 'A Canadian City Problem.' Reprinted in 'Prostitution.' *National Association of Women and the Law Newsletter* (June 1983): 65–72.

Burstyn, Varda, ed. *Women Against Censorship*. Toronto: Douglas and MacIntyre, 1985.

Canada. *The Charter of Rights of Freedoms*. Ottawa: Ministry of Supply and Services, 1982.

– *Report of the Royal Commission on the Status of Women*. Ottawa: Information Canada, 1970.

– *Statutes of Canada*, Criminal Law Amendment Act, assented to May 19, 1972, 21 Elizabeth II.

– House of Commons. *Debates*, Fourth Session, Twenty-Eighth Parliament, Vol. 2, 20 March–5 May, 1972.

– The House of Commons. 'Bill C-15, An Act to Amend the Criminal Code and the Canada Evidence Act,' passed 23 June 1987.

– House of Commons Standing Committee on Justice and Legal Affairs. *Order of Reference Respecting Soliciting for the Purpose of Prostitution*, 83, 11 May 1982.

– House of Commons. Standing Committee on Justice and Legal Affairs. *Seventh Report*, 6 May 1982.

– Minister of Community and Social Services. *On the Rising Incidence of Child Abuse*, Statement to the Legislature by the Hon. John Sweeney, 9 July 1985.

– Minister of Justice. *Bill C-49: An Act to Amend the Criminal Code (prostitution)*, First reading, 2 May 1985.

– Minister of Justice. *Proposed Act to Amend the Criminal Code* 25849. Ottawa.

– Special Committee on Pornography and Prostitution. *Pornography and Prostitution in Canada* (The Fraser Report). Ottawa: Ministry of Supply and Services, 1985.

– Special Committee on Pornography and Prostitution. *Pornography and Prostitution: Issues Paper*. Ottawa: Supply and Services, 1983.

– Special Committee on Sexual Offences Against Children and Youths. *Sexual Offences Against Children* (The Badgley Report). Ottawa: Ministry of Supply and Services, 1984.

– Supreme Court of Canada. *In the Matter of the Constitutional Questions Act, Being Chapter C-180*. C.C.S.M., 31 May 1990.

Canadian Advisory Council on the Status of Women. *Prostitution in Canada*. Ottawa: Ministry of Supply and Services, 1984.

Caulfield, Jon. *The Tiny Perfect Mayor: David Crombie and Toronto's Reform Aldermen*. Toronto: James Lorimer, 1974.

– *City Form and Everyday Life: Toronto's Gentrification and Critical Social Practice*. Toronto: University of Toronto Press, 1994.

Center for Disease Control, Atlanta. *AIDS Weekly Surveillance Report*, (26 September 1988).

'Children Involved in Prostitution.' Report by the Task Force on Children Involved in Prostitution. Calgary (28 January 1997).

Chua, Beng-Huat. 'Democracy as a Textual Accomplishment.' *Sociological Quarterly* 20, no. 4 (Autumn 1979): 541–49.

Cohen, Stanley. *Folk Devils and Moral Panics*. London: MacGibbon and Key, 1972.

– *Visions of Social Control*. Oxford: Polity Press, 1985.

Cole, Susan. 'Whispering Out Loud.' *Broadside* 10, no. 4 (February 1989): 3.

– *Pornography and the Sex Crisis*. Toronto: Amanita, 1989.

Concerned Residents of the West End. 'Appendix "Just-37,"' Submission to the Standing Committee on Justice and Legal Affairs. *Order of Reference Respecting Soliciting for the Purpose of Prostitution* 83 (11 May 1982).

Cooke, Amber. 'Stripping: Who Calls the Tune?' In *Good Girls/Bad Girls*, edited by Laurie Bell. Toronto: Women's Press, 1987.

Corrigan, Philip. 'On Moral Regulation: Some Preliminary Remarks.' *Sociological Review* 29, no. 2 (May 1981): 313–37.

Cote, James, and Anton Allahar. *Generation on Hold: Coming of Age in the Late Twentieth Century*. Toronto: Stoddart, 1994.

Coward, Rosalind. *Patriarchal Precedents*. London: Routledge and Kegan Paul, 1983.

Crook, Nikita. *Report on Prostitution in the Atlantic Provinces*, Report No. 12 for the Special Committee on Pornography and Prostitution. Ottawa: Ministry of Supply and Services, 1984.

Dalla Costa, Mariarosa, and Selma James. *The Power of Women and the Subversion of Community*. Bristol: Falling Wall Press, 1973.

D'Emilio, John. *Sexual Politics, Sexual Communities*. Chicago: University of Chicago Press, 1983.

Delacoste, Frederique, and Priscilla Alexander, eds. *Sex Work*. Pittsburgh: Cleiss Press, 1987.

Doherty Social Planning Consultants. *A Study of the Services Required by Youths Admitted into Cassatta-Warrendale*. 28 July 1986.

Dwight-Spore, Margaret. 'Speaking Up for Our Sisters: Decriminalization of Prostitution.' *Fireweed* 1 (Autumn 1978), 23–6.

Ehrenreich, Barbara. *Re-making Love*. New York: Anchor Press, 1986.

– *The Hearts of Men*. New York: Anchor Press, 1984.

– *Fear of Falling: The Inner Life of the Middle Class*. New York: Pantheon, 1989.

Eisenstein, Zillah. *The Radical Future of Liberal Feminism*. New York: Longman, 1981.

Elizabeth Fry Society. 'What's Happening on the Streets?' Public Forum, Toronto, 15 October 1986.

Engels, Frederick. *The Origin of the Family, Private Property and the State*. Moscow: Progress, 1977.

Ericson, Richard. *Reproducing Order: A Study of Police Patrol Work*. Toronto: University of Toronto Press, 1982.

Ericson, Richard, Patricia Baranek, and Janet Chan. *Negotiating Control: A Study of News Sources*. Toronto: University of Toronto Press, 1989.

Federal-Provincial-Territorial Working Group on Prostitution. *Dealing with Prostitution in Canada: A Consultation Paper* (March 1995).

Foucault, Michel. *Discipline and Punish*. London: Allan Lane, 1978.

– *The History of Sexuality*, Volume 1. New York: Vintage, 1978.

Garner, Hugh. *The Intruders*. Toronto: McGraw-Hill Ryerson, 1976.

Gauntlet. 'Special Issue: In Defense of Prostitution,' no. 7 (1994).

Gilroy, Paul. *'There Ain't No Black in the Union Jack': The Cultural Politics of Race and Nation*. Chicago: University of Chicago Press, 1987.

Gordon, Linda. *Heroes of Their Own Lives: The Politics and History of Family Violence*. New York: Viking, 1988.

Griffith, Alison, and Dorothy Smith. 'Constructing Cultural Knowledge: Motherhood as Discourse.' In *Women and Education*, edited by Jane Gaskell and Arlene Tigar McLaren. Calgary: Detselig, 1987.

Grossberg, Lawrence. 'Rock and Youth.' In *We Gotta Get Out of This Place*. New York: Routledge, 1992.

Gusfield, Joseph. *The Culture of Public Problems*. Chicago: University of Chicago Press, 1981.

Hall, Stuart. *Policing the Crisis*. London: MacMillan, 1978.

– 'The Rediscovery of "Ideology": Return of the Repressed in Media Studies.' In *Culture, Society and the Media*, edited by Michael Gurevitch, Tony Bennett, James Curran, and Janet Wollacott. London: Methuen, 1982.

– 'Reformism and the Legislation of Consent.' In *Permissiveness and Control*, edited by the National Deviancy Conference. London: Macmillan, 1980.

Hannon, Gerald. 'The Anatomy of a Sex Scandal.' *The Body Politic*, no. 25 (July/August 1976): 10–11.

Haug, M., and M. Cini. *The Ladies (and Gentlemen) of the Night and the Spread of Sexually Transmitted Diseases*. Working Papers on Pornography and Prostitution, Report #7. Ottawa: Department of Justice, 1984.

Highcrest, Alexandra. 'Communicating for the Purposes of ...,' *Rites: Supplement on the Faces of AIDS Prevention* 7, no. 4 (Oct. 1990): 10.

– *At Home on the Stroll: My Twenty Years as a Prostitute in Canada*. Toronto: Alfred A. Knopf, 1997.

Hoegg, Lois. 'Summary of Case Law on Soliciting.' *National Association of Women and the Law Newsletter* 5, no. 2 (June 1983), 39–42.

Housten, Susan. 'Waifs and Strays of a Late Victorian City: Juvenile Delinquents in Toronto.' In *Childhood and Family in Canadian History*, edited by Joy Parr. Toronto: McClelland and Stewart, 1982.

Hunt, Alan. 'The Politics of Law and Justice.' In *Politics and Power: Law, Politics and Justice* 4, edited by Alan Hunt. London: Routledge and Kegan Paul, 1981.

Industrial Development Institute. 'Table 5.' In *Manufacturing Matters: Conference Proceedings and Research Papers*. Conference to Consider the Deindustrialization of Metro Toronto. Toronto: Our Times, 1988. 80.

Jackson, Ed, and Stan Persky, eds. *Flaunting It!* Toronto: Pink Triangle Press, 1982.

Jaget, Claude, ed. *Prostitutes: Our Life*. London: Falling Wall Press, 1980.

Jefferson, Christie. 'The Promise of Equality.' *LEAF Letter* 7 (Summer 1989).

Kinsman, Gary. 'The Metro Toronto Police and the Gay Community.' *Atkinson Review of Canadian Studies* 1, no. 2 (Spring 1984): 27–34.

– 'Official Discourse as Sexual Regulation: The Social Organization of Sexual Policing of Gay Men.' PhD dissertation, Ontario Institute for Studies in Education, 1988.

– *The Regulation of Desire*. Montreal: Black Rose Books, 1987.

– 'Whores Fight Back: An Interview with Valerie Scott.' *Rites* 3, no. 1 (May 1986): 8.

Kochendorfer, Diane. *Toronto Street Youth Project Initial Status Report*. Submitted to the Ministry of Community and Social Services for CASATTA Ltd., September 1985.

Komos, Maged E. *Canadian Newspaper Coverage of Prostitution and Pornography, 1978–1983*. Ottawa: Department of Justice, 1984.

Kuhn, Annette. 'Public versus Private: The Case of Indecency and Obscenity.' *Leisure Studies* 3, no. 1 (January 1984): 53–65.

Labour Canada. *Women in the Labour Force, 1986–1987*. Ottawa: Minister of Supply and Services, 1987.

Lacombe, Dany. *Ideology and Public Policy*. Toronto: Garamond Press, 1988.

– *Blue Politics: Pornography and the Law in the Age of Feminism*. Toronto: University of Toronto Press, 1994.

Lau, Evelyn. *Runaway: Diary of a Street Kid*. Toronto: HarperCollins, 1989.

Li, Peter. *The Making of Post-War Canada*. Toronto: Oxford, 1996.

Lombroso, Cesare, and Enrico Ferrero. *The Female Offender*. New York: D Appleton (orig. 1895) 1900.

Lowman, John. 'Geography, Crime and Social Control.' PhD dissertation, University of British Columbia, 1982.

– 'Prostitution in Vancouver: Some Notes on the Genesis of a Social Problem.' *Canadian Journal of Criminology* 28, no. 1 (January 1986): 1–16.

Lucchini, Riccardo. 'Street Children: A Complex Reality,' Paper No. 224, World Health Organization. Translated by Daniel Stocklin. July 1993.

Lynch, Michael. 'Media Fosters Bigotry with Murder Coverage.' *The Body Politic* 36 (September 1977), 1.

Maroney, Heather Jon. 'Using Gramsci for Women: Feminism and the Quebec State, 1960–1980.' *Resources for Feminist Research* 17, no. 3 (Sept. 1988): 26–30.

Marx, Karl. *Economic and Philosophic Manuscripts of 1844*. Moscow: Progress, 1977.

Mathews, Fred. *Familiar Strangers: A Study of Adolescent Prostitution*. Toronto: Central Toronto Youth Services, Autumn 1987.

McCaskell, Tim. 'The Bath Raids and Gay Politics'. In *Social Movements, Social Change: The Politics and Practice of Organizing*, edited by Frank Cunningham, Sue Findlay, Marlene Kadar, Alan Lennon, and Ed Silva, 169–88. Toronto: Between the Lines, 1988.

McLaren, John. 'The Fraser Committee: The Politics and Process of a Special Committee.' In *Regulating Sex: An Anthology of Commentaries on the Findings and Recommendations of the Badgley and Fraser Reports*, edited by John Lowman, M.A. Jackson, T.S. Palys, and S. Gavigan. Vancouver: School of Criminology, Simon Fraser University, 1986.

McLeod, Eileen. *Women Working: Prostitution Now*. London: Croom Helm, 1982.

Metropolitan Toronto Police Commission. *Neighbourhoods Committee Meeting*. Toronto, 5 November 1987.

Morgan, Robin. *Going Too Far*. New York: Vintage, 1978.

National Deviancy Conference, ed. *Capitalism and the Rule of Law*. London: Hutchinson, 1979.

Newman, Frances, and Paula Caplan. 'Juvenile Female Prostitution as Gender Consistent Response to Early Deprivation.' *International Journal of Women's Studies* 5, no. 2 (1982): 128–37.

Ng, Yvonne Chi-Ying. 'Ideology, Media and Moral Panics: An Analysis of the Jacques Murder.' Master's thesis, University of Toronto, 1981.

Pearl, Julie. 'The Highest Paying Customers: America's Cities and the Cost of Prostitution Control.' *Hastings Law Journal* 38, no. 4 (April 1987): 769–800.

Pheterson, Gail, ed. *A Vindication of the Rights of Whores*. Seattle: Seal, 1989.

Platt, Anthony. *The Child Savers*. Chicago: University of Chicago Press, 1969.

'Prostitution.' *National Association of Women and the Law Newsletter: Special Issue* 5, no. 2 (June 1983).

Quebec. Commission of Inquiry into the Administration of Justice in Criminal and Penal Matters in Quebec. *Report, 1968–1970*. 1970.

Ramirez, Judy. 'Hookers Fight Back.' *Wages for Housework Campaign Bulletin* 2, no. 1 (Fall 1977): 1.

Report of the Committee on Homosexual Offenses and Prostitution. New York: Stein and Day, 1963.

Research Committee for the Calgary Community. *Handbook for Action Against Prostitution of Youth in Canada*, 1996.

Roberts, Nickie. *Whores in History*. New York: HarperCollins, 1992.

Rodrigues, Gary P., ed. *Pocket Criminal Code*. Agincourt, Ont.: Carswell Legal Publications, 1987.

Rosen, Ruth. *The Lost Sisterhood*. Baltimore: Johns Hopkins University Press, 1982.

Rozovsky, L.E., and F.A. Rozovsky. *Legal Sex*. Toronto: Doubleday, 1982.

Rubin, Gayle. 'Thinking Sex: Notes for a Radical Theory of the Politics of Sexuality.' In *Pleasure and Danger*, edited by Carol Vance. Boston: Routledge and Kegan Paul, 1984.

Russell, Stuart. 'The Offence of Keeping a Common Bawdy-House in Canadian Criminal Law.' *Ottawa Law Review* 14 (1982): 270–313.

St. James, Margo. 'The Reclamation of Whores.' In *Good Girls/Bad Girls*, edited by Laurie Bell. Toronto: Women's Press, 1987.

Shannon, Esther. 'Vancouver Prostitutes Fear Increasing Violence.' *Kinesis* (September 1986): 3.

Shaver, Fran. *Prostitution: A Critical Analysis*. Brief Prepared for the Special Committee on Pornography and Prostitution, May 1984.

Shearer, Rev. J.G. 'Canada's War on the White Slave Trade.' In *Fighting the Traffic in Young Girls or War on the White Slave Trade*, edited by E.A. Bell, 1910. Toronto: Coles Reprint, 1980.

Shearing, Clifford. 'Subterranean Processes in the Maintenance of Power: An Examination of the Mechanisms Coordinating Police Action.' *Canadian Review of Sociology and Anthropology* 18, no. 3 (August 1981): 283–98.

Shearing, Clifford, and Philip Stenning. 'Private Security: Implications for Social Control.' *Social Problems* 30, no. 5 (June 1983): 493–506.

Smart, Carol. *Feminism and the Power of Law*. London: Routledge, 1989.

– 'Law and the Control of Women's Sexuality: The Case of the 1950's.' In *Controlling Women*, edited by Bridget Hutter and Gillian Williams, 40–59. London: Croon Helm, 1981.

– 'Legal Subjects and Sexual Objects: Ideology, Law and Female Sexuality.' In *Women in Law*, edited by Julia Brophy and Carol Smart. London: Routledge and Kegan Paul, 1985.

Smart, Carol, and Julia Brophy. 'Locating Law: A Discussion of the Place of Law in Feminist Politics.' In *Women in Law*, edited by Julia Brophy and Carol Smart. London: Routledge and Kegan Paul, 1985.

Smith, Dorothy. 'The Active Text: A Textual Analysis of the Relations of Public Textual Discourse.' Paper presented at the World Congress of Sociology, Mexico, 1982.

– *The Everyday World as Problematic*. Toronto: University of Toronto Press, 1987.

– 'No-One Commits Suicide: Textual Analysis of Ideological Practices.' *Human Studies* 6, no. 4 (1983): 309–59.

– 'The Social Construction of Documentary Reality.' *Sociological Inquiry* 44, no. 4 (1974): 257–68.
– 'Textually Mediated Social Organization.' *International Social Science Journal* 36, no. 1 (1984): 59–75.
Smith, N., and P. Williams. *Gentrification of the City.* Boston: Allen and Unwin, 1986.
'Special issue on the sex trade.' *Social Text*, no. 37 (Winter 1993).
Stace, Michael. 'Legal Forms and Moral Phenomena: A Study of Two Events.' PhD thesis, York University, 1980.
Strange, Carolyn. 'The Toronto Social Survey Commission of 1915 and the Search for Sexual Order in the City.' In *Patterns of the Past: Interpreting Ontario's History*, edited by Roger Hall, William Westfall, and Laurel Sefton MacDowell. Toronto: Ontario Historical Society, 1988.
Street Outreach Services. 'Programme Overview, and Description of Street Youth in Prostitution, Service Statistics and Outcomes.' Toronto, May 1987.
Street Prostitution: Assessing the Impact of the Law, Synthesis report, Research Section. Ottawa: Department of Justice, 1989.
Sullivan, Terry. 'Juvenile Prostitution: Moral Disturbance or Job Creation Strategy?' Ontario Social Development Council. *The Reporter* 30, no. 1 (March/April 1985): 12–13.
Taylor, Ian. *Crime, Capitalism and Community.* Toronto: Butterworths, 1983.
– 'Martyrdom and Surveillance: Ideological and Social Practices of Police in Canada in the 1980s.' *Crime and Social Justice* 26 (1986): 160–73.
Terkel, Studs, ed. *Working.* New York: Avon, 1975.
Tong, Rosemarie. *Women, Sex, and the Law.* New Jersey: Rowman and Allanheld, 1984.
Toronto, City of. *Report of the Special Committee on Places of Amusement*, July 1977.
Toronto Street Youth Project. *Report on the Toronto Street Youth Project Reception Centre, May–November 1985.* Submitted to the Ministry of Community and Social Services, 12–13.
Toronto Street Youth Project Steering Committee. *Terms of Reference*, n.d.
Toronto Wages for Housework Committee. 'Fact Sheet on the Yonge Street Crackdown.' Toronto: Canadian Women's Movement Archives, Fall 1977.
Tremeerar's Criminal Annotations, 1971–1982. Toronto: Carswell, 1982.
Valverde, Mariana. *Sex, Power and Pleasure.* Toronto: Women's Press, 1985.
Valverde, Mariana, and Lorna Weir. 'The Struggles of the Immoral: Preliminary Remarks on Moral Regulation.' *Resources for Feminist Research* 17, no. 3 (September 1988): 31–4.
Visano, Livy. *This Idle Trade.* Concord: VitaSana Books, 1987.

Vorenberg, E., and J. Vorenberg. 'The Biggest Pimp of All.' *Atlantic Monthly* (January 1977): 27–38.

Voumvakis, Sophia, and Richard Ericson. *News Accounts of Attacks on Women: A Comparison of Three Toronto Newspapers*. Research report, Centre of Criminology, University of Toronto, 1984.

Vogt, Markus, Donald Craven, David Crawford, David Witt, Roy Byington, Robert Schooley, and Martin Hirsch. 'Isolation of HTLV-III/LAV from Cervical Secretions of Women at Risk for AIDS.' *The Lancet* (8 March 1986): 525–27.

Wachtel, Andy. 'Some Reflections on the Badgley Report.' In *Regulating Sex: An Anthology of Commentaries on the Findings and Recommendations of the Badgley and Fraser Reports*, edited by John Lowman, M.A. Jackson, T.S. Palys, and S. Gavigan. Vancouver: School of Criminology, Simon Fraser University, 1986.

Webber, Marlene. *Street Kids: The Tragedy of Canada's Runaways*. Toronto: University of Toronto Press, 1991.

Weeks, Jeffrey. *Sex, Politics and Society*. London: Longman, 1981.

– *Sexuality and Its Discontents*. London: Routledge and Kegan Paul, 1985.

Weir, Lorna. 'The Medicalization of Sexual Danger: Sexual Rule, Sexual Politics, 1830–1930.' PhD thesis, York University, 1986.

Wheeler, Glen. 'Reporting Crime: The News Release as a Textual Mediator of Police/Media Relations.' Master's thesis, University of Toronto, 1986.

Wofsy, Constance. 'Isolation of AIDS-Associated Retrovirus from Genital Secretions of Women with Antibodies to the Virus.' *The Lancet* (8 March 1986): 527–29.

Women Endorsing Decriminalization. 'Prostitution: A Non-Victim Crime?' *Issues in Criminology* 8, no. 2 (Fall 1973): 137–62.

Wynter, Sarah. 'Whisper: Women Hurt in Systems of Prostitution Engaged in Revolt.' In *Sex Work*, edited by Frederique Delacoste and Priscilla Alexander. Pittsburgh: Cleiss Press, 1987.

Yaworski, Carol. *Mandated Services to Teen Prostitutes*. Moberly House, Toronto, 1986.

'"Zelda": Some Information on Stripping in Toronto.' Paper presented at 'Challenging Our Images: The Politics of Pornography and Prostitution' conference, Ontario Institute for Studies in Education, Toronto, November 1985.

Index

38, 39, 41, 43, 47, 59, 160; of prostitutes, 54, 124, 139–40

National Action Committee on the
Status of Women (NAC), 24, 94,
159, 175
National Juvenile Prostitution Survey,
102, 108–13
National Population Survey, 102,
111–12
Native Child and Family Services, 131
Native people: street youth, 131–2,
181; prostitutes, 8, 140
Native Youth Outreach Program, 131
neighbourhood associations (*see* resi-
dents' organizations)
Nevada, 7–8
Ng, Yvonne, 32, 38
Niagara Falls, 45, 47, 54–5, 58
Nova Scotia, 53, 124 (*see also* Halifax)
NOW, 84, 168–9

Ontario, 32, 97, 128 (*see also* Niagara
Falls, Ottawa, and Toronto); Attor-
ney General, 84; County Court, 50,
51; Court of Appeal, 52; Family and
Child Services Act, 129, 131; Human
Rights Commission, 38
organized crime, 33, 52, 63–4
Ottawa, 36, 53, 58

Parkdale, 89, 90, 92, 94, 140
pimping, 8, 83, 95, 96–7 107, 121–6,
127, 132, 134, 181–2 (*see also* procuring)
Playboy, 25
police, 4, 5, 6, 8, 9, 11, 12, 21, 25, 27, 29,
37, 38, 44–7, 48, 49, 55, 59, 71, 75, 76,
78–95, 117, 119, 121, 129, 134, 141,
143, 144, 169, 172, 174; arrests, 3, 5,

30, 52, 55, 56, 64, 78–82, 90–1, 94,
171, 172, 174; Canadian Association
of Police Chiefs, 46, 60, 90; entrapment, 45, 80, 168–9; as experts, 10,
83, 95, 118, 122–3, 124–5, 126, 136,
175; Morality Squad, 78–80, 84, 87,
91; Niagara Falls, 54; Nova Scotia,
53; Toronto, 31–4, 39, 52, 86–7, 89,
90–1, 93–4, 145, 178; Vancouver, 142
pornography, 5, 10, 23, 24, 25, 36, 48,
62, 63, 65, 74, 77–8, 83, 102
Prevost Commission, 27
private/public distinctions, 28–9, 61–2,
69–71, 75–7, 145
procuring, legislation, 9, 50, 51, 67–8,
107, 144
prostitutes: as activists, 11, 12, 14, 52,
74, 137–8, 141; ages of, 52, 79,
119–21; arrests of, 3, 5, 30, 52, 55, 56,
64, 78–82, 90–1, 94; clientele, 7, 11,
18, 19–21, 49, 52, 54–5, 78–82, 85, 86,
88–91, 94, 105, 106, 107, 126, 127,
139, 142, 148–50, 171, 172; definition
of, 50–1, 151, 153; double standard
for, 6–7, 29; earnings, 8, 15, 17,
18–19, 122; families, 16, 53, 79, 81;
murder of, 54, 124, 139–140; non-
activist, 11, 24; organizations, 22–4,
41, 56, 59, 79–82, 87–8, 98, 133, 158,
161, 169, 171, 175–6; as professionals, 88; stigma, 11, 18, 42, 94, 139;
and welfare, 3, 19, 56, 57, 81, 176;
working conditions, 7–8, 11, 13–15,
19–22, 23, 88, 137–8, 146; young
people as, 48–9, 79, 101–16, 140, 167
Prostitutes and Other Women for
Equal Rights (POWER), 81
Prostitutes Safe Sex Project (PSSP), 87
prostitution: areas of concentration,
50–3, 82, 92–3, 94, 121, 130–1,